Literature, Literacy, and Comprehension Strategies in the Elementary School

Literature, Literacy, and Comprehension Strategies in the Elementary School

Joy F. Moss
Harley School, Rochester, New York
University of Rochester

National Council of Teachers of English
1111 W. Kenyon Road, Urbana, Illinois 61801-1096

To our grandchildren, Daniel, Rachel, Aaron, Yonah, Adam, Julia, Joshua, Tamar, and Emily, who inspire their parents and grandparents.

Staff Editor: Bonny Graham

Manuscript Editor: L. L. Erwin

Interior Design: Doug Burnett

Cover Design: Pat Mayer

NCTE Stock Number: 29900

It is the policy of NCTE in its journals and other publications to provide a forum for the open discussion of ideas concerning the content and the teaching of English and the language arts. Publicity accorded to any particular point of view does not imply endorsement by the Executive Committee, the Board of Directors, or the membership at large, except in announcements of policy, where such endorsement is clearly specified.

Every effort has been made to provide current URLs and e-mail addresses, but because of the rapidly changing nature of the Web, some sites and addresses may no longer be accessible.

Library of Congress Cataloging-in-Publication Data

Moss, Joy, F., 1937-
Literature, literacy, and comprehension strategies in the elementary school / Joy F. Moss.
    p. cm.
Includes bibliographical references and index.
ISBN 0-8141-2990-0 (pbk.)
1. Literature—Study and teaching (Elementary) 2. Language arts
   (Elementary) 3. Children—Books and reading. I. Title.
LB1575.M678 2005
372.64—dc22
    2005020711

Contents

Acknowledgments

This book could not have been written without the students and teachers with whom I have worked over the years. Their contributions are gratefully acknowledged. I am especially appreciative of the involvement of two teachers, Marilyn Fenster and Valerie Myntti, who spent many hours recording children's responses to the literature introduced in the read-aloud/think-aloud sessions featured in this book.

I want to thank Kurt Austin for his support and encouragement from the very beginning of this project, as well as the reviewers whose valuable suggestions were incorporated into the revisions of the early drafts of the manuscript.

I am deeply grateful for the thoughtful and enthusiastic involvement of my family as I worked on this book, and I want to take this opportunity to express my appreciation to our children and their spouses, Kathy and Jeff, Debbie and Keith, and Abby and David, who are raising avid readers and passing on their love of story to their own children; to our grandchildren, Daniel, Rachel, Aaron, Yonah, Adam, Julia, Joshua, Tamar, and Emily, whose remarkable love of reading and writing has strengthened my own conviction about the value of literature in the lives of children; and to my husband, Arthur, with a very special thank-you for his endless patience, his understanding, and his love.

1 Theory into Practice

This book is about teaching reading-thinking strategies to elementary school children in the context of authentic literature experiences that include rich interpretive dialogues and provide the support children need to become engaged, thoughtful, and independent readers and writers. The rest of this chapter explains and expands on these central concepts.

Reading Comprehension Instruction: A Historical Perspective

The reading comprehension instruction practiced in most American schools today evolved out of instructional methods and programs grounded in behavioral and task-analytic theories of learning that flourished during the early and middle parts of the twentieth century. Reading was viewed as a skill that could be divided into a set of subskills involved in both decoding and comprehension. Reading instruction was based on the assumption that reading could be improved by teaching students each of these subskills (Guthrie, 1973; Rosenshine, 1980; N. B. Smith, 1965). Once a reader mastered the skills, he or she was considered a proficient reader who could comprehend any text. In this view of reading, readers were assumed to be passive recipients of the information or meaning that resided in the text. In the 1970s and 1980s, basic and applied research in reading resulted in new understandings of the reading process and a different view of what is important to teach.

A classic study by Dolores Durkin (1978/1979), "What Classroom Observations Reveal about Reading Comprehension Instruction," called attention to the need for change in comprehension instruction. Durkin found that most of the questions that teachers asked students during reading instruction required only literal responses, and she observed that very little comprehension instruction was actually taking place in elementary school classrooms. In the late 1980s the National Assessment of Educational Progress (Applebee, Langer, & Mullis, 1987) recommended that reading instruction should emphasize thinking skills and strategies that would enable readers to engage in higher-level interpretive responses to texts. Since Durkin's study, reading researchers have studied the strategies expert readers use as they read and how to improve readers' understanding of text through comprehension strategy instruction. Allan Collins and Edward Smith (1982) were among the first to provide a framework for using these strategies as an integral part of comprehension instruction. They categorized reading strategies into two general classifications: comprehension monitoring and hypothesis generation, evaluation, and revision. That is, they suggested that readers construct meaning in response to an unfolding text by integrating textual information with their prior knowledge to generate predictions, inferences, and questions about the piece. Readers build a "working hypothesis" about the meaning of the text as it unfolds, and as they encounter new information or activate relevant knowledge they confirm, revise, or reject initial predictions, assumptions, or interpretations. Readers monitor comprehension as the text unfolds by evaluating their working hypothesis to identify gaps or problem areas that need rethinking and revision. The instructional plan presented by Collins and Smith featured teacher modeling and student engagement. That is, the teacher models both comprehension monitoring and hypothesis generation while reading a text aloud. Then the teacher invites student participation in these strategic activities. The goal is for students to internalize these strategies so they can use them as thoughtful, independent readers.

Strategy instruction was also a central part of the studies in "reciprocal teaching" conducted by Annemarie Sullivan Palincsar and Ann L. Brown (1984; 1988), who focused on teaching four comprehension-monitoring and comprehension-fostering strategies. What was unique about this plan was the use of dialogue to help students internalize the strategies. The teacher supports the students as they work in small groups interacting with a text and engaging in a dialogue about the text. Their dialogue is guided by the use of the four basic strategies: asking questions, identifying sections in the text that require clarification, summarizing the text, and making predictions about it. The reciprocity of the dialogue emerges as the students take turns assuming responsibility for leading the group. This work reflected the shift from identifying and teaching discrete skills to focusing on students' efforts to make sense of ideas or to build their own understanding of text and their own active involvement as readers as they construct meaning in a social context.

The research of the 1970s and 1980s served as a point of departure for further studies of strategy instruction, and other researchers have expanded on this earlier work. For example, Michael Pressley and his colleagues (1992) used the term *transactional strategies instruction* to describe an approach in which students are taught to coordinate a repertoire of strategic processes and "teachers and students jointly construct understandings of the text as they interact with it" (p. 516). This collaborative construction of meaning results in a "small interpretive community" (p. 516). The long-term goal is for students to internalize the strategies used in the group setting and to use these strategies as independent readers. "The thought processes that were once interpersonal become intrapersonal" (p. 516). That is, students internalize these processes: development and practice of a repertoire of reading strategies; regular discussion of metacognitive information, such as when, where, and why to use particular strategies; building a nonstrategic world knowledge base; and motivation to use the strategies and world knowledge being learned (p. 517). The term *transactional* as applied to this approach is based on the reader-response theory of Louise Rosenblatt (1978). Her transactional theory of reading will be discussed later.

The new view of reading that evolved out of the research of the 1970s and 1980s emphasized the cognitive and interactive nature of the reading process and the constructive nature of comprehension (Rumelhart, 1980; Spiro, 1980). This research highlighted the active role of readers as they engage in cognitive and affective transactions with text and generate meaning by bringing their prior knowledge and experience to the text (Adams, 1977; Golden, 1986; Goodman, 1967, 1985; Rosenblatt, 1982; Rumelhart, 1976; F. Smith, 1978, 1988). Frank Smith introduced the term *nonvisual information* to refer to this prior knowledge used to construct meaning (1978, p. 5). According to Smith, "The meaning that readers comprehend from text is always relative to what they already know and to what they want to know" (1988, p. 154). He refers to organized knowledge or cognitive structures as "the theory of the world in our heads," which enables readers to make predictions as they interact with a text (1988, p. 7). "Prediction means asking questions, and comprehension means being able to get some of the questions answered. . . . There is a *flow* to comprehension, with new questions constantly being generated from the answers that are sought" (1988, p. 19). In the interpretive dialogues featured in this book, the children were encouraged to develop their own questions to guide the reading-thinking process as they encountered literary texts. The authentic literature experiences that formed the core of the literary/literacy program described in this book were cumulative, and, as such, provided opportunities for the children to expand and revise the *theory of the world in their heads* and to build new cognitive structures (or prior knowledge) to bring to and enrich each new experience with literature.

These authentic literature experiences set the stage for readers to engage in cumulative meaning-making processes. According to Judith

Langer, reading as a meaning-making process involves *envisionment building*:

> I use the term envisionment to refer to the understanding a reader has about a text—what the reader understands at a particular point in time, the questions she has, as well as hunches about how the piece will unfold. Envisionments develop as the reading develops. Some information is no longer important, some is added, and some is changed. What readers come away with at the end of the reading, I call the final envisionment. This includes what they understand, what they don't, and the questions they still have. The final envisionment is also subject to change with time, as the result of conversations with others, the reading of other works, or pondering and reflection. (Langer, 1990, p. 812)

> Envisionments are text-worlds in the mind, and they differ from individual to individual. They are a function of one's personal and cultural experiences, one's relationships to the current experience, what one knows, how one feels, and what one is after. (Langer, 1995, p. 9)

In the context of the interpretive dialogues described in this book, children were invited to articulate their initial understandings or envisionments of a text and to revise or extend these envisionments as they gained new information from the unfolding text. The children were encouraged to use their prior knowledge in conjunction with text knowledge to explore possible meanings, perspectives, and interpretations and to reflect on their own understandings in light of their life experiences and their "conversations with others, the reading of other works, or pondering and reflection."

Rosenblatt also focuses on the nature of readers' responses to unfolding texts, and her transactional theory of reading provides a framework for exploring a reader's responses to literature. According to Rosenblatt, reading is a "transaction, a two-way process, involving a reader and a text at a particular time under particular circumstances" (1982, p. 268). The nature of this transaction is determined by the reader's stance or "mental set," which is related to a reader's expectations and the way he or she approaches the text. Rosenblatt uses the term *aesthetic* to refer to a stance that allows a reader to focus on the "lived through" experience of reading. She argues that the most effective way to read fiction and poetry is from an aesthetic stance. The aesthetic reader enters into the story world and "lives through" it as a personal and emotional experience. Rosenblatt uses the term *efferent* to refer to the stance of the reader who focuses on accumulating information to use in the real world. Thus, nonfiction texts are most effectively approached from an efferent stance by readers who are interested in facts and knowledge to be "carried away at the end of the reading" (p. 269). According to Rosenblatt (1991), readers can switch stances while reading, and stance can move along the efferent/aesthetic continuum within a single reading event (p. 446). Most reading is predominantly, rather that solely, one or the other. Rosenblatt observes that teachers need to be clear about the different purposes of efferent and aesthetic reading, and that different purposes lead to different modes of reading. Thus the teacher needs to decide whether the emphasis is on verifiable information or practical application or whether the purpose is literary (p. 447). Rosenblatt calls for literature instruction that emphasizes aesthetic reading: "Precisely because every aesthetic reading of a text is a unique creation, woven out of the inner life and thought of the reader, the literary work of art can be a rich source of insight and truth" (p. 277).

During the read-aloud sessions described in subsequent chapters, the children entered into the story world and shared their spontaneous personal responses to this experience. They were also invited to step back from this aesthetic experience and to explore the story objectively as a literary text, and to engage in reflection, analysis, and interpretation. The term *critical/analytic* has been used to refer to a third stance, which is defined as a "focus on a major dilemma or problem facing a character, a consideration of reasons for different courses of action, and appeals to the text for evidence and for interpretive context" (Chinn, Anderson, & Waggoner, 2001, pp. 381–82). By stepping back from the text, the children shifted from the aesthetic stance to the critical/analytic. Over time, they learned to adopt the stance appropriate to their purposes in their transactions with texts.

Langer (1994) also distinguishes between a literary orientation and reading to gain information:

> A literary orientation . . . can be characterized as *exploring a horizon of possibilities.* It explores emotions, relationships, motives, and reactions, calling on all we know about what it means to be human. . . . A literary orientation is one of exploring horizons—where uncertainty is a normal part of response, and new-found understandings provoke still other possibilities. When the purpose of reading is primarily to gain information (as when students read science and social studies texts), the reader's orientation can be characterized as "maintaining a point of reference." (pp. 204–5)

James Baumann and Gay Ivey (1997) conducted a yearlong study featuring strategy instruction integrated within a rich literature-based environment. They conceptualized their study in terms of two of what

Hudelson and Lindfors (1993) call *delicate balances*: "a curriculum balance between literature envisionment (Langer, 1995) and skill/strategy instruction, and an instructional balance between teacher-initiated instruction and instruction responsive to students' needs and interests" (Baumann & Ivey, 1997, p. 244). They used Langer's concept of literary envisionment as the framework for promoting literary appreciation and response. An analysis of the results of this study revealed that "students developed into readers . . . [,] became engaged with literacy . . . [,] grew in word identification ability and reading fluency . . .[,] became better at comprehending what they read . . . [, and] grew in written composition proficiency" (p. 269).

In the preface to their book, *Improving Comprehension Instruction: Rethinking Research, Theory, and Classroom Practice* (2002), Cathy Collins Block, Linda B. Gambrell, and Michael Pressley state: "Reading comprehension is an urgent national priority whose time has come! No other body of knowledge is the foundation for all content knowledge" (p. xvii). They express their concern about the absence of effective comprehension instruction in many of today's schools: "Even as recently as 1998, many students left primary and secondary schools having experienced very little training in cognition and metacognition and very little teaching of how to process text independently. Most so-called comprehension lessons consisted merely of a teacher's direct questions about material that students were supposed to have comprehended. Educators did not explain, model, or demonstrate how to understand" (p. xv). A survey of studies of comprehension instruction conducted between 1984 and 1997 revealed that "teaching comprehension strategies based on reading research benefits and increases students' comprehension. Across these studies, strategy instruction increased students' willingness to read difficult material, discover meaning in text, and react to and elaborate on text meaning" (p. 12).

Dixie Lee Spiegel's survey (1998) of the research on the benefits of reader-response approaches to literature revealed that students who participate in peer discussions and respond in journals grow in many ways: these researchers found that students increase their repertoire of responses to literature and "move to higher levels of thinking in their responses" (p. 45). They make personal connections between literature, their own lives, and the world (p. 44). "Students develop an appreciation for multiple interpretations of literature, with tolerance for and even an expectation of ambiguity; and a need for rethinking one's initial responses" (p. 44). Researchers found that these students also grow as readers, in general: "They gain confidence in themselves as readers; they develop an ability to monitor their own reading and learning; and they gain strategies that will enable them to read, respond to, and understand a variety of texts" (p. 46). Several of the studies in Spiegel's survey have shown that these students do better on standardized achievement tests than do students in more teacher- and text-dominated programs (Nystrand & Gamoran, 1991; Swift, 1993; and Raphael & McMahon, 1994).

Comprehension Instruction: Teaching a Repertoire of Cognitive Strategies

Subsequent chapters will describe examples of literary experiences that provide a context for teaching cognitive strategies used by proficient readers and examples of ways teachers model and explain these strategies to students so they can eventually internalize and use them to enhance their comprehension as independent readers. Janice Dole and her colleagues (1991) offer distinguishing features of *strategies:*

> Strategies emphasize intentional and deliberate plans under the control of the reader. Strategies emphasize reasoning; readers use reasoning and critical thinking skills as they construct and reconstruct evolving meaning from the text.
> Strategies are inherently flexible and adaptable. Readers modify strategies to fit different kinds of texts and different purposes.
> Strategies imply metacognitive awareness; good readers can reflect on what they are doing while they are reading. They are aware of whether they understand or do not understand, and this awareness usually leads to regulation and repair. (p. 242)

Researchers in reading comprehension have identified a number of different *reading-thinking strategies*, outlined in Figure 1.1, used by proficient readers to comprehend text:

1. Engaging in cover-to-cover study of new texts: The *cover-to-cover* study of literary texts involves a careful examination of the front and back covers, dust jacket, endpapers, front matter such as the dedication and title pages, author's notes, and other text and pictures that precede or follow the story text. According to Margaret Higonnet (1990), French critics use the term *peritext* to refer to these peripheral features as well as the illustrations that surround or enclose the verbal narrative in picture books or in illustrated chapter books. A study of the peritext enables readers to discover clues to make inferences or predictions about the story during the prereading phase, or it may help them to activate relevant prior knowledge or trigger questions about some-

---

Reading-Thinking Strategies

1. Engaging in cover-to-cover study of new texts

2. Activating and using prior knowledge

3. Drawing inferences

4. Making predictions

5. Determining importance

6. Summarizing, analyzing, and synthesizing

7. Evoking mental imagery

8. Generating questions

9. Using text structure and story grammar

10. Monitoring comprehension

11. Making connections between the text and other texts, oneself, and the world

12. Engaging in metacognition

13. Thinking aloud

Figure 1.1

thing that is not part of their prior knowledge or that seems puzzling to them. Readers can use the peritext to identify the genre or to learn something about the story or the author that will influence their transaction with the text. Readers can use the peritext to study the artist's craft: What choices did the artist make? How do the illustrations enrich the story as a whole? During and after interaction with the text, readers return to segments of the peritext to evaluate their initial responses and to confirm or revise their earlier predictions, or to answer questions posed earlier, or to build understanding and enrich the meaning making process by integrating new information in the unfolding text with clues in the peritext.

2. Activating and using prior knowledge: Readers who bring relevant prior knowledge to a text are able to generate more meaning than readers who do not possess this prior knowledge (Anderson & Pearson, 1984). Reading comprehension programs in the elementary school can provide opportunities for students to build rich prior knowledge through extensive reading of high-quality literary and nonfiction texts and to learn how to activate relevant prior knowledge to bring to their transactions with new texts. The more a person reads, the more knowledge of language, literature, the natural world, and the human experience that person has to bring to the text. Readers elicit prior knowledge before, during, and after the reading event.

3. Drawing inferences: Readers use their prior knowledge and experience and textual information to draw conclusions and develop interpretations and opinions as they interact with a text. Lea M. McGee (1996) used the term *gap-filling activities* to describe children's inferential thinking as they move beyond the literal level of understanding toward interpretations of the story as a whole (p. 196). Narrative writers usually include implicit information that requires readers/listeners to make inferences and to fill in the gaps in the story, that is, to focus on what is not in the story. Inferential thinking is required to identify literal/figurative distinctions, motivations of characters, and logical relationships among events in the story. "When we read, we stretch the limits of the literal text by folding our experience and belief into the literal meanings in the text, creating a new interpretation, an inference" (Keene and Zimmermann, 1997, p. 147). According to Jean Anne Clyde, readers can "step inside the story world" by generating the subtext, the thoughts and emotions behind the action in the story (2003). Clyde observed that readers who created subtext were able to "think deeply about characters' emotions and motives . . . . [and] to appreciate multiple viewpoints" (p. 156–57).

4. Making predictions: Readers think about what will happen next as a story unfolds; they develop an anticipatory attitude toward text and learn to predict their way through the text. "Prediction means asking questions, and comprehension means being able to get some of the questions answered" (F. Smith, 1988, p. 19). Readers use textual knowledge in combination with prior knowledge and experience to make predictions. As the text unfolds and they encounter new information, readers confirm, revise, or reject initial predictions.

5. Determining importance: Readers identify main ideas and significant themes as they read. They use these ideas and themes to determine the difference between important and unimportant ideas. Determining importance of ideas or information in a text is a critical factor in summarizing, analyzing, and synthesizing that text.

6. Summarizing, analyzing, and synthesizing: Summarizing (or review) involves allocating attention to the major content and checking for understanding (Palincsar & Brown, 1984, p. 120). Readers integrate important ideas and information in the text and ignore unimportant or irrelevant information in order to review the content or retell a narrative. Readers engage in analysis by examining basic elements of a text, its structure, or its story grammar. Readers analyze the author's craft by examining his or her language, literary techniques, and style and posing questions about the choices the author made in composing the text. According to JoAnn Portalupi (1999), "We build our knowledge of craft each time we engage in discussion of literature" (p. 5). Synthesis goes beyond what happened in the story to what it's about, the key themes. Readers move from analysis to synthesis by integrating text knowledge and their own prior knowledge to create new insights or understandings or larger meanings that reach beyond the single text. Synthesis of multiple texts enables readers to expand insights and understandings.

7. Evoking mental imagery: Allan Paivio (Paivio, 1971, 1986) uses the term *dual-coding system* to refer to the coding of knowledge in both verbal and nonverbal representations. Readers use all five senses and their emotions to construct their own mental images as they read. These images evolve out of readers' prior knowledge and personal experience, and they clarify and enrich readers' comprehension as they interact with a text. "For readers, the mental images derived from what they've read connect them personally to the texts, over time coalescing into a self-awareness, complexity, and depth which is at the core of being human" (Keene & Zimmermann, 1997, p.141). According to Rosenblatt, the aesthetic reader is able to "savor the images, the sounds, the smells, the actions, the associations, and the feelings that the words point to" (1991, p. 447). Research on mental imagery reveals that comprehension improves when students are taught to use mental imagery (Anderson, 1971).

8. Generating questions: When students pose and answer their own questions before, during, and after reading, they become more actively and deeply involved in the reading process, and they can identify gaps in comprehension and points in the text that need clarification or hypotheses that need to be rethought (Palincsar & Brown, 1984). Questions may lead to predictions or inferences or to a focus on the important elements in the text. Other readers' questions during dialogue may challenge students' interpretations and stimulate new questions and inquiry, enhancing understanding of the text.

In a critical literacy program, students are encouraged to adopt a questioning stance in response to socially conscious literature that exposes them to issues of equity, justice, and power. Students' questions set the stage for inquiry that takes them *beyond* the texts to gain new understandings and insights about social issues and prepares them to take action against injustices and inequities they encounter in their own worlds.

9. Using text structure and story grammar: Knowledge of text structure is an important factor in reading comprehension. "Successful readers are aware of differences between narrative structures and expository structures, and they use this knowledge to guide and monitor their comprehension" (Reutzel, Camperell, & Smith, 2002, p. 325). In the 1970s, researchers identified an internal structure for simple stories, referred to as *story grammar* (Mandler & Johnson, 1977; N. L. Stein, 1978). This inner structure is made up of a network of categories and the logical relationships among them, and provides a systematic way to analyze stories (Leondar, 1977; N. L. Stein, 1978). By listening to and reading a variety of narratives, children develop a *story schema,* an implicit knowledge of story grammar or story structure that can be used to comprehend and recall narratives. Stories are organized into sequences of events in which the main characters pursue goals and overcome obstacles (Graesser, Golding, & Long, 1991; Mandler & Johnson, 1977). Readers use their story schemata to become aware of the logical and purposive behaviors that characterize well-formed stories (Leondar, 1977; N. L. Stein, 1978). Comprehending stories requires readers to infer characters' motives and to identify themes. In her discussion of story grammar research, April Nauman (1990) states that "a basic understanding of story structure enables readers to predict what kinds of things will happen next and to infer certain information not stated explicitly—skills that improve comprehension. An understanding of story structure also enables young writers to recognize what kinds of experiences make good stories and to select what details to use. We can use the work of story grammarians to help children become more sophisticated readers and writers" (p. 58). Story grammar research provides evidence that children use their knowledge of story structure to understand and recall stories, to make predictions about stories, and to generate their own stories. Researchers have also demonstrated that explicit teaching of story structure improves comprehension of stories (Fitzgerald & Spiegel, 1983) and helps students compose better-organized stories (Fitzgerald & Teasley, 1986).

Cognitive theorists have demonstrated that the quality of reading comprehension is determined in large part by the quality of prior knowledge or nonvisual information the reader/listener brings to the text. This knowledge is organized; the term *schema* is used to refer to one's organized knowledge or mental model of the world, just as the narrower term *story schema* above refers to a mental model of the way stories work. In terms of schema theory, readers comprehend a text when they are able to retrieve relevant schemata from their memory stores and make appropriate connections to new information in the text. One of the most effective ways to improve comprehension is to activate relevant knowledge stored in these memory banks before reading.

Proficient readers identify the genre of the text they are reading, and use their knowledge of genre to generate meaning. In the seventh edition of *A Critical Handbook of Children's Literature* (2003), Rebecca Lukens defines *genre* as "a kind or type of literature that has a common set of characteristics" (p. 13). An awareness of genre enables a reader to draw from a set of expectations associated with a particular genre in his or her transaction with a particular literary text.

Knowledge of story grammar and genre for narrative texts and knowledge of organization or overall structure for expository texts has been found to be especially valuable for helping readers differentiate important from unimportant information as well as for helping them recall information (Meyer & Rice, 1984).

10. Monitoring comprehension: Proficient readers know when they understand the text they are reading, and they know when it does not make sense. In order to repair comprehension problems, they identify the source of the problem (such as an unfamiliar word or concept or text structure, or segments of the text that are confusing or unclear), and then they decide how to solve the problem (by consulting a dictionary, rereading the passage, searching for missing details, or drawing from prior knowledge). Finally, the reader refines or revises his or her understanding or interpretation of the text.

11. Making connections between the text and other texts, oneself, and the world: Proficient readers think about their own world knowledge, their literary histories, and their personal experiences as they read, and they make connections between the text they are reading and the thoughts it triggers. These connections generally take three forms:

> Text-to-text connections;
>
> text-to-self connections; and
>
> text-to-world connections. (Keene & Zimmermann, 1997)

Readers' transactions with a new literary text often trigger thoughts of personal experiences, memories, and associations as well as relevant world knowledge. Readers also find connections between a new text and previous texts. Students are encouraged to identify and use *intertextual links* to generate meaning. The term *intertextuality* was first coined by Julia Kristeva (1984) to describe the process a reader uses to comprehend one text by means of a prior text. In his research on the way readers understand texts, Richard Beach (1990) found that "the more stories they [the students in this study] read, the richer their intertextual links, which, in turn, related to the quality of their interpretation of the story" (p. 70). The results of this study are consistent with other studies of intertextual linking which, taken together, suggest the value of "continually relating current texts to past texts so that students build a sense of their own histories as readers" (Wolf, 1988). In an *"intertextually rich environment"* (Hartman, 1995, p. 528), children develop the habit of reading intertextually and engaging in comparative analysis as a natural dimension of literary study.

Text-to-world connections include the world knowledge readers bring *to* a text to generate meaning as well as the understandings and insights about the world that readers gain *from* their transactions with a text. When a text prompts reflection about complex social issues, readers look beyond the text to probe more deeply into an issue and consider ways to translate concerns and insights into action in their own world.

12. Engaging in metacognition: "Research has confirmed what teachers of reading may have observed in themselves and in their students, namely, that thoughtful, active, proficient readers are *metacognitive:* they think about their own thinking during reading" (Keene, 2002, p. 84). When teachers articulate and demonstrate reading-thinking strategies and focus instruction on the mental processes that underlie reading, their students develop an awareness of their own thought processes as they read. By engaging in metacognition, readers can take control of their transactions with texts; they can plan what strategies to use, monitor the effectiveness of these strategies, and revise their plans to solve comprehension problems. Proficient readers know what they are doing when they read.

13. Thinking aloud: *Think-alouds* refer to talking about thinking processes used during reading or listening to a text. James Baumann and his colleagues define think-alouds as "overt, verbal expression of the normally covert mental processes readers engage in when constructing meaning from text" (Baumann, Jones, & Seifert-Kessell, 1993, p. 185), and they list think-aloud strategies as "asking questions, drawing on prior knowledge, assessing comprehension by asking, 'Does this make sense?'; predicting and verifying, inferring unstated ideas, retelling, and rereading and reading on to clarify meaning" (p. 187). Linda Kucan and Isabel Beck (1997) reviewed the research on thinking aloud in reading comprehension and found that think-alouds were also being used to promote social interaction. "Current efforts to engage students in constructing meaning from text in collaborative discussions seem to indicate a new direction for thinking aloud research, one in which social interaction assumes increased importance" (p. 271).

Think-alouds can provide teachers with a vehicle for demonstrating the reading-thinking strategies used by proficient readers as they respond to unfolding texts. *Mosaic of Thought: Teaching Comprehension in a Reader's Workshop,* by Ellin Keene and Susan Zimmermann (1997), is about "lively talk in [literature-rich] classrooms and what happens when children develop an awareness of their thought processes as they read" (p. 11). In this book the authors describe classroom instruction that is based on the conviction that "reading comprehension could be taught by showing children what proficient readers thought about as they read, and teaching children to use those same strategies themselves" (p. 24). The authors comment: "As we worked with the strategies, it became clear that metacognition—thinking about one's own thinking—was an umbrella under which the other strategies fell. Each strategy was a variation of metacognition" (pp. 24–25).

In "Using the Think-Aloud for Reading Instruction," Leslie Oster (2001) describes her use of think-aloud strategies for instruction as well as assessment. Her students' think-aloud comments, shared in group discussion or in writing, revealed their strengths and weaknesses as readers. These comments helped Oster plan instruction to meet specific learning needs and helped her students develop metacognitive awareness by focusing on patterns in their own think-aloud comments.

The Literary Context

For many years researchers have demonstrated that children who are immersed in rich, authentic literary experiences become highly engaged in literature and develop literary awareness and appreciation (Clark, 1976; Durkin, 1961; Routman, 1988, 1991; Short, 1995; Walmsley, 1992). Baumann and Ivey (1997) studied the impact of a combined program in which teacher-led strategy instruction was embedded in a literature-based framework. Their data demonstrated that the students in their study "became more proficient in reading and writing abilities . . . and . . . they grew in knowledge, interest, and attitudes toward reading, writing and literature" (p. 272). Like the findings in a study by Block (1993), the results of the Baumann and Ivey study reveal that "elementary students can acquire reading and thinking strategies within a literature-based environment" (p. 270). The authors conclude that: "The immersion in literature and the embedded strategy instruction created a kind of symbiotic, synergistic relationship in which each program characteristic contributed to and fed off the other" (p. 272). Claude Goldenberg (1992/1993) uses the term *instructional conversation* to describe "discussion-based lessons geared toward creating richly textured opportunities for students' conceptual and linguistic development" (p. 317). Goldenberg's model is designed to "weave instruction and conversation into a seamless whole: The conversation is instructional, and the instruction is conversational" (p. 319).

According to Langer (1998), literature is thought-provoking and "literature classrooms are particularly good environments not only for the learning of literary works . . . but also for the development of literate thinking, intelligent reasoning, and human sensitivity" (pp. 16–17). Literature has the power to touch the minds and hearts of aesthetic readers and to transform readers who enter into the lives of literary characters. Readers who respond with empathy and compassion make emotional connections, and they imagine beyond the boundaries of their own experience and gain new insights and perspectives about what it means to be human and about the universality of human experience and the uniqueness of individual human beings. According to Langer (1995): "All literature . . . provides us with a way to imagine human potential. In its best sense, literature is intellectually provocative as well as humanizing, allowing us to use various angles of vision to examine thoughts, beliefs, and actions" (p. 5).

Literature and Critical Literacy

Critical literacy "transcends conventional notions of reading and writing to incorporate critical thinking, questioning, and transformation of self or one's world" (McDaniel, 2004, p. 472). This idea of transforming oneself and one's world through language is rooted in Paulo Freire's philosophy of transformative education (2000). Langer has called attention to the "intellectually provocative [and] humanizing" nature of literature and its transformative power, and using selected children's literature in the classroom is one way to support critical literacy and transformative education. Critical conversations begin when teachers encourage children to adopt a questioning stance in response to literary texts and to consider ways to translate insights about issues of equity and power into social action to change their worlds. Christine Leland and Jerome Harste draw from Luke and Freebody's (1997) theoretical model of critical literacy to develop criteria for selecting books that invite readers to engage in critical analysis, i.e., searching for the particular views that are represented in the text as well as those that are silenced and "[being] conscious of the assumptions that are embedded in the text" (Leland and Harste, 2000, p. 3). For example, they selected books that "don't make difference invisible, but rather explore what differences make a difference . . . . [;] help us question why certain groups are positioned as 'others' . . . . [; and] show how people can begin to take action on important social issues" (p. 4). The authors note: "Engaging children in conversations about the pernicious effects of 'otherness' can help them begin to see and understand the world in new ways" (p. 5). Children respond with compassion and empathy as well as righteous anger as they encounter injustice and inequity in socially conscious literature. When these emotional responses are interwoven with a growing understanding of social issues, students are prepared to practice social justice and to take action against injustices they encounter in their own worlds.

Reading Aloud

The first chapter of *For Reading Out Loud: Planning and Practice* (Fisher & Medvic, 2003) is entitled: "Why Read Aloud?" The authors begin this chapter with an answer: "We read aloud to children because it is the best way we know to help them learn to love reading. Reading aloud to children forms the foundation of literacy learning" (p. 1). In their classic text, *Children's Literature in the Elementary School* (8th ed., 2004), Charlotte Huck and Barbara Kiefer also emphasize the powerful connection between reading aloud and learning to read. Children who hear books read aloud on a regular basis discover the patterns of narrative and expository texts and learn to understand the meanings of the texts. As they become immersed in rich literary experiences in these read-aloud sessions, children learn about themselves, about others, and about the world, and they learn to think critically and creatively. The literature children hear is reflected in their writing. "Whether consciously or unconsciously, children pick up words, phrases, textual structure, even intonation patterns from books they know" (p. 11). In addition, children build on the ideas found in narratives and expository texts as they engage in writing, drawing, drama, and art activities. In the social context of the read-aloud sessions, children learn to collaborate in responding to, exploring, and studying the shared texts. Susan Hepler and Janet Hickman (1982) use the term *community of readers* to describe children working together to become readers of literature and to explore and build meanings together.

Shelby Barrentine (1996) uses the term *interactive* to describe the kind of read-aloud style that encourages students to engage in discussion and response *during* the reading of the story. Grover Whitehurst and his colleagues (1994) use the term *dialogic* to refer to the interaction that occurs as the text unfolds in a read-aloud session. Lawrence Sipe studied storybook read-alouds and the role of the teacher in promoting critical thinking and thoughtful literary interpretation (2003), conducting an in-depth study of a single teacher as she interacted with her students during the reading of stories over a nine-month period. Sipe observed that this teacher was interjecting her own comments as she read aloud the author's words. "She is not only expanding on the text and interpreting it; she is connecting emotionally to the text and personalizing it" (p. 165). In addition, the teacher served as an "emotional bridge between the children and the story . . . she let her storybook reading be determined, in part, by her audience . . . . [S]he encouraged different kinds of responses to the story, including the children's own stories[,] . . . . socio-dramatic play, dramatic re-enactments, and journal writing as extensions of the readalouds" (pp. 165–66). Sipe uses the term *storytelling style* to describe the teacher's role as reader and storyteller and the "synergy developed between the teller's words and the interjected comments of the audience" (p. 164).

The authors of *Reading Aloud and Beyond: Fostering the Intellectual Life with Older Readers* (Serafini & Giorgis, 2003) envision "the read aloud as the foundation of the reading curriculum, the launching point for the study of the language arts and the content area disciplines" (p. xi). They emphasize the central role of literature in the curriculum: "Literature is the driving force behind the curriculum we construct with our students . . . . Literature is used as a lens to understand the world" (p. 3). The authors also highlight the use of the picture book with older students: "We believe that the length and format of the picture book make it a perfect resource, one that often goes untapped in the intermediate and middle grades" (pp. xii–xiii). They use the metaphor "teacher as docent" to describe the role of the teacher during a read-aloud experience (p. 4). Like the museum docent, the teacher can serve as a guide in the world of literature. The teacher invites personal responses and helps his or her students build new understandings, construct new interpretations, gain new insights, and view the literary text from multiple perspectives as they enter into it together and explore its meanings.

Interpretive Dialogues

This book is about literary discussion that evolves before, during, and after a story is read aloud and that promotes literary understanding and provides a context for strategy instruction. As a teacher of young children for over thirty years, I have had the good fortune to participate in lively discussions about literature with my students over those years (Moss, 1982, 1984, 1990, 1998, 2000, 2002; Moss & Fenster, 2002).

Subsequent chapters in this book include excerpts from actual literary discussions that evolved in the context of cumulative read-aloud/think-aloud sessions in which children listened to and discussed shared texts. Students were invited to talk about their unique, personal, and emotional responses to the aesthetic experience (Rosenblatt, 1978) and to share their understandings, interpretations, and questions as they listened to the texts. They considered the contributions of others and constructed new meanings together in the social context of the classroom. These literary discussions were an integral part of the read-aloud sessions. Discussion began with comments, questions, and predictions triggered by the book's title and the front and back covers and other components of its peritext; the cumulative discussion continued during the unfolding of the story and after its conclusion. Thus the children entered the story world together, building understanding, cover to cover, in an ongoing, shared reading experience. They were actively involved in the collaborative construction of meaning and interpretation *as each text unfolded.* At the conclusion of the shared reading of particular texts, the children were invited to step back from the text to adopt a critical/analytic stance. Deborah Wells (1995) uses the term *grand conversations* to describe literature discussion groups in which children engage in genuine dialogue to explore important ideas and issues. In her book *Knee to Knee, Eye to Eye: Circling in on Comprehension* (2003), Ardith Cole writes: "Literature conversations provide a platform for deep, rich comprehension of text. By developing these classroom structures for talk, teachers can help students collaborate, substantiate their ideas, and negotiate" (p. xiv). According to Cole, literature conversations not only foster deeper comprehension of text, they also have a "positive influence on social interaction, relationships, and community spirit" (p. xv).

Most readers know that independent reading can be meaningful and enjoyable. They also know that sharing reading experiences with others can enrich and extend their solitary transactions with texts. When students have opportunities to talk about books and to share their personal responses, interpretations, and opinions with others in the social context of the classroom, these shared thoughts often trigger further ideas from other participants. As they listen to one another, students discover diverse personal responses to a single shared text as well as multiple perspectives and interpretations. In the process, they learn from others and about others as unique individuals. These literary discussions—whether in response to stories read aloud in a group setting or to stories read independently and then shared—are an integral part of the reading experience in the classroom. Our responsibility as teachers is to introduce students to a rich world of language, ideas, and human experience in the form of poetry, fable, myth, legend, folk and fairy tale, modern fantasy, contemporary and historical realism, biography and autobiography, and informational books. As teachers, we can set the stage for enjoyable literary experiences that enhance the quality of students' responses to and appreciation of literature; that challenge them to stretch their minds and imaginations and open their hearts; and that provide the linguistic and literary knowledge and cognitive strategies needed to generate deeper meanings. Literary selections that invite students to engage with the text and to search for understanding offer the kinds of reading experiences that readers want to share with others (Moss, 2002). Rich interpretive dialogues evolve as students enter into the world of literature, think deeply about the ideas embedded in texts, and engage in a collaborative construction of meaning in the social context of the classroom.

The cumulative read-aloud/think-aloud group sessions also developed students' ability to respond to each new text in light of previous texts. These group sessions formed the core of literature units, and, from one session to the next, students gradually accumulated literary knowledge as well as reading-thinking strategies that enriched their transactions with new texts. As students explored intertextual links, they cycled back to previous texts with new ways to understand subtle meanings and literary patterns and themes in these earlier texts. Each of the literature units described in this book was an integral part of a larger literary/literacy curriculum that included a series of literature units for a given school year in the elementary school. As students became immersed in each successive unit, they carried with them strategies, understandings, and insights gained in previous units. The opportunity to revisit diverse genres and recurring patterns and themes enabled students to probe more deeply into the literary texts they discussed in the group sessions or selected for independent reading.

Scaffolding

Teachers can offer support, or *scaffolding,* to help students learn to use higher-order thinking strategies. The concept of scaffolding is derived from the developmental theories of Lev Vygotsky (1978), a Soviet psychologist who proposed that an adult's assistance enabled a child to function in the "zone of proximal development," an area between what the child can accomplish independently and what the same child can accomplish with assistance. Scaffolded instruction helps children bridge the gap between what they know and what they need to know to become independent learners. To help students learn the reading-thinking strategies used by proficient readers to generate meaning, teachers may model a particular strategy. For example, in order to teach a strategy for using the title and covers of a new text to activate relevant prior knowledge, to fill in gaps in prior knowledge, and to make predictions about the story, the teacher may ask prereading questions such as these:

- What do you think the title means? How do you know that?
- Do you have any questions about anything in the title?
- What do you notice about the illustrations on the front and back covers?
- What clues do you find in the title or in the illustrations that will help you predict what the story is about?
- Why do you think the artist chose that picture for the back cover? Why do you think that?

After modeling prereading questions prior to reading aloud several new books, the teacher gradually withdraws this support and allows the children to assume responsibility for using the title and covers to activate prior knowledge, identify unfamiliar ideas, and make predictions about the story to initiate the meaning-making process. At this point, the teacher may simply hold up the book to show the front and back covers and to read the title as a cue for the children to respond on their own. Next, the teacher may introduce other parts of the peritext with specific questions until the children have internalized the cover-to-cover strategy and will be able to use it when they read independently.

Another type of scaffolding involves thinking aloud. As the teacher reads a story to the students, he or she thinks aloud as the story unfolds to demonstrate strategies he or she, as a proficient reader, uses to generate meaning. For example, the teacher shares his or her inner thoughts in reaching a segment of the text that is confusing and decides to backtrack in order to find a detail that might provide clarification. By externalizing these thinking strategies, by thinking aloud, the teacher allows the students to observe a critical part of the reading process that is usually hidden from them. The teacher gradually withdraws support and invites the students to engage in "think-alouds" themselves as they construct and reconstruct evolving meanings from the unfolding text, in a collaborative interpretive dialogue.

The interpretive dialogue, or "instructional conversation," serves as a context for scaffolding. The teacher helps the students develop a repertoire of reading-thinking strategies through such scaffolding techniques as modeling, thinking aloud, explaining, prompting, rereading key segments of text, asking students to provide textual support for position or interpretative statements, coaching in how to use a strategy to read a new text, constructing visual representations, or sharing information from nonfiction resources to build the background knowledge necessary to comprehend a literary text. As the students gradually internalize the reading-thinking strategies, they assume responsibility for using them to generate meaning in a collaborative dialogue or during independent reading. As students become increasingly active as participants in the social construction of meaning, the teacher gradually becomes a partner or co-participant in the meaning-making process.

Teachers also provide scaffolding by *selecting* texts to read aloud in this social context or to recommend for independent reading. They select texts that foster reader engagement and lively discussion; stimulate critical dialogue about complex social issues of race, class, and gender; facilitate discovery of intertextual links and literature-life connections; and provide opportunities for children to gain insights about the human experience and to learn about literature and the craft of authors and artists. Scaffolding can also be supplied by a learning environment in which peers work collaboratively to solve problems or complete projects. Students provide scaffolding for classmates as they help one another understand a new concept or otherwise serve as resources for one another as they confront challenging tasks together.

In *Lessons in Comprehension: Explicit Instruction in the Reading Workshop* (2004), Frank Serafini features the reading workshop as context for scaffolded instruction. He offers a series of minilessons that teachers can use to help their students learn the strategies they need to understand literature and informational texts. In discussing the nature of "a quality comprehension lesson," Serafini writes: "It is sharing our reading lives, making our literate abilities visible, and maintaining the quality of the learning experience as students assume responsibility for their reading that is the basis for the reading comprehension lessons we provide in our classrooms" (p. 6).

Reading Engagement

Engagement during reading is a state of deep involvement and sustained personal commitment to creating understanding while one reads (Nystrand & Gamoran, 1991). The reader is totally absorbed in the task and is intrinsically motivated to enter into the transaction with the text (Rosenblatt, 1978). Readers who are cognitively engaged use metacognitive and self-regulatory strategies. "That is, students are seen as being cognitively engaged when they are able to regulate their attention and effort, relate new information to existing knowledge, and monitor their comprehension" (Almasi, McKeown, & Beck, 1996, p. 107). John T. Guthrie and his colleagues (Guthrie, Alverson, & Poundstone, 1999) studied students' motivations for reading and noted: "Behind the book-circulation figures in any school is a story of reading engagement. Engaged students are possessed by the desire to find books, dwell in them, and share them with friends" (p. 8).

Janice Almasi and her colleagues (1996) conducted a yearlong study of the nature of engagement in the literature discussions in two fourth-grade classrooms. Their data analysis revealed that students and teachers became cognitively engaged as various tools were used to construct meaningful interpretations of the text: relating the content of the text to personal experiences, movies, or other books; using the text to support ideas or verify or reject earlier predictions; and piecing information together about aspects of the text such as character motives, character actions, or text events (p. 113). They also found that "engagement occurred when teachers provided an environment in which students felt free to ponder or question the text's meaning, content, character motives, text events, or author's craft" (p. 113). They discovered that students' questions played an important role in creating engagement and lively discussion and that students became highly engaged and stimulated when they responded to and challenged one another's interpretations in the course of discussion, or challenged the author's style, or questioned the meaning of the text. Stimulating texts also played an important role in promoting active engagement.

In a discussion of children's literary responses during read-aloud experiences, Sipe (2002) identified a type of expressive engagement in which children "talk back" to the story or characters (p. 477). According to Sipe, "talking back to the story and addressing characters directly begins to blur the distinction between the story world and the children's world. For a moment the two worlds become superimposed—one transparent over the other" (p. 477). Sipe adds that such responses are evidence of children's deep engagement in the story world and that these responses are *"deeply pleasurable* for children" (p. 479, italics in original).

Independent Readers and Writers

The ultimate goal of the comprehension strategy instruction featured in this book is to provide the support students need to become engaged, thoughtful, and independent readers and writers. A review of research focusing on strategy instruction since 1984 (following Palincsar and Brown, 1984) revealed that "across these studies, strategy instruction increased students' willingness to read difficult material, discover meaning in text, and react to and elaborate on text meaning" (Block, Gambrell, & Pressley, 2002, p. 12). In most of these studies, teachers modeled, demonstrated, or explained reading-thinking strategies used by proficient readers and provided opportunities for students to practice and internalize these strategies in a social context in which students collaborated to construct meaning in response to authentic literature. Once the students had internalized these strategies, they could use them to engage in independent reading transactions.

Reading and writing are complementary processes of meaning making and communication. Studies of the relationship between reading and writing demonstrate that readers construct meaning by using their prior knowledge in conjunction with authors' cues, and writers construct meaning by using their prior knowledge in conjunction with their assumptions about the prior knowledge their readers bring to the text. Reading and writing are social activities. "Readers think about authors, and writers think about readers" (Shanahan, 1990, p. 11). Readers can be influenced and informed by an author; writers can influence and inform readers. "Such notions of authorship and audience can only be developed fully when students have available to them the perspectives of both reading and writing . . . . The fusion of reading and writing in the classroom offers children the possibility of participating in both sides of the communication process and, consequently, provides them with a more elaborate grasp of the true meaning of literacy" (p. 4). Once students grasp the close relationship between reading and writing, they will be able to draw from their growing repertoire of reading-thinking strategies to generate meaning as writers.

In classrooms where reading and writing are taught and practiced together in the context of a literature-rich environment, children are given opportunities to record their experiences as aesthetic readers and their responses and interpretations in personal response journals, and to draw from their literary transactions to write their own narratives and poetry and essays. As they extend their reading experiences into writing, children become actively involved as learners and thinkers. Literature has the potential for bringing out what is in the minds and hearts of readers and writers; writing enables them to give voice to thoughts, feelings, opinions, and memories triggered by their reading experiences and to reflect on interpretations, meanings, and questions generated in response to literary texts.

Sandra Stotsky (1983) reviewed the findings from correlational and experimental studies of reading-writing relationships and concluded that "reading experience seems to be a consistent correlate of, or influence on, writing ability. Thus, it is possible that reading experience may be as critical a factor in developing writing ability as writing instruction itself" (p. 637). In an article entitled, "Reading Like a Writer," Frank Smith explains: "To learn to write we must read like a writer . . . . To read like a writer we engage with the author in what the author is writing. We anticipate what the author will say" (1984, pp. 52–53). Smith notes that reading like a writer is the only way to acquire "the intricate complexity of a writer's knowledge" (p. 51). That is, the knowledge that writers require resides in texts, so reading like a writer helps students build a store of writer's knowledge. Children also need to write like readers. According to Smith (1982), the writer becomes a reader during the rewriting phase of the composing process. "Rewriting is the writer's own response to what has been written" (p. 127). Young writers need to become critical readers of their own writing from the viewpoint of their potential audiences. This view of the reading-writing relationship blurs the boundaries between these two aspects of literacy.

Further evidence of the validity of teaching reading and writing together can be found in story grammar research discussed earlier. Nancy Stein (1978), for example, used story grammar in her investigations of children's understanding of stories. By listening to and reading a variety of narratives, children develop a story schema, an implicit knowledge of story grammar or story structure. Stein demonstrated that children use their story schemata both to comprehend and to compose narratives.

Writing can be used as a prereading activity. In a review of writing-to-reading research, Bena Hefflin and Douglas Hartman (2002) describe a variety of practices in which writing is used prior to reading. For example, the *K-W-L model* (Ogle, 1986) was designed as a "framework to elicit students' prior knowledge and engage interest before, during, and after reading expository text" (Hefflin and Hartman, 2002,

p. 205). This model includes a three-step procedure in which the students engage in brainstorming about the topic to identify what they *know;* formulate questions to identify what they *want* to know; and record what they *learned* in response to these questions.

Another procedure, *semantic mapping,* has been used to "organize brainstormed ideas graphically, indicating relationships among ideas and key concepts by labeling lines, boxes, circles, and other geometric shapes with words that are strategically positioned to represent their semantic syntax" (Hefflin and Hartman, 2002, p. 205). In *Webbing with Literature: Creating Story Maps with Children's Books* (1996), Karen Bromley focuses on the use of semantic webbing or mapping as a way of sharing literature with children and fostering greater understanding and appreciation of literature.

The *language experience approach* has been used by teachers of young children since it was introduced by Sylvia Ashton-Warner (1958, 1963), Russell Stauffer (1970), and Roach Van Allen (1976). Children draw from their own personal experiences and interests to create stories that they dictate to the teacher. The children use these dictated stories as reading material that is predictable and readable because it uses their natural language and their own experiences. These dictated experience-stories may also be prompted by an object, event, or topic introduced by the teacher to serve as a stimulus for story development.

Dialogue journals are used as vehicles to establish ongoing written conversations between teachers and students (Staton, 1980). Children are invited to write about their experiences, feelings, thoughts, and questions. In responding to each entry the teacher focuses on the writer's message, not the mechanical aspects of the writing. Teachers encourage more written expression by answering children's questions; by introducing questions and comments that support and extend children's topics; by introducing new or related topics; by expressing appreciation, empathy, understanding, admiration, and other appropriate human responses; and by sharing their own personal thoughts, feelings, and experiences. By responding to the children, teachers show their acceptance of children's ideas and at the same time model accepted conventions of written language in a meaningful context. The dialogue journal provides a context in which reading and writing can be taught as complementary processes of meaning making. The dialogue journal also provides teachers with valuable information about their students as unique individuals and as learners, and can also be used as a vehicle for written literature conversations between the teacher and individual students and among students themselves. The children are invited to write about their reading experiences and to share their responses, in-sights, and interpretations. The teacher or peer-partner responds to each new entry and shares his or her own understandings and interpreta-tions. Oral discussions during the group read-aloud sessions set the stage for written conversations about literature. The literary dialogue journal enables students to respond to authentic literary experiences and to engage in authentic writing intended for a real audience. For chil-dren who are reluctant to contribute to the oral literary discussions, these private written conversations often pave the way for more active par-ticipation in the public arena. The teacher's supportive responses serve to encourage these students to take the leap and to share their ideas and opinions in the social context of a whole class dialogue. This writing-to-reading exchange can even occur through e-mail among students in the same school or among students who live in other parts of the United States or outside.

The *writing workshop* (Atwell, 1987; Calkins, 1986, 1994; Graves, 1983, 2003; Ray, 1999, 2002; Ray & Cleaveland, 2004; Ray & Laminack, 2001) is a predictable time set aside in the school day for students to become actively involved in writing their own texts so they can see themselves as authors. The teacher provides minilessons to focus on procedures or rules for working together in the workshop; literary com-ponents such as setting, characters, problem or plot, and theme; and transcription skills such as punctuation and spelling. Children are en-couraged to read and reread what they write during the composing process so they can monitor their meaning making. They are invited to talk about their writing with a partner or in a small group during the composing process. When children are allowed to think aloud during writing, they help one another clarify meanings by asking questions, making suggestions, or providing relevant information (Cazden, 1981). While the children are working on their pieces, the teacher holds con-ferences with individual children. The children regularly share their work-in-progress with classmates as part of *share sessions* (Calkins, 1994, p. 190). In this context, they gradually develop a sense of audience. The more they think about a potential reader, the more attention they pay to what the reader needs to know or what might be interesting or hu-morous for the reader. *Publication celebrations* are held when students are ready to publish and share their finished work (p. 190).

Looking Ahead

In this book I focus on teaching reading-thinking strategies in the context of authentic literature experiences in which elementary school students respond to literary texts in peer discussions and journals. In subsequent chapters I describe a literary/literacy program in which strategy instruction is woven into literature study experiences. Each chapter includes excerpts from some of the lively discussions that evolved in the course of the cumulative read-aloud/think-aloud group sessions that formed the core of the literature units described in this book. These excerpts illustrate students' personal responses to literary texts and the way they practiced and internalized reading-thinking strategies as they engaged in literary study and collaborated to construct meaning in response to shared literary texts, to explore multiple perspectives, and to elaborate on these meanings through critical thinking and literary interpretation.

The literature units described in this book highlight elements of comprehension instruction embedded in a literary/literacy program designed to help elementary school students discover the joy of literary learning as they engage in the process of becoming thoughtful readers and writers. Teachers who read this book are invited to create their own literature units to fit their unique teaching styles and curricular goals and to meet the diverse needs and interests of their students. They are encouraged to use literature units as a framework for teaching and practicing reading-thinking strategies. "Comprehension instruction is a creative process, and no two teachers will approach it exactly the same way . . . . The creative instruction students receive in learning how to comprehend during elementary school will accrue over time in heightened reasoning abilities as they make their way through the grades to high school and beyond" (Barton & Sawyer, 2003/2004, p. 346).

2 Text Sets in the Kindergarten

Cumulative Literary Experiences

Text sets are collections of books that are conceptually related in terms of themes, genres, topics, and text types (Short, Harste, & Burke, 1996). When children are given an opportunity to listen to or read a series of conceptually related texts, they are likely to identify interesting connections and to generate questions that lead to inquiry and discovery. This chapter features two examples of cumulative literary experiences or "literature units" structured around text sets. Each text set was created to provide a context for generating cumulative literary discussions, demonstrating and practicing reading-thinking strategies, and exploring literary concepts.

A Text Set Featuring Traditional and Modern Retellings of "Goldilocks and the Three Bears"

Objectives for This Literature Unit

1. To introduce children to a traditional tale that has been retold by diverse writers and artists over the years

2. To provide opportunities for children to respond to each new text *as it unfolds* in a read-aloud/think-aloud group session

3. To provide opportunities for children to compare each new text with previous texts read aloud in a series of read-aloud/ think-aloud group sessions and to identify similarities and differences among these retellings

4. To introduce children to modern retellings of this traditional tale

5. To provide opportunities for children to discover the ways modern writers and artists have revised and changed this traditional tale and to reflect on the reasons for these changes

6. To provide opportunities for children to discover some of the reading-thinking strategies used by experienced readers in their transactions with literary texts

7. To provide opportunities for children to engage in independent reading experiences at school and at home

---

> 8. To provide an opportunity for children to engage in a collaborative writing project to compose their own modern retelling of this traditional tale
>
> 9. To provide opportunities for children to reflect on the choices made by the central character and to consider alternative choices

Session 1

Traditional and modern retellings of "Goldilocks and the Three Bears" were read aloud and discussed in a series of group sessions that formed the core of this literature unit.[1] *The Three Bears* retold and illustrated by Paul Galdone (1972) was introduced in the first group session. Although many of the children said they knew this story, they were not familiar enough with this traditional tale to retell it as a cohesive narrative. The children were invited to examine the front and back covers of the book and to comment on what they noticed. This invitation set the stage for the children to engage in a cover-to-cover study of this shared text (Strategy 1):

> "It looks like a bear family. The father bear has his arm around the mother bear."
> "She's holding the baby, and the baby has a teddy bear!"
> "The father bear is really big and scary-looking."
> "But, look, he's smiling!"
> "That girl on the back cover is smiling, too. Is that Goldilocks?"

When the teacher showed them the title page, the children shared what they noticed:

> "There's an arrow sign. It has the title printed on it."
> "I think it's pointing to the forest—that must be where the three bears are."

The children were invited to continue to share their observations *as the story unfolded.* For example, they noticed that the size of the print corresponded to the size of each bear as it was mentioned in the text. However, one child was surprised to see that in the picture of the three bears sitting in their chairs, the baby bear is reading a large book, the mother is reading a middle-sized book, and the father is reading a small book. Another child recognized that the picture of Goldilocks sitting in "the chair of the Little Wee Bear" was the same as the picture on the back cover. The text ends with the words: "And she ran away as fast as she could, never looking behind her. No one knows what happened to Goldilocks after that. As for the Three Bears, they never saw her again."

The teacher asked: "Why do you think Goldilocks ran away?" This question prompted the children to engage in think-alouds (Strategy 13) as they inferred unstated ideas in this story (Strategy 3):

> "She knew she wasn't supposed to be in their house!"
> "She was probably scared when she saw them looking at her."
> "She thought they were going to chase her."
> "But the bears just looked *surprised* to see someone in their house. They didn't look mad."
> "And it didn't say they were mad at her. They seemed like nice bears."
> "*We* know they're nice, but *Goldilocks* didn't know that."

The teacher encouraged metacognition (Strategy 12) by asking: "How do you know the bears are nice?"

> "Because on the front cover, they were smiling and they looked like a happy family."
> "And the big bear was pushing the baby bear on the swing. And when they went for a walk, he carried the baby bear on his shoulders. He's a nice daddy."
> "And when they saw the mess she made, they just seemed surprised. Their eyes were round."

Then the teacher observed: "That was a good clue you used to figure out how the bears felt about their uninvited visitor. How did you know how Goldilocks felt?"

> "Probably her mom told her not to just go in someone's house. That's what my mom says to me. You have to wait to get invited in."
> "I think she felt scared because she knew she did something wrong."
> "I think she was scared because her mom must have told her to stay away from bears, and she didn't know it was the bears' house. When we go camping in the woods, we have to watch out for the bears!"
> "But it doesn't say anything like that in the story. We didn't get to meet her mom."
> "I wonder what her mom is going to say when she comes home."
> "Maybe she won't even tell her mom what she did."
> "I guess we have to just imagine it."

The teacher responded: "You have used some of your own experiences to figure out how Goldilocks felt when she woke up and saw the bears. This is just what good readers do! They look for clues and use their own experiences or their imaginations to figure out what is *not* included in the stories they listen to or read."

This excerpt from the children's comments about this story suggests that they had "stepped inside the story world" and were generating a subtext as they imagined the thoughts and feelings of the characters (Clyde, 2003).

Session 2

Goldilocks and the Three Bears (Brett, 1987) was introduced in the second group session. After the children examined the front and back covers, they were asked to compare this book with Galdone's book. They noticed that, unlike Galdone's bears, who were not wearing clothes, Brett's bears were wearing colorful clothing. They also noticed that Brett included Goldilocks in the title and there was a picture of Goldilocks at the top of the front cover instead of on the back cover. After a careful examination of the family of bears on the front cover, the children identified the bear pictured on the back cover as the baby bear ". . . because he's wearing the same blue shirt the baby bear is wearing on the front cover." When the children recognized Goldilocks featured on the title page and the three bears in the frame surrounding this double-page spread, they decided that Jan Brett had changed the illustrations to fit the title:

> "She has Goldilocks in the title, so she shows her right away . . . picking flowers. In the other book, we didn't see her until after the bears left their house."
> "And in this story, Goldilocks has braids instead of curls."
> "And she [Brett] put some mice in that picture. I wonder if she's going to have mice on the other pages, too."
> "I have a book by this author, and she has things happening all around the pictures . . . like in this book. Even on the cover, there's Goldilocks sleeping on the top."

At this point, the teacher pointed to other examples of illustrations surrounded by frames and inserted a comment about the craft of this artist: "Jan Brett often has interesting *frames* or borders around her pictures. Her frames often tell more of the story." This prompted children's comments:

> "So it's like a picture frame [he pointed to a framed picture on the wall]. But it's different because a lot of her [the artist's] frames have pictures *on* them!"
> "She [Brett] usually draws fancy clothes in her books, and this house is fancier than the other one [in Galdone's retelling], but the furniture is made out of logs like that one."

"You can tell it's a happy bear family like in the other one [points to the picture of the father bear playing with the baby bear]."

"And on the last page the bears are all snuggling together."

"The ending is the same as the other one—the same words. And it doesn't say anything about the mom and dad or what happened when she got home."

"I think her mom will say 'Where have you been?' and Goldilocks will say she was chased by bears!"

"I noticed something! When the bears are walking out of their house, you can see Goldilocks in the woods . . . in the frame. And when Goldilocks is in their house, you can see the bears in the woods . . . in the frame." [This observation prompted the children to return to the illustrations with the dual settings.]

"I noticed something else. The color of the bowls match their shirts!"

"And this story is like the other one . . . .Big size is for Big Bear, medium size is for Mama, and little size is for Baby Bear. [This child had just figured out this one-to-one correspondence as a pattern and was delighted with her discovery. Throughout this read-aloud session, she focused on the repetitive patterns.] And in both stories, each page copies itself! Like 'just right, just right.'"

The teacher responded with the word for this discovery: "Yes, many of the old stories have *patterns* that are repeated again and again." She also reinforced the notion that good readers compare each new story they hear or read with other stories they already know. She added that good readers look carefully at all parts of the book, from cover to cover, in search of clues that would help them understand and enjoy the story. The teacher concluded: "Your comments about this story show that you are doing just what good readers do!"

At the end of the second session, the teacher held up Valeri Gorbachev's retelling of *Goldilocks and the Three Bears* (2001). The children noticed that the three bears on the front cover were wearing clothes and sitting in front of "a regular house" and that Goldilocks was on the back cover.

"She's peeking in the window at the three bowls of porridge."

"And there she is walking through the forest all by herself [she pointed to the endpapers]. It's like the other book with Goldilocks in the title! The artist shows her inside the book even before the bears."

"I like the picture on the first page of the story. The big bear is playing on a little violin, and the mother is reading a book, and the little bear is eating honey!"

"Bears like honey. Remember in that one [he pointed to Brett's retelling] there was a beehive on the first page [the first title page], and then there was that other little picture of Baby Bear carrying a beehive?"

"Here it is . . . it's in a frame" [she found the picture in Brett's book].

"And he has a teddy bear—like in that one" [he pointed to Galdone's retelling, on display by the story circle with the other texts they had heard].

Session 3

David McPhail's small illustrated edition of *Goldilocks and the Three Bears* (1995) was introduced in the third session, and the children initiated the cover-to-cover study of this book. They commented on the small size of the book and then identified the three bears on the front cover and Goldilocks on the back cover and "the three bowls of porridge on the first title page" and "the three bears' cottage on the next title page." As the children listened to the story unfold and examined McPhail's illustrations, they noticed that this Goldilocks had straight golden hair instead of curls. But they were especially surprised to hear the text opposite the picture of Goldilocks walking along the path through the forest: "You might say that Goldilocks was a spoiled child because she always got her way. Her mother and father were good people, but they couldn't bear to say *no* to her. So Goldilocks grew up thinking she could have whatever she wanted" (n.p.). The children immediately responded to this new segment in a now-familiar text:

"He [McPhail] added something!"
"I think he's trying to explain *why* Goldilocks just walked in the bears' house without even being invited!"
"Whenever my little sister screams she gets what she wants."
"Maybe that's what Goldilocks did."
"So she got spoiled. Spoiled kids get mad when they don't get their way."

Two pages later, McPhail expands the traditional text again: "The bears—who trusted everyone and were very trustworthy themselves—never locked their door, and on this day, had not even bothered to latch it." The children decided that McPhail added these words to explain why the bears had not locked their door when they went out for a walk. The next pages of the story are similar to the traditional retellings. By this time the children were ready to chime in with the familiar patterns to help tell this story. However, McPhail adds two new pages of text *after* the traditional ending: "Despite their experience with Goldilocks, the three bears went on as before, and to this day, they still don't lock their door." The picture under this text shows the bears setting out on another walk. The text on the last page reads: "As for Goldilocks, she learned a lesson she never forgot, and she never again entered anyone's house without first being invited" (n.p.). The picture below this text reveals the little bear standing at the door talking with Goldilocks. The children used the clues in the text to figure out the meaning of this illustration:

> "I think the baby bear is inviting her into his house" [he pointed to the illustration in which the baby bear is beckoning to Goldilocks].
> "She was waiting to be invited."
> "I think he's asking her, 'Why did you break my chair? Why did you eat my porridge?'"
> "Maybe she's going to apologize. I think they're going to be friends."
> "Maybe she's not going to be so spoiled now."

After the children talked about the changes in McPhail's retelling, the teacher asked: "Why do you think Mr. McPhail decided to add these new parts to this very old story?"

> "I think he wanted to *explain* things."
> "In the other stories, it doesn't say *why* she just walked in. That really didn't seem right!"
> "Maybe *he* thought the same thing when *he* heard the story, so he fixed it."
> "Maybe he wanted to make sure kids didn't copy Goldilocks. Maybe he wanted to teach them not to just walk into someone's house!"
> "I like this new ending. It answers our questions."

By this time, the children were discovering that different artists illustrated this old tale in different ways and that some retellers, such as McPhail, chose to make small, but significant, changes in the traditional text. In subsequent group sessions, as the children listened to additional retellings, the teacher invited them to look for other changes made by different artists and retellers.

Session 4

Armand Eisen's retelling of *Goldilocks and the Three Bears* (1987) was read aloud in the fourth session. At this point in the cumulative experience, the children were ready to engage in an ongoing think-aloud as they responded to the pictures and helped to tell this familiar story. One child noted the beehive on the page prior to the two title pages and recalled that Jan Brett had included a beehive on one of her title pages. The teacher responded to this discovery by returning to Brett's retelling, pointing to the beehive on the first title page, and asking: "Why did these artists decide to place a beehive at the beginning of the book?"

> "It's because bears like honey! Remember in that book [he pointed to Gorbachev's book], it shows the baby bear eating honey."

In response, the teacher reached for Gorbachev's book and turned to the page with this picture and read the text. She asked, "How do you know he's eating honey? It doesn't say that in the story."

> "I don't know—I just thought it was honey."
> "I figured it out because bears like honey and the little bear looks happy in that picture."
> "And anyway, we have a honey pot just like that one! So it probably *is* honey."

The teacher observed: "So, many of you used clues from your own experiences and what you already knew about bears to figure this out. That's just what good readers do when they read stories!" Throughout this cumulative experience with diverse retellings of a single traditional tale, the teacher talked about the kinds of strategies good readers use to generate meaning. The previous excerpt illustrates the children's use of metacognition to figure out how they used their prior knowledge to fill in gaps in a literary text and to make inferences as they interacted with this text (see Strategies 2, 3, and 12). The teacher's remarks prompted additional interpretations. For example, one child commented on the picture of the three bowls of porridge on the major title page:

> "The big one has steam coming out of it—that's because it was too hot! And the little one is empty, so it shows that Goldilocks already ate it all up!"

Another child pointed to the dedication page, which includes a picture of a toy bear sitting next to a bowl and holding a spoon, and predicted that the baby bear would have a toy bear in this story "just like that one." (He pointed to Galdone's book.) As each new retelling was read aloud, it was added to the book display next to the story circle. The children pointed to particular texts as they engaged in comparative analysis and made intertextual comments.

As Eisen's retelling unfolded, one child noticed something interesting in the picture opposite the page in which Goldilocks is introduced: "She's holding a doll that looks just like her!" This comment prompted several students to search for and point out this doll in other pictures. They noticed that when Goldilocks is shown asleep in Baby Bear's bed, she is holding a toy bear, and the doll is shown in the frame. It seems to be sitting on the floor leaning against the wall. Several children responded to this illustration:

> "Did she drop her doll when she went to sleep?"
> "Maybe she thought the teddy bear was more cuddly. That must be the bear that Baby Bear sleeps with."
> "That's what I thought when we saw that picture of the toy bear sitting next to the bowl!" [He was delighted to be able to confirm his earlier prediction.]

The last page of text reads: "Just then Goldilocks woke up to see the three bears looking down at her. Do you know what she did then? Why, Goldilocks sprang out of bed and ran down the stairs and out the front door. She did not stop until she was all the way home. And the three bears never set eyes on Goldilocks again." On the bottom of this page is a picture of Baby Bear holding the doll. The children were eager to talk about the changes made by the reteller and artist:

> "It's the same words at the end, but he [Eisen] sort of sounds like a teacher."
> "That's what I thought. Like when we're listening to a story, you [the teacher] say, 'What do you think is going to happen next?'"
> "In the picture, it looks like Baby Bear found Goldilocks's doll. I think maybe Goldilocks took his bear home with her."
> "So they can remember each other!"
> "Remember in that one [he pointed to McPhail's retelling]? They got to be friends."

The framed picture on the final page of the book reveals Goldilocks hugging her mother. There are no words on this page, and the picture prompted the children to wonder what Goldilocks is telling her mother and to answer their own question (Strategy 8):

> "I think she's telling the whole story of how she went into the forest to pick flowers and how she found this house and no one was home and she went in . . . ."
> "I don't think she told *everything* that happened."
> "It looks like her mom is asking her why she came home so late."
> "I bet Goldilocks never tells her all the stuff she did. Her mom will never find out."
> "Unless she reads this book!"

Session 5

Lorinda Bryan Cauley's *Goldilocks and the Three Bears* (1981), introduced in the fifth session, is another example of a retelling with new details added to the traditional text. The children again initiated a cover-to-cover study of this book:

> "The bear family is on the front, and Goldilocks is on the back, reading a book."
>
> "There's Little Bear looking at an empty bowl [she pointed to the front flap]. I think he must be sad because his porridge is gone."
>
> "There's the bear family again! [The teacher held up the first page.] But this time the father bear is reading, and the mother is sewing, and the little bear is reading, too. So he must not be a baby if he can read!"

On the next page Goldilocks and her mother are introduced, and the text reads: "That morning her mother sent her out to pick flowers to keep her out of mischief. (Goldilocks was *always* getting into trouble)" (n.p.). The next page suggests what kind of mischief she gets into. The children compared this segment with McPhail's description of Goldilocks:

> "Both of them [Cauley and McPhail] added stuff to explain *why* Goldilocks messed up the bears' house!"

The children noticed another change in this text. When Goldilocks tries out the three chairs in the bears' house, the small chair breaks because "she rocked and she rocked and she rocked until the bottom fell out, and down she came, bang, on the floor!"

> "In the other stories the chair broke when she sat down. But in this one she rocked too hard. I guess she got into mischief again!"

They also noticed that the reactions of the bears to Goldilocks's mischief were more intense than in the other stories:

> "In this story, the papa bear 'growled' and the mama bear 'scowled' and the baby bear 'wailed.'"
>
> "Their faces look angry. In the other stories, they looked sort of surprised."
>
> "And the big bear makes his fist like this [a clenched fist] to show he's mad."

To reinforce their observations, the teacher read the next page, in which the bears decide to go upstairs: "Papa Bear was in a rage, wondering who would dare come into their house without being invited. So huffing and puffing, up the stairs they all went to see if anyone was there" (n.p.). After she is discovered, Goldilocks runs through the woods, "but it seemed as if the woods were full of wild bears, so she ran faster and faster." The children examined Cauley's illustration and noticed the ghost-like bears in the forest and the trees with eyes that seem to be looking at Goldilocks. Several children interpreted this scene:

"I don't think there're *really* ghosts there. I think maybe she's so scared, she *thinks* she sees them."

"But she sees those eyes staring at her—and she *knows* she's in trouble."

" She knows she did something wrong. Maybe the ghosts know it, too."

"But it could be her imagination. Those eyes are really knot-holes in the tree."

On the last page, there is a picture of Goldilocks and her mother, and her mother is holding her on her lap. The text reads: "When Goldilocks was safe at home, her mother gave her a scolding she did not soon for-get. And she made up her mind never again to make herself quite so much at home as she did in the house of the three bears" (n.p.). This ending prompted a number of interesting comments:

"So in *this* story, she must have told her mom the whole story. That's why she got scolded."

"In that other one [Eisen's retelling] we don't know if she told the whole story. It doesn't say she got scolded. We just don't know. This one is different."

"This one gives you more clues to figure things out."

"These stories [she pointed to the retellings of Cauley and McPhail] tell more about Goldilocks and her mom . . . and Goldilocks learned a lesson . . . like she probably wouldn't just go in houses when she's not invited."

"In the stories we heard first, they didn't tell what happened *after* she ran away."

"I remember another clue in this one [Cauley's retelling]! See on the back cover, it shows Goldilocks reading a book? Maybe she's learning not to be so mischievous. It looks like she can sit quietly and read a book like the little bear—remember that first picture of Little Bear reading?"

At this point the teacher articulated for the children what strategies they had used to respond to these stories: "You have been using *clues* in the words and the pictures to figure out what is *not* included in the story. And I noticed you went back to the book to find more clues, such as that picture on the back cover! This is just what good readers do when they listen to or read a story. Also, I noticed the way you compared all these stories and found interesting connections and differences. Good readers do this, too."

Session 6

Leola and the Honeybears: An African-American Retelling of Goldilocks and the Three Bears (Rosales, 1999) was introduced in the sixth session. For this new version of "Goldilocks and the Three Bears," Melodye Rosales draws from her own family memories. She retells this old tale from the viewpoint of Leola, an African American girl who lives with her grandmama "in a small, cozy cottage not far from the Pine Hollow Woods" (p. 8). Her grandmama warns her: "Don't go straying off anywhere. And don't go talking to any strangers" (p. 7). However, Leola doesn't pay attention to her grandmama and sets off on her own, saying, "'I'm going to do what I want to'" (p. 8). She chases some milkweed pods until she suddenly discovers she has entered the Pine Hollow Woods and is lost. These woods are the home of a family known as the Honeybears, who own an inn frequented by "woodland folks from far and near" (p. 12). When Leola reaches the "deepest, darkest part of Pine Hollow Woods" (p. 16), she encounters Mister Weasel, who wants to eat her. Leola runs away from him and discovers a little house in a large clearing. At this point, the story follows the familiar pattern of tasting the food, trying the chairs, and finally falling asleep in "Lil' Honey's little bed" (p. 26). When the Honeybears return to their home and find a stranger in Lil' Honey's bed, Mama Honeybear says to Leola: "Didn't your folks teach you any manners?" (p. 32). Leola tells them about her Grandmama and Mister Weasel and finishes her story with: ". . . and I was so scared and hungry I didn't think anyone would mind, *just this time*" (p. 32). Mama Honeybear forgives Leola, gives her "a tender good-bye bear hug" (p. 35), and asks Miss Blackbird to guide her home. The story ends with these words: "From that day on—even when she wanted to do what she wanted to—Leola always listened to her Grandmama. (Well . . . most of the time.) And she never strayed too far from home again" (p. 37).

The children initiated a cover-to-cover study of this book by talking about the title and the pictures on the front cover and the first few pages:

> "The title doesn't have Goldilocks in it, and it has Honeybears instead of three bears, and the girl on the cover has black curls instead of yellow hair, and she has a doll that looks like her."
> "There's a blackbird with a purple hat on the cover . . . and it's on the first two pages, too. We should look for that bird on the other pages."
> "The bears are different colors, and on the back cover the bears are with *other* animals. I think this must be a different story."

As the children listened to the story unfold, they entered into it and responded emotionally to Leola. For example, several children called out, "She's spoiled!" when they heard that Leola did not pay attention to her grandmother and said, "I'm going to do what I want to." One child pointed to the McPhail retelling on display near the story circle and said, "She's just like Goldilocks in *that* story!" When Leola chases the milkweed pods, one child said: "Oh no . . . she's going into the forest . . . she's going to get lost!" When Leola meets Mister Weasel, another child cried out: "I bet he wants to eat her! She better run away!" After this scene, the child who responded to the cover with "This must be a different story" observed: "Leola is on the cover in front of the bears, and this story is really all about *her.* I don't think this *is* the three bears' story!" Several children focused on the blackbird with the purple hat that reappeared as the story unfolded. They noticed that the picture inside the Honeybears' inn shows the blackbird wearing a red hat. Some thought it was the same bird with a new hat; others said there were two birds with different hats. They also discovered that part of this picture was on the back cover, and they found the answer to their question about the other animals. When Leola enters the Honeybears' house to escape from Mister Weasel, the children immediately recognized the familiar elements of "The Three Bears" story and chimed in with the repetitive patterns about the food, chairs, and beds. When Mama Honeybear asks Miss Blackbird to guide Leola to her home, the children's eyes lit up with recognition: "Look! It's the purple hat bird!"

The illustration opposite the last page of text shows Leola sitting on her grandmother's lap. This scene prompted a number of responses:

> "There's Miss Blackbird flying away!"
> "I think Leola didn't tell her grandmama she went into the woods."
> "Me too. I think she told a lie."
> "I think she's telling the truth to her grandma."
> "Leola said, 'I will listen to you.'" [This child paraphrased the lines in the text, but she was providing textual support for the child who speculated that Leola was telling the truth.]
> "And she's helping. She's folding the laundry [she pointed to the small picture on the last page]. And they're both smiling!"
> "Grandma loves Leola and was worried about her. Grandma and Leola must have worked things out after Leola told her what happened." [This comment was offered by the boy who said earlier, "I think she told a lie." He had apparently revised his interpretation after hearing the comments of the other children.]

At the conclusion of their discussion about this story, the children were eager to talk about the differences between this retelling and the earlier stories introduced in the previous sessions:

> "In this story, the *reason* she goes into the three bears' house is

different. She got lost and got chased by Mister Weasel. He was going to eat her! So she *couldn't* go home!"

"I think it was okay to go in the house to hide from the weasel, but she shouldn't have eaten the food and stuff."

"It was pies instead of porridge. That was different! And it was an inn, not a cottage."

"In this one you knew what Leola was thinking, and she talked to the bears."

"That part was different—she *explained* to them why she walked in their house!"

"I liked the ending in this one. The mother bear was nice. She gave Leola a hug and a basket of food and asked Miss Blackbird to take her home so she wouldn't get lost again."

"She forgave Leola for making such a mess, and it says they're friends."

"I bet Leola goes back to visit them—maybe with the bird. It's like that one that shows Little Bear talking to Goldilocks on the last page" [McPhail's retelling].

"This one is *much* different from the other stories. This one was scary—when that weasel came and was going to eat her."

"I like this one better than the other ones. It has more action."

"And Leola was more interesting than Goldilocks. I liked the way she changed in the end. I think she was glad Mama Bear was nice to her."

Session 7

Heidi Petach's *Goldilocks and the Three Hares* (1995) is a humorous modern revision of the traditional tale. When it was introduced, in the seventh session, the children noticed the wordplay in the title and the amusing details in the illustrations on the front and back covers. They observed that on the back cover the words EIGHT MICE are printed on the other side of the sign with the title on the front cover and that EIGHT MICE is printed so it can be read if the book is turned upside down. As the story was read aloud, the children were delighted to discover all the changes made by this author/artist. For example, they noticed that the hare family lives in an underground home and that a family of mice lives below them. The mice carry on a running commentary filled with jokes and puns and remarks about the artist. One child commented: "So the back cover is about the second story—the eight mice!" Another child noticed: "All the characters talk in 'speech bubbles'!"

The children noticed that when the mama hare burns the oatmeal and the hare family goes out for breakfast, Goldilocks is playing ball above them. The ball rolls down the rabbit hole, and Goldilocks looks for it and falls into the hole . . . "Like *Alice in Wonderland!!*" When she finds herself in the hares' house, she tries their oatmeal, chairs, and beds.

The children discovered a parallel story in the pictures: While Goldilocks is in the hares' house, the mice are trying to escape from two weasels by hiding in the hare house. They manage to outsmart the weasels and tie them up with yoyo string. When the hares return and realize that someone has been in their home, they call the police, who find the weasels, a famous robber gang! The robbers are arrested, and Goldilocks wakes up and appears to think she's Dorothy in *The Wizard of Oz*. The children who were familiar with this story identified the clues:

> "When Goldilocks talked to Mama Hare, she called her Auntie Em!"
> "And then she said she would fix the chair she broke and called it Toto's chair. That was Dorothy's dog!"

Session 8

Prior to the eighth session, the children were introduced to additional retellings of this traditional tale and invited to choose one of these new books to read independently or with a partner at school or to share with their parents at home. These new books along with the shared texts made up the complete text set that was displayed near the story circle. After the children had had an opportunity to select one of these books and to read it at school or at home, they gathered together for the eighth session to share what they had discovered about each of the books they had selected.

> *Goldilocks and the Three Bears,* by Janet Stevens (1986), triggered the following comments:

> > "She [the reteller] didn't change much—except at the end when Goldilocks ran away and said she wasn't going to wander alone in the forest anymore, and Papa Bear locked the door!"
> > "In this one the bears looked mad when they saw that someone had been eating their porridge and sitting in their chairs."

> *Goldilocks and the Three Bears* (Watts, 1985). The children who selected Bernadette Watts's *Goldilocks and the Three Bears* noticed the Bear family on the front cover and the mama bear painting on the back cover:

> > "It looks like she's painting the flowers that are on the endpapers!"
> > "On the title page, the three bears are looking at Goldilocks. I wonder if they knew her before she came into their house."
> > "I noticed something. When Goldilocks was walking in the woods, she was carrying a butterfly net. When the bears were walking home, the net was on the ground. On the next page, the net is against the door."

"On the front cover and the back cover Little Bear is holding the net, so maybe he found it and brought it home."

"Or it could be that she found *his* net!"

"On the last page, it says she never went back to the bears' cottage. So they didn't get to be friends like in the story about Leola."

The Rebus Bears (Reit, 1989, 1997) is one of the Bank Street Ready-to-Read series designed for children who are beginning to read independently. The children who selected this book were delighted to be able to read this tale on their own with the help of a familiar narrative and the rebus pictures. They also enjoyed sharing the pictures in this session.

Goldilocks and the Three Bears (Marshall, 1988) was selected by children who were already familiar with James Marshall's humorous picture books. They brought the book to the group session so they could share their favorite parts. For example, they asked the teacher to read aloud the opening lines: "Once there was a little girl called Goldilocks. 'What a sweet child,' said someone new in town. 'That's what you think,' said a neighbor" (n. p.). The children responded:

"She's like the Goldilocks in some of the other stories. Her mother *warned* her not to take the shortcut because of the bears, but Goldilocks didn't pay any attention because she always did what she wanted to do—like Leola."

"Here's the picture of her going into the forest. The big sign says SHORTCUT and the little signs say Danger and Turn Back and Not a Good Idea!"

"My favorite picture is Baby Bear's bed. You can hardly see it under the toys and books and stuff. It looks like my bedroom!"

Deep in the Forest (Turkle, 1976) is a wordless book about a curious bear cub that visits the cabin of a pioneer family out for a walk in the forest. The children enjoyed reading this humorous modern revision of the traditional tale. They were delighted to be able to provide the text throughout the story and to identify Goldilocks when she and her family return to their cabin and discover the little bear!

The Three Bears Rhyme Book (Yolen, 1987) includes fifteen poems that feature the three bears and their friend Goldie as they take a walk, eat porridge, have a birthday party, and engage in other activities. Each poem is told in the first person by Baby Bear, who calls his friend "Goldie." One child brought the book to the group session to share some of her favorite poems. She also pointed to the title page, which shows Goldie sitting outside with Little Bear, who is next to her watching as she writes in a notebook, and to the back cover, which shows Goldilocks sitting under a tree holding a book. She shared her interpretation: "I think that's her writing book, and she's writing the poems that Little Bear is telling her because they're his poems in the book but he doesn't know how to write yet." [Later, the teacher read aloud some of these poems to inspire the children to write or draw and dictate original poetry or prose about these story characters in their own writing books or journals.]

Goldie and the Three Bears (Stanley, 2003) is a contemporary revision of this traditional tale that features Goldie, a young girl who "knew exactly what she liked—and what she didn't" (n.p.). Her search for a friend ends with success when she encounters Baby Bear. The child who read this book with her parents compared it with McPhail's retelling. This child observed that Stanley's retelling is the only one in which Baby Bear is a girl, who seems to be about the same size and age as Goldilocks.

Goldilocks and the Three Bears (Aylesworth, 2003) features bowls, chairs, beds, and a beehive hidden in the frame of the picture on the front cover. The same frame on the back cover includes a recipe for "Mama Bear's Porridge Cookies." A child who selected this book observed that the picture on the dedication page, in which Goldilocks is standing with her hands on her hips, was a clue that this story would be like the "other stories with a spoiled and selfish Goldilocks." This child explained that she knew her prediction was right as soon as her mom read the first page! Another child noted that the problem with Goldilocks in this story was "she was just too curious so she forgot what her mom told her!" A third child compared the last page with the conclusions in other retellings: "This one shows her with her mom like in those stories [he pointed to Eisen's retelling and to Cauley's retelling], and it says she's going to remember to do what her mom tells her. So in this one Goldilocks learns a lesson!"

Goldilocks Returns (Ernst, 2000). In this humorous sequel, Goldilocks returns to the home of the three bears fifty years after her initial visit. This time, she decides to "set things right" (n.p.). One child who shared this book explained that Goldilocks had changed because she wanted to do something nice for the bear family. But two other children who read this book disagreed, and identified clues in the text that suggested she was "still doing what *she* wanted to do!"

Goldilocks and the Three Martians (Smith, 2004). The artist, Michael Garland, uses colorful computer graphics for this humorous, outer-space revision of the traditional tale, which inspired a number of children to create their own illustrations to portray Goldilocks' adventures in other settings.

Stella Louella's Runaway Book (Ernst, 1998). As Stella looks for the book she must return to the library that day, a growing group of people who have enjoyed reading the book join in the search. As the characters share their favorite parts of the book, the reader discovers that it is *The Three Bears*. The children who selected this book identified the clues they had used to figure out the title of the book Stella had lost, and they also noted that the story of Stella's search was like the story of *The Gingerbread Man*.

The children's spontaneous comments about the books selected for independent reading demonstrated that they had internalized the cover-to-cover strategies introduced during the group read-aloud sessions. They used terms such as *endpapers* and *title page* to talk about the stories. They drew from their growing repertoire of reading-thinking strategies to focus on clues in the text, illustrations, and intertextual links to generate meaning in response to these retellings and revisions.

Dramatic Play

After the children had had an opportunity to share their thoughts about the books they had selected, the teacher placed four hand puppets, Goldilocks and the three bears, on the display table with the text set and invited the children to use these for dramatic play during Choice Time. The titles in this text set continued to be available for the children to read or reread independently or with a partner in the classroom or with members of their families at home throughout the school year.

Collaborative Writing Project

This study of diverse retellings and modern revisions of the traditional tale "Goldilocks and the Three Bears" concluded with a collaborative writing project in which the children worked together to create their own illustrated revision of this story. In preparation for this creative process, they were invited to review the stories introduced in the group sessions by identifying the recurring patterns in these stories as well as the changes made by different retellers and artists. The findings from this story review were recorded on a wall chart under the headings "Same" and "Different." The teacher explained that their own story should include the basic story parts listed under "Same," but they could decide what would be new or different in their own story. Then they worked together to create a *story map* for their new story by responding to the teacher's questions: What is the setting (or settings) in your story? Who are the characters in your story? What is the problem (or problems) in your story? How will the problem(s) be solved? How will your story end? The children's revision of this old tale was entitled: "Goldilocks and Leola and the Bear Families." After they voted on which new elements they would include in their story, the children dictated a collaboratively constructed narrative, and then each child chose a scene he or she wanted to illustrate. When the text and pictures were ready to be put together into a bound volume, the children decided what to include on the covers, title page, dedication page, and authors' biographies at the end of the story. The finished product was shared with other classes and displayed with the books by professional writers and artists featured in this literature unit. Copies of this illustrated story were made available for each child to take home.

Looking Back

The primary purpose for developing this cumulative literary experience structured around a text set was to expose the children to a traditional tale that is an integral part of their literary heritage and to introduce them to diverse writers and artists who have retold and revised this old tale over the years. By engaging in a comparative study of these diverse retellings, the children had an opportunity to discover the ways modern writers and artists have retold, revised, and changed this traditional tale and to reflect on the reasons for these changes. The children noticed that some of these retold and revised tales focused on the choices made by the central character and challenged readers to consider alternative choices. They identified and discussed stories in which the central character is more fully developed and changes her attitudes and behavior at the end of the story. In the tradition of Paulo Freire's (2000) "transformative education," the children engaged in critical analysis that led to a growing awareness of their own power to transform themselves.

In the course of this study of a single traditional tale, the teacher discovered significant gaps in the children's knowledge of other traditional tales that, at one time, had been shared as a regular part of bedtime read-aloud routines for many preschool children. In order to fill in these gaps in their literary backgrounds, the teacher decided to introduce some of these traditional tales to the children and to add them to the display of the retellings of "The Three Bears." She selected tales retold and illustrated by Paul Galdone: *The Three Little Pigs* (1970b), *The Three Billy Goats Gruff* (1973b), *The Little Red Hen* (1973a), *Henny Penny* (1968), *The Gingerbread Boy* (1975), *Rumpelstiltskin* (1985), *Cinderella* (1978), *Hansel and Gretel* (1982), *The Elves and the Shoemaker* (1984), *Little Red Riding Hood* (1974), *The Magic Porridge Pot* (1976), and *Androcles and the Lion* (1970a). Charlotte Huck, an emeritus professor of education at Ohio State University and authority in children's literature, and Barbara Ziefer emphasize the value of folk literature for young children: "Traditional literature is a rightful part of a child's literary heritage and lays the groundwork for understanding all literature . . . ." (2004, p. 238).

The exploration of the stories in the text set featuring "The Three Bears" described above was also designed to introduce the children to some of the reading-thinking strategies used by experienced readers in their transactions with literary texts. A survey of the group sessions reveals that the children had begun to use a number of these strategies as they responded to each new text and as they engaged in an ongoing comparative study of the diverse retellings of "The Three Bears." For example, the children initiated a "cover-to-cover study" of each new text as described in the explication of Strategy 1 in Chapter 1. The children searched for clues in the peritext that enabled them to make predictions (Strategy 4). During and after the read-aloud experience, the children returned to relevant segments in the peritext as well as the narrative text to confirm or revise these predictions and to deepen their understandings and explore multiple meanings (Strategy 10).

Throughout the cumulative discussions about these diverse retellings, the children engaged in think-alouds (Strategy 13) as they verbalized their thoughts about each story. Thinking aloud in these read-aloud/think-aloud sessions enabled the children to externalize their thinking processes as they constructed and reconstructed evolving meanings in response to the unfolding text. The children were learning to do what proficient readers do *in their heads* in response to literary texts. The children drew from their prior knowledge and the text information to make predictions and inferences and to generate questions (Strategies 2, 3, 4, and 8). They made connections between the text and their own lives and identified intertextual links between the new text and prior texts to construct meaning in response to these texts (Strategy 11). In response to teacher-initiated questions such as "How do you know the bears are nice?" the children learned to engage in metacognition: to think about their own thinking and to figure out and articulate how they generated meaning as the story unfolded (Strategy 12). By the time they were ready to select additional retellings and revisions for independent reading at school or at home prior to Session 8, the children were able to apply what they had learned about traditional and modern literature and to use their growing repertoire of reading-thinking strategies to engage in thoughtful transactions with these new texts.

A Text Set Featuring Literary Themes in Traditional and Modern Stories

A second text set formed the core of another literature unit in which children were invited to study literary themes. The first stories introduced to the children in the group read-aloud sessions were fables. The fable, a traditional literary genre, is defined as "a very brief story, usually with animal characters, that points clearly to a moral lesson. The moral, an explicit and didactic or preachy theme, is usually given at the end of the story and is the reason for the existence of the fable" (Lukens, 2003, p. 24). Literary themes are abstract ideas that are the central meaning in a narrative. In most stories, the themes are implied, and readers are required to engage in inferential thinking to discover significant truths about the human experience as they interact with literary texts. In fables, these truths or themes are usually explicitly stated, and are often more accessible to young children than implied themes.

Objectives for This Literature Unit

1. To introduce children to diverse literary genres such as traditional and modern fables, traditional and modern folktales, and modern animal fantasies

2. To provide opportunities for children to respond to each new text as it unfolds in a read-aloud/think-aloud group session

3. To provide opportunities for children to compare the stories in the text set in terms of the literary themes or lessons featured in these stories

4. To provide opportunities for children to practice some of the reading-thinking strategies used by experienced readers in their transactions with literary texts

5. To provide opportunities for children to engage in independent reading experiences at school and at home

---

Session 1

One of the stories in this text set, Aesop's "The Lion and the Mouse," was introduced in the first group read-aloud/think-aloud session. According to some scholars, Aesop was a Greek slave and storyteller who was born about 600 BCE. Fables attributed to Aesop had appeared in India and Egypt long before his birth, but his name continues to be associated with the wonderful fables first written in Greek and later translated into Latin and many other languages over the centuries. Today, there are a wide variety of illustrated editions of single fables as well as fable collections. This text set includes several different versions of "The Lion and the Mouse."

This ancient fable features a theme of kindness rewarded and reciprocity that is found in many traditional tales told around the world.

It is a theme that children will encounter in traditional as well as modern stories in kindergarten and beyond as they continue to explore the world of literature. After explaining that fables are stories that were told long ago to teach lessons about loyalty and kindness and other virtues, the teacher read aloud "The Lion and the Mouse" found in a collection, *Fables from Aesop*, adapted and illustrated with colorful fabric collages by Tom Lynch (2000). Before reading the moral at the end of this brief tale, the teacher asked the children: "What lesson do you think this fable teaches?" After the children articulated their own interpretations of the meaning of this fable, the teacher read aloud the moral or lesson given at the end of this fable: "So remember! No act of kindness, however small, is ever wasted" (n.p.).

At the end of this group session, the teacher called attention to a display of other versions of this fable in collections and single illustrated editions and explained that the books on this display table would be available for them to enjoy during the quiet reading time in the classroom or to share with their families at home.

> *Aesop's Fables* (Aesop & Pinkney, 2000). A child who shared with her family "The Lion and the Mouse" in this collection communicated her thoughts about this fable in a group session: "It sounded like the one we read in school but the lesson at the end was different." (Pinkney's retelling ends, "Even the strongest can sometimes use the help of the smallest" [p. 41]). The teacher recorded both lessons on a wall chart so the children could compare them and discuss the differences. This prompted the children to examine the lessons at the end of other retellings and to bring them to the teacher to be recorded on this chart.

> *The Lion and the Mouse: And Other Aesop's Fables* (Orgel & Aesop, 2000), includes a retelling of "The Lion and the Mouse" that ends with the words, "Someone very small can sometimes help in a big way" (n.p.).

> *The Lion and the Mouse* (Watts & Aesop, 2000), ends with the lion articulating what he has learned: "I will never again laugh at someone weaker or smaller than myself" (n.p.). The child who chose this retelling especially liked the last line: "And so the lion and the mouse remained the best of friends until the end of their days." She also shared her discovery of an interesting difference found in this retelling: "When the lion first met the mouse, he was just a young cub!"

> *The Lion and the Mouse* (Herman & Aesop, 1998, 2003). This retelling, intended for beginning readers, concludes with the words, "Always Help Others."

The Lion and the Rat (La Fontaine, 1963, 1984, 1999) concludes with the words: "So the little rat, by patience and hard work, was able to do what the lion, in all his strength and rage, could not" (n.p.). The child who selected this picture book found the familiar theme of reciprocity embedded in the response of the rat after the lion allows him to escape: "One day I shall repay you for your kindness" (n.p.).

"Androcles and the Lion" (included in Pinkney's collection, pp. 28–29) concludes with this lesson: "Gratitude is not limited to humankind" (p. 29). The children who discovered this fable were invited to read *Andy and the Lion,* by James Daugherty (Daugherty, 1938, 1989), a humorous retelling of this ancient fable. The 1989 edition includes a subtitle that suggests the lessons to be taught: "A tale of kindness remembered or the power of gratitude."

Session 2

In the second group session, the teacher read aloud a modern revision of the traditional fable *The Lion and the Mouse* (Jones, 1997). The children identified similarities and differences as they compared this version with Tom Lynch's adaptation of this fable as well as the other retellings they had selected for independent reading. For example, they noted the new characters, settings, and problems added to the plot. They observed that Jones created detailed pictures of the mouse and his family and portrayed them wearing clothes and engaged in human activities. Jones also includes a peephole in the center of many of the pages of this modern revision, and the children enjoyed peeking into the hole and predicting what would happen to Mouse. In this story, Mouse leaves his family and his home in a sailing ship to seek adventure. After escaping from Cat on the ship's deck and falling into the ocean, Mouse ends up in a jungle where he encounters new dangers. His life is saved when Monkey rescues him from the jaws of Crocodile, but later in his journey through the jungle Mouse manages to save himself from the jaws of Lion. He begs for his life with the words, "If you spare my humble life I'll promise to repay your favor. . . . Small creatures are capable of great deeds" (n.p.). The King of the Jungle rejects the notion that a tiny mouse could ever help him but responds: "Still, I admire your courage. You are a brave little fellow, so I'm going to set you free" (n.p.). As in the traditional fable, Lion is later ensnared in a hunter's trap, and Mouse gnaws through enough ropes to set him free. When Lion thanks his rescuer, he says: "Small creatures are capable of great deeds" (n.p.). When the children heard these words as the story unfolded, they decided that Lion had learned a lesson and that these words should be added to the list of "lessons" on their wall chart. The final page of this picture book shows separate portraits of Lion and Mouse, their tails linked together, and the caption: "One good deed deserves another" (n.p.). This final page prompted a lively discussion. The children identified this theme statement as a "new lesson" that should be added to their list. Some demonstrated their grasp of this concept by sharing examples of reciprocity in their own lives. The children seemed to especially like the way Jones concluded her story:

> "I liked the way they became friends . . . like when Lion gave him a ride on his back . . . and when Lion called Mouse 'little friend'!"
>
> "I liked the part when Lion got the other animals to help Mouse get back home."
>
> "It seemed that all the animals wanted to help when they found out Mouse was Lion's friend!"
>
> "It even *shows* they're friends in that last picture. . . See how their tails curl around each other? Remember . . . we learned the sign for 'friend.' See? It's just the same!" [This student demonstrated the sign for friendship.]
>
> "I think the artist must know sign language, too!"
>
> "And that's what friends do [he pointed to the lesson chart] . . . they help each other."

Session 3

In the third group session, the teacher read aloud *Amos and Boris* (Steig, 1977), a modern fable about an unusual friendship between Amos, a mouse, and Boris, a whale. One night, after setting out to sea in a homemade boat, Amos rolls off the deck of the boat and into the sea. When he discovers that his boat is gone and he is all alone in the "middle of the immense ocean," Amos begins to "wonder what it would be like to drown" (n.p.). Fortunately, Boris appears, rescues Amos, and agrees to take him home. In the course of the journey they learn about each other and develop a deep friendship based on mutual admiration. When they finally part, Amos says: "I will always be grateful to you for saving my life and I want you to remember that if you ever need my help I'd be more than glad to give it!" (n.p.). As Boris sets out for the Ivory Coast of Africa, he laughs to himself: "How could that little mouse ever help me? Little as he is, he's all heart. I love him, and I'll miss him terribly" (n.p.). Years later, Boris "was flung by a tidal wave and stranded on the very shore where Amos happened to make his home . . . . Just as Amos had once felt, all alone in the middle of the ocean, Boris felt now, lying alone on the shore . . . . And just as he was preparing to die, Amos came racing back with two of the biggest elephants he could find" (n.p.). Thus, Amos, a tiny mouse, is able to help Boris, a huge whale, just as he had promised. At the end of this story, the children compared it with Aesop's "The Lion and the Mouse" and identified the two central lessons (recorded on their chart) that would fit this story:

> "Small creatures are capable of great deeds."
> "One good deed deserves another."

Session 4

King Solomon and the Bee (Renberg, 1994) was introduced in the fourth group session. This is a legend of ancient Israel about a bee who helps the great King Solomon when the Queen of Sheba tests the king's wisdom. Before reading aloud this picture book, the teacher called attention to the setting of this legend and the central characters. Two of the children had heard stories about King Solomon and shared what they knew about him. In this story, a bee stings the king's nose, but before the king has time to punish the bee it pleads with him: "Do not be angry with me; do not punish me. Who knows? Maybe one day, my lord, my king, I will be able to repay you with a favor" (n.p.). Of course, the king is amused and lets the bee go free. Later, when the Queen of Sheba challenges the king to solve difficult riddles and puzzles, he is able to solve each one until the last test. The queen sets before him many bouquets of beautiful flowers. Only one bouquet is made up of real flowers; the other bouquets have artificial flowers. King Solomon is unable to tell them apart until a little bee flies in through the open window and, without anybody else noticing except for the king, lands on the bouquet of real flowers. "And that is how the little bee repaid the king" (n.p.).

The children immediately compared this old legend with the traditional and modern fables read earlier:

> "It's just like the other ones. The bee is like the little mouse, and the king is like Boris the whale and the lion in the other stories."
> "And the lion is the *king* of the jungle, so he's like King Solomon!"
> "In these stories they all help each other, and one's little and one's big!"
> "This story is like a fable—the lesson is One Good Deed Deserves Another!"

Session 5

Nobiah's Well: A Modern African Folktale (Guthrie, 1993) was read aloud in the fifth group session. This is the story of a young boy, Nobiah, who lives with his mother and sister in a dry land in a small hut that is a long way from the nearest well. One day Nobiah is sent on the long journey to the well to fill their clay jar with water. On his way home, he shares this treasured water with the thirsty animals he encounters. When he returns to the hut, there is only enough water for his sister and mother to each take a drink. Nobiah goes to bed thirsty and sad, but he is awakened by the animals he had helped. They urge him to dig a well by his hut and work with him until water finally begins to come from deep within the hole. Now Nobiah and his family and all the villagers will no longer have to travel long distances for water. At the end of this beautiful tale, one of the children observed: "Nobiah helped the animals, and they helped him—just like in the other stories." In response to this comment, the other children chanted in unison: "One good deed deserves another!" Another child pointed to the wall chart and noted that this tale also teaches the lesson that "someone small can sometimes be a big help." After further discussion in which the five shared stories were compared, one child made an interesting discovery: "These stories are in different places. So maybe these same exact lessons are taught all over the world!"

The teacher reinforced the validity of this discovery and told the children that as they listened to and read more and more stories from around the world they would continue to find these lessons.

At the conclusion of the fifth group session, the teacher called attention to a display of the books selected for this literature unit. The children were invited to choose one or more of these books to enjoy in school or at home. They were given an opportunity to draw pictures about their favorite story characters or scenes and to share their drawings and their responses to these self-selected books in the sixth group session, the final session for the cumulative literary experience structured around this text set. In addition to the stories read aloud in the group sessions and the "Lion and the Mouse" stories, this text set included:

> *The Hungry Otter* (Ezra, 1996), a modern animal fantasy about the reciprocity between an otter and a crow.
>
> *One Gift Deserves Another* (Oppenheim, 1992), an adaptation of a Grimm brothers tale.
>
> *Just Rewards, or, Who Is That Man in the Moon and What's He Doing Up There Anyway?* (Sanfield, 1996), a retelling of a Chinese folktale in which an act of kindness is rewarded and an act of greed is punished. The children who read this story identified the different motives behind the deeds of two neighbors in their "book

talks" during the sixth group session. One child explained the difference between the man who helped a wounded sparrow because he *cared* about the little bird and his neighbor, who decided to help a bird, too, ". . . but for a different *reason!* He just wanted to get a reward!" Another child noted that the greedy neighbor said kind words, "but his *thoughts* were mean." The child drew a picture of this character, using speech and thought bubbles to reflect this contradiction. His picture also portrayed the way the character was punished for his greed at the end of the story.

The Ant and the Elephant (Peet, 1972), a modern animal fantasy in which a grateful ant rescues his rescuer, an enormous elephant. A child who read this book noted: "It was like the story about the mouse and the lion . . . in the end the lion understood what the mouse felt like when he was trapped!"

The Full Belly Bowl (Aylesworth, 1998), a modern fantasy in which an old man does a kind deed and, in return, receives a magical bowl that reproduces whatever is placed in it.

The Mean Hyena: A Folktale from Malawi (Sierra, 1997), a story of revenge for an unkind deed. This tale concludes with the words of the storyteller within the story: "So, you see, don't play a trick on someone unless you want an even bigger trick played on you." One child who chose this book compared it with the others and noted that the lesson could be: "One mean trick deserves another."

The Old Woman Who Lived in a Vinegar Bottle (Godden, 1972), an English folktale about a poor old woman who is rewarded for her kindness to a little fish.

The Dancing Pig (Sierra, 1999), an Indonesian folktale about two sisters who are rescued from an ogress by the animals they have fed and entertained with their dancing.

Room on the Broom (Donaldson, 2001) is the story of a witch who is rescued from a dragon by the animals she has treated with kindness.

Koi and the Kola Nuts: A Tale from Liberia (Aardema, 1999). In this African folktale, the son of the chief is able to make his way in the world with the help of the creatures with whom he has shared his resources.

Sitti and the Cats: A Tale of Friendship (Bahous, 1993). In this Palestinian fairy tale, a poor old woman receives generous gifts in return for her kindness to a cat and manages to teach her selfish neighbor the value of kindness as well.

Celia and the Sweet, Sweet Water (Paterson, 1998) is a modern tale of a young girl's quest for a cure for her mother's illness. She gets help from those she meets on her journey because of her kindness to them.

Assessment

The text set featuring diverse retellings of "The Three Bears" was introduced to kindergarten children during the beginning of the first semester of the school year. The text set featuring diverse stories with common literary themes was introduced to the children at the end of the second semester of the same year. The literary experiences structured around the first text set were designed to introduce the children to reading-thinking strategies that would be used in subsequent literary experiences throughout the school year. At the end of the year, the children's responses to new literary texts were evaluated in terms of their ability to use reading-thinking strategies to build understandings and generate meaning. For example, the teacher found evidence that most of the children were actively involved in initiating a cover-to-cover study of each new text and used clues to make predictions and inferences and to activate relevant prior knowledge to enrich the meaning-making process in their transactions with these texts. She also found evidence that the children often monitored their own comprehension as they confirmed, revised, or rejected initial predictions and identified comprehension problems. They took advantage of the conceptual relationships among the stories in the text sets to engage in comparative analysis of these texts and to use intertextual links to generate meaning and enrich the quality of their interpretation of the stories. Although a few of the children spontaneously engaged in metacognition, for the most part the children articulated the basis for their own interpretations in response to teacher-initiated questions.

A follow-up study of these children revealed that many of them continued to use these strategies beyond their kindergarten year. In addition, for many of these students, the content of these literary experiences had become an integral part of their literary backgrounds and the prior knowledge they used to make predictions and generate meaning in response to increasingly complex texts. For example, as first-grade students, these children discovered the themes of kindness rewarded or reciprocity in stories such as *Sirko and the Wolf: A Ukrainian Tale* (Kimmel, 1997). In this folktale, a farmer and his wife decide to get rid of their faithful sheepdog, Sirko, when he is too old to guard the sheep. A wolf finds Sirko alone and starving and helps him carry out a secret plan to convince his owners to change their minds about Sirko. Their plan works, and Sirko is taken back as a beloved pet. Later, Sirko finds a way to repay the wolf's kindness when he hears the wolf howling with hunger during the first snowfall. When *Crackers,* by Becky Bloom (2001), was introduced to these first graders, this story reminded them of the reciprocity in "The Lion and the Mouse." Crackers the cat is kind to mice, and, in return, the mice manage to help Crackers when he is in trouble.

As second graders, these children were introduced to *The Magic Stove* (Ginsburg, 1983). When an old man shares his last piece of bread with his rooster, one child exclaimed, "It's the rooster that's going to give him the magic stove. I just know it!" When asked to explain this prediction, he replied, "Because this is like those stories you read to us before. This is the kind of story about someone doing a kind deed and getting rewarded. It's like 'one good deed deserves another!'" This child had demonstrated his use of prior literary experiences to make predictions about a new text and his use of metacognitive strategies to explain this prediction.

As third graders, the children identified this theme in stories such as *The Golden Sandal: A Middle Eastern Cinderella Story* (Hickox, 1998), an Iraqi variant in which the heroine is rewarded for her kindness to a little red fish who later becomes her "fairy godmother." Each of these stories prompted the children to engage in an ongoing dialogue—from cover to cover—that was remarkably similar to the internal dialogue a critical reader generates in the course of transacting with a literary text.

Throughout these experiences with literature in kindergarten and beyond, the children were invited to respond to literary texts by engaging in critical thinking, questioning, and reflecting on characters' choices and considering alternative choices. A review of the excerpts from the dialogues recorded in this chapter yields evidence that the careful selection of "intellectually provocative [and] humanizing" literature (Langer, 1995, p. 5) can support critical literacy and set the stage for transformative education as envisioned by Freire.

Note

1. The group sessions for these two units were held in the school library and were led by Moss. Valerie Myntti, a kindergarten teacher, recorded the children's responses in the first literature unit and read to these children in the classroom some of the other traditional tales that were not part of their literary histories.

3 Cat Tales

Cats in Literature: Past and Present

The Cat Tale Literature Unit described in this chapter was originally developed in response to the many cat-lovers in a first-grade classroom. However, since a remarkable number of traditional and modern stories as well as nonfiction texts featuring felines are available for children of diverse ages, this literature unit can be adapted for use with older children in the elementary school. For centuries cats have appealed to storytellers and artists who have tried to capture the variable qualities of these creatures: alternately languid and lively, mischievous and composed, independent and affectionate, from the sophisticated and dignified Siamese to the ragged stray. The ancient Egyptians worshiped them, dancers have imitated them, musicians and poets have celebrated them. Cats have symbolized grace and beauty as well as evil and witchcraft. Thus, the literature collected for the Cat Tale Unit features a wonderfully diverse cast of characters.

The Cat Tale Literature Unit

Objectives for This Literature Unit

1. To provide opportunities for children to form a "community of readers" and to enjoy literature together in read-aloud/think-aloud group sessions

2. To introduce children to feline characters featured in a variety of traditional and modern tales, fiction, poetry, and nonfiction, and in stories from diverse cultures

3. To provide opportunities for children to learn about literature, the language of literary analysis, and the craft of authors and artists

4. To provide a context in which children practice the reading-thinking strategies used by proficient readers to respond to literary texts

5. To provide opportunities for children to study literature with a "writer's eye" (Portalupi, 1999, p. 6) in order to enrich their comprehension and composition of literature

6. To use the literary experiences in the read-aloud/think-aloud group sessions as the springboard for literacy experiences in reading and writing workshops

---

Continued on next page

> 7. To provide opportunities for children to discover new possi-
>   bilities for independent reading and writing

Session 1

The teacher wrote "Cat Tales" at the top of the chart by the story circle
and held up the picture book, *Ruby* (Emberley, 1990) to introduce the
new literature unit. She initiated a cover-to-cover study of this text by
inviting the children to talk about the title and the picture on the front
and back covers (Strategy 1):

> "The title is 'Ruby.' That's like a diamond but it's red."
> "Ruby could be the name of that little mouse with the red
> hood."
> "That mouse looks like Little Red Riding Hood!"

The teacher had placed a copy of this traditional tale on the easel to help
the children make the connection with this familiar tale (Strategy 11).
Then the teacher held up a card with the word "surprise" printed on it.
Several children decoded it and explained its meaning. The teacher said:
"Authors and illustrators often put surprises in the stories they create.
Let's look for the surprises in the stories we read in this unit." One child
asked: "But isn't there supposed to be a cat in this story?" Another child
responded: "We better keep looking." As the children examined the front
and back covers, the endpapers, and the title page of the book, they were
asked to look for clues to identify the *setting* for this story. (These children had been introduced to this literary term prior to this session.) One
of the children responded: "I see big buildings, cars, signs . . . It's in a
city. The other one [he pointed to the book *Little Red Riding Hood*] was
in a *forest.*"

  When the children examined the first double-page spread, they
noticed Ruby sitting in a big chair reading a book. They were delighted
to discover that the title of the book was *Red Riding Hood.* At the beginning of this story, Ruby's mother asks her to take a bag of triple cheese
pies to her granny and to her granny's neighbor, Mrs. Mastiff. The
teacher explained that a mastiff is a very large dog.

> "So the granny is a mouse and the neighbor is a big dog?"
> "That's a surprise! Granny's friend is a huge dog!"

As the story unfolds, Ruby sets out on a journey to visit her granny and
encounters a cat who offers to escort her to her granny's apartment.
Ruby rejects this offer but gives an address to the cat, 34 Beacon Street.

Then she tells the cat she's going to call her granny and goes off to make a phone call. The cat hops in a taxi and gives the address to the driver. At this point in the narrative the children were asked to try to figure out whose address Ruby gave to the cat and whom she had called.

> "I don't think she gave the cat her granny's real address. I think she gave a fake address so the cat wouldn't eat her."
>
> "I think she gave the neighbor's address because it's that huge dog!"
>
> "So maybe Ruby called the *neighbor* to tell her the cat's coming!"

In the text, Ruby arrives at 34 Beacon Street and rings the bell, but the children gasped when they saw in the illustration what appeared to be the *cat* at the door. They were very relieved to see on the next page that it is Mrs. Mastiff wearing the cat's hat and jacket. They also noticed a bone sticking out of her purse. At the conclusion of the story, the children were invited to talk about the surprises in this story (Strategy 6).

> "The first surprise was a little mouse and a big dog are friends."
>
> "*We* were surprised when the door opened and we thought it was the cat!"
>
> "But it was just the way the artist did it. It was really the neighbor. The dog ate the cat! But the *cat* must've been surprised to see that big dog!"
>
> "He thought granny's neighbor would be a mouse!"

Then the teacher asked: "Why do you think Michael Emberley (the author/artist) decided to include these surprises in his story?"

> "It makes it funnier."
>
> "It makes it more interesting because it's not what you expect."
>
> "It's fun . . . like a surprise party."
>
> "*We* were surprised and the *cat* was surprised!"
>
> "I think it would be sort of boring if there weren't any surprises."

The teacher's next question was: "What is a *villain*?"

> "A bad guy!"
>
> "In this story it's the *cat*. The cat is the villain because he was going to eat Ruby and her granny . . . *and* the neighbor!"
>
> "In that story [she pointed to *Little Red Riding Hood*] the villain is the wolf . . . but Ruby was smarter."
>
> "She tricked the cat when she gave him the neighbor's address so she'd eat *him*!"

The children responded to two more questions: "Who was the *heroine*?" and "What kind of story is this: fantasy or realism?" They identified Ruby as the heroine because she tricked the cat and saved her granny and herself with the help of Mrs. Mastiff. They identified the story as fantasy "because the animals talk and wear clothes like people." When the teacher read aloud the back flap, the children were delighted to hear that 34 Beacon Street in Boston could be the home of the author!

In this introductory session, the teacher reinforced the use of literary terms such as *setting*, *villain*, and *heroine*; she called attention to the genre and parts of the peritext such as the covers, endpapers, and title page; and she introduced surprise as a technique authors and artists use as part of their craft. Further reinforcement occurred in writing workshops that followed the read-aloud/think-aloud sessions.[1] For example, in the first workshop, the children created pictures of diverse settings and then created characters that they cut out and pasted on these setting pictures. In this workshop an ongoing discussion was initiated in response to the question, "What makes a story a story?" Throughout the school year, the writing workshop provided a context in which children studied narrative elements and developed an awareness of story structure and authors' craft (Strategy 9). For example, in some workshops the children focused on the problems (or conflicts) in stories; in other workshops they focused on character development. In one workshop, the children talked about the element of surprise in stories and in their own lives. They drew pictures of someone *showing* surprise in response to an event in a story or in response to a real-life event and then composed the text to accompany each of these "surprise pictures."

Session 2

The children examined the covers of *Brave Babette and Sly Tom* (Elzbieta, 1989) and initiated a cover-to-cover study of this second picture book. They identified the setting as Paris—"because you can see the Eiffel Tower!" One child gave an extensive definition of the word "brave"; another child explained the word "sly." The children predicted that the mouse on the cover was Babette and identified the genre as fantasy— "because the mouse is wearing a coat, and she has an umbrella, and she's walking on two legs instead of four." One child wondered if the mouse was pregnant or just fat. They looked at the title page and noted a small mouse flying on the back of a blackbird. They wondered who that was.

As they listened to the story unfold, the children were able to answer some of their initial questions:

"So the mouse on the cover *isn't* Babette. It's the mother mouse, and she *is* pregnant!"

"And the mouse on the title page is Babette, her new baby."

"And the blackbird is taking care of her because her mom got chased away by that mean cat . . ."

"That's Sly Tom! He's sneaky just like C. said."

"So the cat is the villain! It's just like the cat in *Ruby!*"

"And the mom escaped on that red balloon!"

The children enjoyed the part in the story in which Babette manages to avoid being eaten by the cat by tricking him and revealing his cowardice. They also identified narrative elements and intertextual links:

"Ruby and Babette are both heroines, and both are smart!"

"Both stories have helper characters—Mrs. Mastiff and the blackbird."

Toward the end of the story the children's eyes widened with recognition when they heard the words: "One Sunday afternoon . . . a red balloon floated down into the park" (n.p.). The children responded in unison: "It's the mom! She got home to her Babette!" And the children were pleased to hear that Babette's mom and the blackbird get married: "Now Babette has a mom and a dad!"

After the children had an opportunity to share their personal responses to the story, the teacher asked: "What were the surprises in this story?"

"I was surprised when the mom came floating down!"

"The surprise for me was that she went all over the world in the balloon."

"I was surprised when the *cat* was scared of the mouse!"

"Me, too. I thought he was so fierce, but he was just a coward!"

"He *believed* Babette when she said she had magic powers."

"He was fierce when he was attacking the little animals that were afraid of him. But Babette made *him* scared of *her!*"

"There's a bully on our street who always picks on the little kids."

"Like Sly Tom. He was a scaredy cat!"

Finally the teacher introduced a question to call attention to another element in the story structure: "What were the *problems* in this story?"

"When the mom got chased away, she couldn't be with her new baby. That was the first problem!"

"The cat *caused* that problem!"

"The blackbird took care of the baby. So he helped with that problem."

"But the cat was a problem for the whole park until Babette tamed him."

"So she solved the problem for everyone in the park . . . because she got him to change from a mean cat to a tame cat."

"But first she had to solve *her* problem . . . the cat was trying to catch her!"

"The title is *Brave Babette and Sly Tom.* . . and Sly Tom was Babette's problem!"

Strategy 9, as explicated in Chapter 1, highlights the use of text structure and story grammar in reading comprehension. According to Stephanie McConaughy (1980), a story is defined as "a series of problem solving episodes centering on the main character's (or characters') efforts to achieve a major goal" (p. 158). Teacher-initiated questions can help students internalize story structure and, in turn, enhance their reading comprehension (Sadow, 1982). Since the plot in *Brave Babette and Sly Tom* includes a series of problems, the children were invited to identify the sequence of problems and solutions for Babette and her mother. Although all the children were familiar with stories featuring a single problem, many of the children were not familiar with stories featuring a series of interwoven problems and needed help to comprehend the plot structure. In the language of story grammar research, the problems in a story are the conflicts that drive the action in the story or the *initiating events* that lead the central character(s) to formulate goals to solve the problems.

The prior knowledge and experience that readers bring to a literary text is organized, and, as we have seen, the term *schema* refers to that organized knowledge or mental model of the world. Schema theorists interested in story comprehension have demonstrated that there is an inherent logical structure or grammar made up of a network of categories and logical relationships in stories (Stein & Glenn, 1979). Although schema theorists label the components of a story differently, a *story grammar* usually includes these categories:

- A *setting* that introduces the characters and the time and place in the story;
- an *initiating event* that leads the main character to formulate his or her major goals and starts the sequence of actions and events;
- the *goal,* which is the major desire of the main character;
- a number of *attempts,* which are the actions of the characters;
- a series of *outcomes,* which are the events or states produced by the character's actions;

- *internal responses,* which are the subgoals, thoughts, and feelings of a character leading to his or her actions;
- *reactions,* which are thoughts or feelings produced by the outcomes of actions, and
- the *resolution,* or final consequence of the story (McConaughy, 1980, p. 158).

These basic components are related causally or temporally. By listening to and reading a variety of stories, children develop a story schema, an implicit knowledge of story grammar. According to the results of story grammar research, children use this knowledge of story organization to comprehend and recall stories, to make predictions about stories and inferences about characters' motives, to become aware of logical and purposive behaviors of the characters, and to generate their own stories. Children with better knowledge of story structure tend to be better readers (Fitzgerald, 1983).

Story grammar provides a conceptual framework for formulating questions that reflect the story as a whole and that focus on its internal logic and pattern of relationships. These questions can be used as teaching tools to strengthen children's awareness of story structure and to demonstrate reading-thinking strategies used by good readers to generate meaning in their transactions with literary texts.

Session 3

The children were invited to look at the front and back covers and the endpapers of the picture book *Crackers* (Bloom, 2001) and to find something that was surprising:

> "The cat and mice are having a picnic together. Usually cats chase mice!"
> "And the mice aren't afraid of the cat!"
> "So—in this story the cat is probably *not* the villain!"
> "On the endpapers it shows the whole town, and you can see the same picture of the picnic, but it's really small in the middle of the town."

As the story unfolded, the children discovered that "Crackers" is the name of a cat who has difficulty keeping a job because he likes mice and does kind deeds for them instead of chasing them. In return, the mice help Crackers find a perfect job at the Squeak and Company Cheese Shop run by mice. This reciprocity prompted the children to return to a story they had heard when they were in kindergarten (Strategy 11):

> "We read a story like this last year! Remember that one with the lion that helps a mouse and then the mouse helps the lion?"

"That was *The Lion and the Mouse* (Jones, 1997) and in the end they were friends and it said 'One good deed . . . ' What was the rest?"

"It was 'One good deed deserves another.' That could have been the ending for *Crackers!*"

"But this story is different because the cat is the hero, and in the other ones the cat is the villain."

"But in real life cats *do* chase mice. So you expected that the cats in those other stories would want to eat Ruby and Babette. But in this story, it's a *surprise* that the cat liked the mice and they're friends."

"So that's Crackers's *problem*! He didn't chase mice, so he got fired."

"But then his problem got solved because he was nice to the mice!"

At the conclusion of this session, the teacher introduced the children to a display of fiction, nonfiction, and poetry featuring cats that had been selected for this literature unit. The children were invited to choose titles they would like to read independently or with a partner at school or with their parents at home. A variety of texts were selected for this collection in order to meet the diverse reading needs and interests represented in this class. (This collection can be found in the "References" segment at the end of this book.) Book talks about particular titles were presented at the end of this session to call attention to stories selected in terms of their connections with the first three shared texts:

> *Anatole and the Cat* (Titus, 1957, 1990). A picture book.
>
> *The Bookstore Burglar* (Maitland, 2001). The characters in this book for beginning readers were first introduced in *The Bookstore Ghost* (Maitland, 1998).
>
> *The Cat's Purr* (Bryan, 1985). A West Indian folktale.
>
> *The Church Mouse* (Oakley, 1972, 1987). A picture book.
>
> *Clarence the Copy Cat* (Lakin, 2002). A picture book.
>
> *Lucky's Choice* (Jeschke, 1987). A picture book.
>
> *Martin's Mice* (King-Smith, 1989). A novel.
>
> *Slim and Jim* (Egielski, 2001). A picture book.
>
> *Solomon: The Rusty Nail* (Steig, 1985). A picture book
>
> *Wanted: Best Friend* (Monson, 1997). A picture book.

Session 4

The children responded to the title and the pictures on the covers and endpapers of *Mouse Trouble* (Yeoman, 1976), introduced in the fourth group session:

"There's a windmill and that man with the bags looks mad."

"Those look like flour bags. He's probably the miller, and the mice probably get into his bags."

"I think he's mad because of all those mice. It [the title] says he's having trouble with the mice."

"The cat on the back cover isn't chasing the mice."

"Maybe this is another story about a cat that's nice to the mice."

As the children listened to the story unfold, they were able to confirm their predictions and discovered that the cat is *not* a good mouser and does not chase the mice. When the miller decides to get rid of this useless cat, the mice trick the grouchy miller and save the cat. At the end of the story, the children looked at the cover and endpapers again and shared further comments about the story:

"I changed my mind about the front cover. I think the miller was mad at the *cat* because he didn't catch the mice."

"I think this is sort of like *Crackers*. The cat in this story didn't chase the mice and then the mice helped the cat . . . like one good deed deserves another!"

"And in the end they all lived together as friends."

"I think that picture on the endpaper [he pointed to a picture of an older mouse talking to five small mice] is a daddy mouse telling his children the story of how the mice saved the cat from the villain—the mean miller!"

"I think the little mice would like the surprises in the story— that the cat wasn't a good mouser and the mice *saved* the cat!"

"I read another story with my mom about a cat that wasn't a good mouser either. It's called *Clarence the Copy Cat*."

"My dad read me a book like that—*Martin's Mice*. It's a really good book!"

Session 5

The teacher introduced the picture book *Newf* (Killilea, 1992) by showing the front cover with a picture of a large black dog and a tiny white kitten and reading from a nonfiction text about Newfoundland dogs: *The Newfoundland* (Wilcox, 1999). This nonfiction text provided the children with relevant information about this dog breed, known for lifesaving and search-and-rescue work. Although the kitten in *Newf* hisses and strikes out at the dog when it first encounters this huge creature, their relationship eventually develops into a friendship. The kitten's playful behavior prompted a number of text-to-self connections as the children described their own experiences with kittens. When Newf rescues the kitten from the ocean and later finds the kitten buried in the snow, the children recalled relevant information they had acquired from the nonfiction text about the nature of the Newfoundland.

At the end of the story, the children were asked: "What kind of a story is this?"

> "It's realism. The artist made the animals look real."
> "They're not cartoons like the other ones."
> "This could really happen in real life, because those dogs do rescue people who are drowning or lost in the snow."
> "*Did* it really happen? Is it a true story?"

In response to this last question, the teacher read aloud the note about the author on the back flap of the book. According to this note, the author and her husband visited the Gaspe Peninsula and "saw one of the giant black dogs. Inquiring about it, Marie was told the legend upon which this story is based." Then the teacher read the information about the story on the front flap that explains that this story is a retelling of "a north country legend about the mysterious black dog who comes in from the sea." She explained that a legend is an old story that often has some basis in actual events in the past.

At the conclusion of this session, the teacher called attention to four other picture books in the collection that featured special relationships between large animals and small kittens.

> *The Dog Who Had Kittens* (Robertus, 1991).
>
> *A Rose for Pinkerton* (Kellogg, 1981).
>
> *Four Hungry Kittens* (McCully, 2001). A wordless picture book.
>
> *Koko's Kitten* (Patterson, 1985). A nonfiction account of a friendship between a gorilla and a kitten.

Session 6

When the teacher read the title and showed the front and back covers and title page of *Katje, the Windmill Cat* (Woelfle, 2001), the children noticed the realistic painting of a cat in the foreground and the sketch of a village dominated by a windmill in the background of the picture on the front cover:

> "This story could be about a miller and a cat like in *Mouse Trouble*."
>
> "But that one had cartoon pictures, and this one has paintings that look more real."
>
> "I think this could be a realism story . . . and maybe not so funny."
>
> "I think the setting could be Holland because they have a lot of windmills there and tulips. There's a picture of a tulip on the back cover."

> "Those little square pictures [on the title page] look like the
> tiles we have in our kitchen."

In response to these predictions and comments triggered by their initial cover-to-cover study of this new text, the teacher shared some relevant background information before reading aloud this story that offers an interesting contrast with *Mouse Trouble.* She confirmed that the setting for this story is a village in Holland and that the blue-and-white tiles on the title page are known as Delft tiles, made in the town of Delft in Holland. She showed other pictures of windmills in Holland found in a nonfiction text and explained the need for dikes to keep out the sea and the use of windmills to pump out the water as well as for grinding grain. She also shared her personal experience in Holland in an old house in a Dutch village. Her host had pointed to the blue-and-white tiles around the fireplace and explained that when the family settled around the fire for a story in the evening, someone would choose one of the tiles and the storyteller would tell the story associated with the picture on that tile. The teacher showed the children actual examples of Delft tiles and then invited them to look at the tiles on each page of the book and to figure out the connection between the tiles and the text on that page. Finally, she read aloud this line from the front flap: "Gretchen Woelfle's heroic tale is inspired by a true story that took place over 500 years ago." After the children had an opportunity to talk about this background information, the teacher began to read aloud the story.

This is the story of Katje the cat who lives with Nico the miller and chases the mice in the windmill. When the children heard the first page, they noted the difference between Katje and the cat in *Mouse Trouble:* "Katje's a *good* mouser! This is what cats do in real life. Cats are *supposed* to chase mice." Katje and Nico live happily together until Nico brings home his new bride, Lena, who does not want the cat in the house. When they have a baby, the tensions increase, and Katje goes off to live in the mill. However, when a storm breaks through the dike that holds back the sea, Katje manages to save the baby during the flood. Her heroic deed earns her a special place in Lena's heart, and Katje lives together happily with Nico and Lena, working as a mouser at the mill during the day and playing with the baby before and after her work day. At the back of the book, an author's note provides further information about *Katje, the Windmill Cat,* which is based on a true story of a brave cat that saved a baby in a terrible flood that occurred on November 5, 1421, in a small village in South Holland. At the end of the story, the children contrasted it with *Mouse Trouble:*

"This one isn't fantasy. It really happened! I like true stories."

"*Mouse Trouble* was funny, but this story is more serious."

"When the flood came it was scary because the baby could've drowned and the mom and dad were afraid they couldn't get to her."

"Katje was a real heroine. She saved the baby from the flood."

"This is more like *Newf* because they're both realism stories, and Newf saved the baby kitten and Katje saved the baby."

"But in *Mouse Trouble* the mice saved the *cat*! That was the surprise!"

"The surprise in this one was that the cat saved the baby!"

Throughout this comparative analysis, several children were waiting patiently to share their personal stories about their pet dogs and cats and kittens. At the conclusion of this analysis, these children were invited to tell their stories. As these stories were shared with the group, others were reminded of stories they wanted to tell. At the end of this delightful storytelling fest, the teacher invited the children to write and illustrate their stories during writing workshop.

Session 7

When the teacher held up *Opera Cat* (Weaver, 2002), the children immediately identified it as "a funny animal fantasy story!" They noted that the cartoon figures on the front cover were like the ones in *Mouse Trouble*, and they predicted that this story would *not* be like *Newf* or *Katje, the Windmill Cat*. Then the children talked about the title:

"An opera is when someone sings in a theater. It's like a story but it sounds like music, but they don't sing real words."

"I think it's real words but it's a different language, and the singers talk to each other in songs!"

"Maybe an opera cat is a cat that howls like an opera singer?"

As the story unfolded, the children discovered that the cat, Alma, belongs to Madame SoSo, an opera singer who lives in Milan. "Alma was no ordinary cat" (p. 11). She has secretly learned to sing all the songs her mistress practices every day. In fact, Alma can sing them as well as the opera singer. On the night of the big premier, Madame SoSo gets laryngitis. Alma reveals her secret talent, and they work out a way to hide the cat in the singer's large hairdo so the cat can sing in place of her mistress. "The audience was mesmerized" (p. 25). They applauded the opera star, unaware that "it was Alma who was singing . . . Alma who was the star!" (p. 26).

After the children shared their personal responses to this humorous story, they were asked to identify the heroine:

"Alma was the heroine. She helped Madame SoSo! Like Katje!"

"Alma saved the day! She knew the opera songs so she could sing and Madame SoSo could lip-sync so everybody thought she was singing!"

"Alma saved her job when she got strep throat!"

"The surprise in this story is that a cat can sing like a person."

"And she could sing in Italian just like Madame SoSo!"

"This story had a surprise and a secret. Alma had a secret because Madame SoSo didn't know the cat could sing like her."

"There was another secret. When the cat was hiding in her hair, the people didn't know it. It was their secret!"

"I think the author made the story interesting with surprises and secrets!"

"I have a book about an opera dog that really did sing on stage with a famous opera singer from Rochester . . . Renee Fleming! At the back of the book there's a copy of the *New York Times* article about it! It's called, *The Dog Who Sang at the Opera* (West & Izen, 2004)."

At the conclusion of this session, the teacher invited the children to choose another book for independent reading and called attention to stories about other heroic cats in the collection.

Blue-Ribbon Henry (Calhoun, 1999)

Dolores and the Big Fire: A True Story (Clements, 2002)

Henry the Sailor Cat (Calhoun, 1994)

High-Wire Henry (Calhoun, 1991)

The Lighthouse Cat (Stainton, 2004)

The Mousehole Cat (Barber, 1990)

New Cat (Choi, 1998)

The Story of the Seagull and the Cat Who Taught Her to Fly (Sepúlveda, 2003)

Tiger Trouble! (Goode, 2001)

Session 8

Like the cover of *Katje, the Windmill Cat*, the cover of *Charlie Anderson* (Abercrombie, 1990) has a realistic painting of a cat, and the children used this clue to predict that this would be "a realism story." The first title page shows the cat walking through a doorway; the major title page shows the cat sitting on a dinner table. The opening lines prompted the children to make a connection between this story and a familiar traditional tale: "One cold night a cat walked out of the woods, up the steps, across the deck, and into the house where Elizabeth and Sarah lived.

He curled up next to their fireplace to get warm. He watched the six o'clock news on TV. He tasted their dinner. He tried out their beds."
  The children responded:

> "It's just like *Goldilocks and the Three Bears!"*
> "The cat came out of the woods, so maybe it's a stray cat."
> "I think it's a wild cat that lived in the woods, and then it got cold so he wanted to be in a house."

As they listened to the story unfold, the children gained new information and confirmed or revised their initial predictions accordingly (Strategy 4). In the story, the cat is taken in by Elizabeth and Sarah, who name him Charlie and feed him dinner and breakfast. Every morning he goes into the woods, but he always returns in time for dinner and to sleep in Elizabeth's bed. On weekends the girls go into the city to stay with their father and stepmother. One day, when they are back in the country with their mother, the girls discover that Charlie has spent his days at the home of a couple who had just moved to a new house on the other side of the woods. The couple explain to the girls that their cat, named Anderson, has lived with them for seven years, and that "he prowls the woods at night" (n.p.). When the girls tell the couple that the cat has a home with them in the evenings, they all understand why the cat is so fat and happy. They decide to call the cat Charlie Anderson. The story ends with the words, "Just like Elizabeth and Sarah, Charlie has two houses, two beds, and two families who love him. He's a lucky cat" (n.p.). The children were invited to explain these closing lines and to discover the parallel plot pattern in this story:

> "The cat eats at both places. He has two families."
> "One family lives on one side of the woods, and the other family lives on the other side of the woods in the new house."
> "It's just like Sarah and Elizabeth. The mom lives in the country, and the dad lives in the city with a new wife. They have two families."
> "The families are in two different settings . . . the city and the country."
> "It's like my family. My mom lives here, and my dad lives in Chicago. I spend all the school vacations with him."
> "I live with my mom and my stepfather. My dad lives in the city, and I get to stay in his apartment on weekends just like Elizabeth and Sarah."
> "In that last picture it shows both families. [She pointed to the framed photographs in this illustration.] There's the mom with the two girls in one picture, and there's the dad with the two girls in the other one."

The teacher's last question "What is the problem in this story?" prompted the children to focus on another element in the structure of this narrative as well as the craft of the author:

> "I think it was when Charlie didn't come home one night. It was a bad storm and Sarah and Elizabeth were so worried."
>
> "They looked everywhere, and then they went to the new house and that's when they found Charlie!"
>
> "That's how they all discovered the cat's secret! This story has a surprise *and* a secret like the one about Alma, the singing cat!"
>
> "So the problem was that he was missing, but when they found him they solved the riddle."
>
> "What riddle?"
>
> "Where did he go after breakfast? And why was he getting so *fat?*"
>
> "Another riddle was the title. When they found Charlie, *we* found out why the title is *Charlie Anderson*!"
>
> "And the characters found out his secret—that he had two houses and two families exactly like Elizabeth and Sarah!"
>
> "The author made it so they [the characters] were surprised and so were *we!* This story has secrets and surprises, too!"

Session 9

As soon as the children were introduced to *Nobody's Cat* (Miles, 1969), they focused on the title, and predicted that the story would be about ". . . a stray cat or a wild cat, but not a pet cat." As they listened to the story, they discovered that the central character is a stray cat in an urban setting. The cat struggles to survive on his own as he searches for food, defends himself against the dangers inherent in city life, and figures out who is a friend he can trust and who is an enemy he must avoid as he encounters humans. The children used their own experiences as cat owners and/or the knowledge they had gained from the stories in this unit to make sense of the cat's behavior and body language in specific episodes in the story (Strategy 3). For example, they talked about their own cats or fictional cats as they interpreted pictures in which the cat is stretching with his claws out, or arching his back, or stalking his prey, or playing with a string. They were all learning to "read" the body language that communicated fear, anger, affection, or contentment. In one scene, after several school children leave food for the cat, he goes after a mouse and leaves the dead mouse on the steps of the school.

> "My cat does that. It's sort of how he says thank you."
>
> "So the cat is thanking the children for giving him food."

"I kept hoping that girl would take him home with her, but the cat went back to his box in the alley."

"Some cats just like to be independent. I think this cat *liked* to be on his own—even though there were a lot of dangers."

"He's just the opposite of Charlie Anderson. Charlie was independent, too—but he had *two* homes. And this cat didn't have any home."

"But I think maybe that box in the alley was like home for him. He seemed to be happy to go there at the end of the day."

"It's like people. Some people like to stay home and some people like to go on dangerous adventures. This cat went out on a dangerous adventure every day."

Session 10

When *Nobody's Cat* (Joosse, 1992) was introduced, the children were surprised to see a second book with the same title, created by a different author and illustrator and published more than two decades later. However, when they looked at the covers and title page and listened to the opening lines, they noticed significant differences between the two stories: In this story, a feral cat lives in the woods with her four babies, who are as hungry as she is. When she has no more milk to give them, the feral cat "went to the people's house. It had been a long time since she had been near people" (n.p.). A boy discovers the cat on their porch, and his mother gives her a dish of cream. The feral cat returns to her nest to feed her babies and then carries one of the kittens to the house and leaves it on the porch.

When one of the children asked: "But why did she do that?" another child responded, "Maybe she couldn't feed all four of the babies." As the story unfolds, the mother cat returns to the porch three more times to leave each of her kittens, and the boy's mother finds homes for them. At the end of the story, the boy decides to keep the feral cat, and she seems to be happy to be his pet. The last lines of the story are: "Now nobody's cat belonged to someone. She wasn't wild anymore." A note about the author at the end of the book reveals that this story is based on her own experience with a wild cat that showed up at her door crying for food one day. And then, "day by day, one by one, the cat's babies appeared on her front porch. Ms. Joosse and her family found homes for both the mother and her kittens, and she was inspired to write *Nobody's Cat*." After hearing that this story is based on "a real cat," the children returned to the question posed earlier: "Why would a mother cat leave her kittens like that?" (Strategy 8).

"I think she gave them all away so they could have better homes."

"I think J. is right. The mother cat knew she couldn't feed them enough."

"I agree with J. and C., and she liked the boy, so she stayed with him."

"But she must've been so sad to have to give up her babies!"

"Maybe we could write a story called *Somebody's Cat* and tell what happened when the feral cat becomes a pet." [Several children volunteered to work with this boy on this project.]

"That other story was about a boy cat, and he only had to get food for himself. But a mother cat has to get food for her babies, too."

"In the city it was easier to find food, but in the woods it's harder. The mother cat was always thinking about her kittens."

"In the other story, the cat liked to be independent, so he didn't go home with that girl at the school. He went back to his box in the alley. But I think the mother cat was too sad to go back to the woods alone."

"I think we should make a happier ending when we write *Somebody's Cat*. Maybe she can have more babies, and she could *keep* them!"

At the conclusion of this session, the children were introduced to stories in the collection that feature cats on their own. Many of these books include authors' notes that explain the inspiration for these stories.

Across Town (Sara, 1992). A wordless storybook.

"Amanda." A poem by Karla Kuskin, in *Cat Poems* (Livingston, 1987).

Annie and the Wild Animals (Brett, 1985).

Cool Cat, School Cat (Cox, 2002). An early chapter book.

Ginger Finds a Home (Voake, 2003).

Goodyear the City Cat (Coats, 1987).

Homebody (McDonald, 1991). "This story is dedicated to the homeless and uprooted, animal and human alike, and to the gray cat on Stark Road."

Mrs. Merriwether's Musical Cat (Purdy, 1994).

One Dark Night (Hutchins, 2001).

The Third-Story Cat (Baker, 1987).

A Traveling Cat (Lyon, 1998).

Session 11

Prior to this session, the teacher set up a display of nonfiction texts about the diverse members of the cat family.

ABC Cats (Darling, 1998)

Amazing Cats (Parsons, 1990)

Bengal Cats (Stone, 1999a)

Big Cats (Simon, 1991)

Cat (Clutton-Brock, 1991)

Cats (Gibbons, 1996)

Cats (Grabianski, 1967)

Cats (O'Neill, 1998)

Cats: In from the Wild (C. Arnold, 1993, 1999)

The Cheetah (Stone, 1989a)

The Cougar (Stone, 1989b)

How to Talk to Your Cat (George, 2000)

The Leopard (Stone, 1989c)

The Life of a Cat (Feder, 1982)

Lion (C. Arnold, 1995)

Pippa, the Cheetah, and Her Cubs (Adamson, 1970)

Safari (Bateman & Archbold, 1998)

Siamese Cats (Stone, 1999b)

Spot a Cat (Micklethwait, 1995)

Tiger Tales and Big Cat Stories (Chancellor, 2000)

Tigress (Dowson, 2004)

The True-or-False Book of Cats (Lauber, 1998)

Wild Cats (Winston, 1981)

A World of Cats (Rowland, 1989)

Young Lions (Yoshida, 1989)

After the children had had an opportunity to explore these texts and to select specific titles to study with a partner, they were asked to draw pictures and write about one of the members of the cat family they had studied. They were also encouraged to use the Internet to search for additional information about this particular member of the cat family. After completing this research project, the children gathered together for Session 11 to share what they had learned about the different kinds of wild and domestic cats they had found in these books and to talk about the connections between domestic and wild cats. They also talked about the way specific authors of fiction had used factual information to develop realistic cat characters in their stories.

Session 12

When the teacher introduced *Tiger* (Allen, 1992), she invited the children who had focused on the tiger for their research project to share what they had learned about this "Big Cat" (Strategy 2). Then the teacher held up the book to show the picture of the large tiger spread across the front and back covers and the picture of a boy holding a duck on the title page. In this story, the villagers hear a rumor that a tiger lives in the woods, and they hire a famous hunter to kill it. Only a young boy, Lee, wants to protect the animal. The children responded to the unfolding text:

> "You can tell Lee loves animals from those pictures—the way he's holding the duck on the title page—and the little pig on this page."
> "That's why he doesn't want them to kill the tiger."
> "What's a rumor?"
> "It's a story that gets told over and over, but no one knows who started it or even if it's really true."
> "So the villagers *heard* about the tiger, but they didn't know if it's true."

As the story unfolds, the hunter follows the tracks of the tiger and then observes the tiger as it hunts, sharpens its claws on the bark of a tree, and enjoys a swim in the river. When the tiger emerges from the water, the hunter gets three shots.

As the children listened to this part in the story about the hunter taking aim at the tiger and shooting, they were clearly disturbed and puzzled by this turn of events. The children had seemed to identify with the boy in the story who wants to protect the tiger, and they did not want the hunter to kill this beautiful creature. As they listened to the text on the next page, the children expressed relief to hear that "the tiger loped elegantly away and out of sight" and that "the hunter packed away his camera and rested for awhile before beginning the trek back to the village" (n.p.). As soon as the children discovered that the hunter was using a camera instead of a gun, they wanted to go back to the beginning of the hunting scene to figure out how the author and artist had given them the impression that the hunter was using a gun. As they listened again to each line and examined each illustration, they were able to figure out the double meanings and wordplay used to lead up to the surprise at the end of this scene. At the end of the story, the hunter returns to the villagers with the news that there is no tiger in the woods. Only the photographer and the boy know the truth about the tiger.

The teacher read aloud the information at the back of the book about tigers and what can be done to save them from extinction as well

as about the South Chinese tiger in this story. After discussing the meaning of "endangered species" and "extinct," the children speculated about
the "hunter" in this story (Strategy 3):

> "I think maybe he took pictures of those animals in case they
> did get extinct, so we could remember them."
>
> "And we could see his photographs in books like in those
> [she pointed to the nonfiction books about animals]."
>
> "The hunter had a secret like in those other stories . . . like
> Charlie!"
>
> "The boy was the only one in the village that knew the secret.
> The hunter smiled and winked at the boy . . . he knew the boy
> would keep the secret."
>
> "This story had a secret and a surprise!"
>
> "The hunter was really a photographer. *That* was a surprise."
>
> "The people wanted to kill the tiger, but the boy didn't. That
> was the *problem* in the story!"
>
> "The villagers just thought about how much money they could
> get from the tiger skin. The boy cared about the tiger. He loved
> animals."

Session 13

When the children examined the picture on the front cover of *Heart of a
Tiger* (M. D. Arnold & Henterly, 1995), they wondered why a big tiger
was behind the little gray kitten. Some compared this picture with the
covers of *Newf* and *A Rose for Pinkerton*. The children also wondered
about the title of this story. Prior to the first page of the narrative, the
author includes some information about a custom among the animals:
"A Name Day Celebration is held and each animal born the previous
spring chooses its own name" (n.p.). The story begins a week before this
Celebration, and Number Four, the runt of a litter of kittens in India, is
worried that he might be stuck with the name "Smallest of All" or "Tiny
Gray Thing." He sets out in search of the Bengal tiger "so I can learn to
be like him and give myself a name like his on Naming Day." When he
finally encounters the tiger, the Bengal responds to Four's desire to learn
from him: "How can one teach wisdom? How can one teach bravery?"
But the small kitten persists and follows Beautiful Bengal day after day.
When Four sees the hunters with their guns, he is able to warn Bengal
and to save his life. Bengal says to Four: "You will never be a Bengal
tiger . . . . But inside, Little Four, you have a heart that will grow in wisdom and power as you grow." When Naming Day arrives, Little Four
chooses the name "Heart of a Tiger."

An author's note at the back of the book explains that although
"the animals' naming custom and celebration in *Heart of a Tiger* are fab-

ricated, many human cultures have similar customs and ceremonies."
The author provides examples of rituals and naming practices in diverse
cultures. For example, the practice of naming children according to birth
order is found in China and Japan, "in the same way the mother cat,
Visvasi, referred to her kittens prior to their name selection" in this story.
One of the children who was familiar with *The Dragon Prince: A Chinese
Beauty and the Beast* (Yep, 1997) noted that the seven daughters in this
variant are named according to their birth order and that Seven is the
heroine or "Beauty."

Session 14

For the final read-aloud/think-aloud session in this literature unit, the
teacher selected a traditional tale, *Puss in Boots,* adapted from Charles
Perrault's version of a French tale (Galdone, 1976). She introduced this
story as a very old tale that had been told and retold by storytellers long
before it was written down by Charles Perrault over three hundred years
ago. The teacher showed the children the number 398.2 printed on the
spine of the book and pointed to the section in the school library where
they would be able to find other old stories from around the world that
have been told and retold by storytellers for hundreds of years. When
she held up this book so the children could see the smiling cat with the
red boots on the front cover, she introduced this cat as a *trickster.* Most
of the children were familiar with another famous trickster, Anansi the
spider, and they were invited to talk about some of his tricks in preparation for entering into the world of Puss in Boots.

The opening paragraphs of this story reveal the problem faced
by the youngest son of the miller who has just died. "[The miller] left
the mill to his oldest son, and the donkey to his second son. To his youngest son he left the cat, Puss" (n.p.). The youngest son is worried that he
will be unable to earn a living with nothing but a cat. Fortunately, the
cat is a remarkable trickster who manages to solve his master's problems by outwitting an evil giant and gaining his fields and castle and
by helping his master win the hand of the King's daughter.

As this complex story unfolded and each new trick was revealed,
some of the children asked questions about the parts of the story that
puzzled them. For example, some wondered about the motivation behind the cat's behavior. Others wondered why the king would give such
fancy clothes to the miller's son. They worked together to figure out how
each of these tricks contributed to the success of the cat's ultimate plan
for his master's future as well as the connections between events oc-
curring earlier and later in the story sequence. By the end of the narra-

tive, the children were able to figure out why the cat planned to get rid of the wicked giant, and they were especially delighted with the clever way the cat outwitted the giant. One of the children noted that this story reminded him of *Do Not Open* (Turkle, 1981). "In this story an old lady says to a huge monster with magic powers, 'I bet you can't change as small as a little mouse' and it does and the lady's cat eats him just like in *Puss in Boots*."

After discussing Puss in Boots as a charming and cunning trickster, the children compared this story with others introduced in this literature unit:

> "This story is like *Opera Cat.* The cat helped her mistress, and Puss in Boots helped his master."
>
> "Katje was another cat that helped the humans. She saved the baby from the flood. But that one was a true story and this one is fantasy . . . like the other trickster stories."
>
> "The surprise was that the *cat* could solve all the problems and get money and a wife for his master!"
>
> "And the *secret* was that the Marquis of Carabas was a fake name for the miller's son!"

At the end of this session, the teacher called attention to several illustrated retellings of this old tale as well as examples of other traditional tales featuring cats, and invited the children to select one for independent reading at school or at home.

> *Jamil's Clever Cat: A Folktale from Bengal* (French, 1998). An Indian version of "Puss in Boots."
>
> *Puss in Boots* (Perrault, 1990).
>
> *Puss in Boots* (Light, 2002). The cat in this text is a female.
>
> *Puss in Cowboy Boots* (Huling, 2002). A retelling of the traditional tale set in Texas.
>
> *A Book of Cats and Creatures* (Manning-Sanders, 1981).
>
> *The Boy Who Drew Cats,* adapted from Lafcadio Hearn's *Japanese Fairy Tales* (Hodges & Hearn, 2002).
>
> *The Boy Who Drew Cats: A Japanese Folktale* (Levine, 1994).
>
> *The Cat and the Rooster: A Ukrainian Folktale* (Malkovych, 1995).
>
> *Catch That Cat! A Picture Book of Rhymes and Puzzles* (Beisner, 1990).
>
> *Cats of Myth: Tales from Around the World* (Hausman & Hausman, 2000).
>
> *The Chinese Story Teller* (Buck, 1971).
>
> *How the Manx Cat Lost Its Tail* (Stevens, 1990).

Mabela the Clever (MacDonald, 2001). An African folktale.

On Cat Mountain (Richard & Levine, 1994). A Japanese folktale.

Petite Rouge: A Cajun Red Riding Hood (Artell, 2001).

Sitti and the Cats: A Tale of Friendship (Bahous, 1993).

Stories to Tell a Cat (Schwartz, 1992). A collection of cat stories drawn from folklore.

Three Samurai Cats: A Story from Japan (Kimmel, 2003).

The White Cat: An Old French Fairy Tale (San Souci & Aulnoy, 1990).

Independent Reading and Writing, Dialogue Groups, and Assessment

Throughout this unit the children were introduced to selected titles in the collection and invited to choose books to read independently or with a partner in school or with their parents at home. The collection included fiction, nonfiction, folklore, and poetry thematically related to the stories shared in the sequence of read-aloud/think-aloud sessions. The children were encouraged to search for connections between the shared texts and their self-selected texts and to share their discoveries of intertextual links in the group discussions. For example, several children identified "cat-villains" such as the one-eyed cats in *Slim and Jim* and *Solomon: The Rusty Nail* and compared them with Sly Tom and "the cat that wanted to eat Ruby." The children who selected *The Church Mouse* noticed that the cover is similar to the cover of *Crackers*: "In both pictures, it looked like the cat and the mice were friends." The children were also invited to record their personal responses to these texts as well as their thoughts about characters, problems, and solutions. Their responses consisted of drawings and written texts, including dictated texts, depending on individual needs. The children kept their work in personal literature folders that they brought to individual conferences with the teacher to discuss their reading and writing experiences. During these conferences, children were often asked to retell or summarize a narrative in order to practice integrating important ideas and information in the story (see Strategies 5 and 6). According to Janice Dole and her colleagues, "The ability to summarize information requires readers to sift through large units of text, differentiate important from unimportant ideas, and then synthesize these ideas or create a new coherent text that stands for, by substantive criteria, the original" (Dole, Duffy, Roehler, & Pearson, 1991). These retellings or narrative reconstructions enabled the teacher to evaluate the child's understanding of the major content and structure of the story and to identify gaps in the meaning-making process. For example, if a child did not spontaneously infer important story ideas during the retelling, the teacher introduced "how" and "why" questions to call attention to implied meanings and to help the child engage in inferential thinking about plot and character development. Many of the children had difficulty with the "internal response category." The teacher's questions were designed to help these children make inferences about a character's motives, feelings, and thoughts and to relate these to the goals and actions that form the plot.

Although significant information can be derived from a child's retelling of a story, it is a time-consuming procedure. When an abbreviated version was necessitated by time constraints, the child was asked to "tell about the most important parts of the story." In a group setting, a round robin retelling of a shared story gave each participant a chance to share in the reconstruction of the story by contributing segments of the total narrative sequence, filling in gaps, or challenging the validity of a prior contribution. This activity served to reinforce and enhance the children's story-comprehension strategies and provided the teacher with clues about the nature of their transactions with a literary selection. Small dialogue groups were established to allow the children to talk about their independent reading with a few classmates who had read/heard the same title or thematically related stories. Jane Hansen, in her book *When Writers Read* (Hansen, 2001), discusses the value of "response sessions" in which children have a chance to share their reading experiences and to invite classmates to respond with comments and questions. Talking about a book helps children clarify their ideas as they think out loud. In the small dialogue groups, the children were not grouped in terms of ability, and the content and direction of the discussion were determined by the children as they talked about books they had chosen for independent literary transactions. Some of the children initiated a dialogue by sharing relevant material in their literature folders. Others initiated discussion by telling about a "really good part of the story" or by reading aloud a strong lead sentence. Some opened with their personal responses to the story or connections to other tales or to personal experiences. Those who had read nonfiction books generally began with what they had learned or something that surprised them or a question that was *not* answered in the book. In the whole-group sessions and in small dialogue groups, the children learned to respond to one another with mutual respect and support. In this context, the children gained self-confidence and the motivation to engage in further reading and sharing experiences.

A Collaborative Writing Project and Assessment

To conclude the Cat Tale Literature Unit, the children were invited to participate in a collaborative writing project to create an original story featuring members of the cat family. In preparation for the composing process, they engaged in a synthesis discussion by reviewing the stories introduced in the group sessions and recorded on the chart next to the story circle. They reviewed each story in terms of basic story elements, specific aspects of the author's craft, and intertextual links. For example, they focused on the central characters such as the hero or heroine, the villain, and the helper character; the problem; the setting; the genre; and the author's use of surprise to develop the plot and elicit reader response. According to Shelby Wolf (2004), "Literature . . . relies on the unexpected" (p. 97). Over the course of this literature unit, the children became increasingly aware of the "unexpected" components of the stories they heard or read independently, and they began to initiate a search for the "surprises" revealed by the author and/or the artist. As the children reviewed the story characters and the intertextual links among these stories, they noticed that cats were the villains in stories such as *Ruby* and *Brave Babette and Sly Tom* and that cats were heroines in stories such as *Katje, the Windmill Cat* and *Opera Cat*. They identified the different kinds of cats they had encountered in the shared texts: cats that talked and behaved like humans in animal fantasies such as *Ruby* and *Puss in Boots;* cats that were friendly to mice in animal fantasies such as *Crackers;* realistic cats in stories such as *Katje, the Windmill Cat* and *Charlie Anderson;* stray cats as in *Nobody's Cat;* pet cats as in *Opera Cat* and *Charlie Anderson;* and wild cats such as the tigers in *Tiger* and *Heart of a Tiger.* The children identified the surprises as well as the secrets in stories such as *Opera Cat, Tiger,* and *Puss in Boots.* This review session reinforced the children's grasp of the narrative elements and patterns in the shared texts introduced in this literature unit, and it enabled the teacher to assess what the children had learned about literature, authors' craft, and cats.

After reviewing the shared texts, the children were ready to think about the basic elements and techniques they would use to create their own story together. They began by suggesting ideas for the setting, characters, problems, and genre and voting for the ideas they liked best for this group-constructed story. In this way, the children eventually reached consensus that their story would be about a family of stray cats that lived in an alley in the city ". . . like the cat in *Nobody's Cat*" (Miles). The idea to feature a mother cat with four small kittens as the central characters was drawn from the story *Heart of a Tiger,* in which the kittens were named, One, Two, Three, and Four. The children decided that these would be the names of the kittens in their own story. After they voted for an urban setting, one child suggested: "We could have *two* settings like in *Charlie Anderson.* So the cats could go from the city to another place." After much discussion, the children decided that the cat family would go to Sea Breeze, a local amusement and water park, and the problem would be that one of the kittens would get lost there. (Later, they added other problems.) Because they wanted their cat characters to have the ability to understand human language and their story to be told from the viewpoint of the cat characters, the children chose to compose a fantasy with some elements of realism embedded in it ". . . like the story, *Opera Cat.*" As their story evolved, the children created the amusement park setting as the antagonist. For the cat family, it was a place of danger and confusion. The conflict in their narrative emerged as the cat family confronted one problem after another in this second setting: the wave pool, the roller coaster, the crowds of people. Several children had identified Miles's *Nobody's Cat* as an example of a story in which the "setting had lots of dangers for a cat." In a chapter featuring the literary element of setting in *A Critical Handbook of Children's Literature* (2003), Rebecca Lukens calls attention to the functions of setting, including the role of "setting as antagonist" and the ways setting can clarify conflict (pp. 153–56). Although the teacher had not taught her young students about the "functions of setting," the children seemed to have discovered the critical role of setting in stories such as *Nobody's Cat,* and they drew from their reading experiences to construct their own story. According to Frank Smith, the knowledge that writers require resides in texts, so to become a writer, one must learn to "read like a writer" (1984). In the context of the cumulative literary transactions in this literature unit, the children explored each new text in terms of its narrative elements and the author's craft. In the process, they were building a store of writer's knowledge that they used to create their own narrative.

The children chronicled the cat family's adventures in the amusement park and chose the wave pool as the scene of the "first problem." At this point in their narrative, they introduced a helper character, the lifeguard, who would play a significant role throughout their narrative. At the conclusion of their story, the children decided to create a happy ending in which the stray cat and her kittens would become the pets of the lifeguard who gives them each a special name. The children referred back to stories they had heard or read independently in which stray cats became pets: *Nobody's Cat* (the Joosse version), *Ginger Finds a Home,* and *Mrs. Merriwether's Musical Cat*.

The children incorporated the element of surprise in their story using the viewpoint of the cat family to describe their adventures. For example, when the mother cat and her kittens are taking a walk in the city, they get caught up in a crowd of people and find themselves in a crowded "house." The cat family is very surprised when it starts to move. Later, they learn that this "moving house" is called a bus, and that it takes people to new places. At the amusement park, the cat family finds another crowd of people lined up, and the mother cat thinks the people are waiting for the "moving house" to take them home. Unfortunately, they decide to follow "green shoes" and end up on a roller coaster ride. This is the most frightening experience of all for the mother cat and her four kittens!

After the children completed the final draft of their story, they each selected a scene to illustrate and then worked together to create a title page and to write a dedication and authors' note. This material was bound together, and their book was barcoded and added to the collection in the school library so other children could enjoy it. Each child was also presented with his or her own personal copy of this illustrated story.

Story Schema: Comprehension and Composition and Assessment

In the context of this literature unit featuring cats in fiction, nonfiction, and poetry, the children were given opportunities to internalize and use knowledge of text structure and story grammar as they engaged in the comprehension and composition of literary texts. According to April Nauman (1990),

> . . . a basic understanding of story structure enables readers to predict what kinds of things will happen next and to infer certain information not stated explicitly—skills that improve comprehension. An understanding of story structure also enables young writers to recognize what kinds of experiences make good stories and to select what details to use. We can use the work of story grammarians to help children become more sophisticated readers and writers. (p. 58)

The literary discussions featured in this chapter and the collaborative story writing project at the end of the cat tale unit revealed the children's use of their growing knowledge of story grammar to engage in comprehension and composition. The diverse literary texts carefully selected by the teacher and introduced in this literature unit apparently provided the "prior knowledge" that the children brought to their transactions with subsequent texts and to the creative process of composing an original literary text. For example, some of the stories included in the text set selected for this literature unit were told from the viewpoint of mice characters; other stories were told from the viewpoint of cat characters; and other stories were told from the viewpoint of human characters. Over time, the children discovered the importance of viewpoint in these narratives. For example, the story *Ruby* is told from the viewpoint of Ruby, a mouse, who grasps the hidden plans of the cat that offers to escort her on her journey to visit her granny and her granny's neighbor. The mouse also understands the cat's belief that the neighbor is also a mouse and a potential meal. Ruby and the reader know that the neighbor is a very large dog. To understand the story fully, the reader must be able to identify the plans and beliefs of both characters. The reader must understand that the mouse knows what the cat is up to and that the mouse engages in a double deception. That is, Ruby pretends to be unaware of the cat's plan and pretends to call her granny, while she is actually calling the neighbor. In order to understand the story, the reader must infer each character's beliefs, motivations, and plans. In story writing, children can use their understanding of characters' points of view, inner thoughts, beliefs, and motivations to create interesting narratives. For example, when the first graders featured in this chapter wrote their own story, they created humor by using the viewpoint and inner beliefs (or misconceptions) of the cat family to tell about their adventures in the "moving house" and in the amusement park.

The nature of the children's responses to the stories introduced in this literature unit and the nature of the story they created together at the conclusion of the unit reflected their growing awareness of story structure and their use of this knowledge to enhance their comprehension and composition of literary texts. In the literature units described in this book, students are exposed to a wide variety of literary texts, and reading and writing are taught and practiced together. In this context students have opportunities to learn to read like writers to become writers.

Note

1. The read-aloud/think-aloud sessions for this literature unit were held in the school library and were led by Moss. Marilyn Fenster, the first-grade teacher, led reading and writing workshops in the classroom and collaborated with Moss to develop this literature unit.

4 Friendship

Connecting Literature and Life

As young children move outside their immediate or extended family, they search for friendships in new social settings. The classroom community can offer a rich learning experience that supports social adjustment and growth and that provides opportunities for children to learn how to establish, build, and maintain friendships. Literature can be a significant resource for learning about oneself, about others, and about the nature of interpersonal relationships. The literature unit described in this chapter was structured around a text set featuring friendship and designed to create a bridge between the story world and the lives of children to foster this social learning.

The titles included in this text set were selected to provide a context for realizing the objectives that guided the development of this friendship literature unit. Although this unit was originally developed for grades 1 to 3, teachers of older students can adapt this plan for their own classrooms by selecting more complex and challenging literature featuring characters who are close to the age of their students.

The Friendship Literature Unit

Objectives for This Literature Unit

1. To provide opportunities for children to explore social relationships in diverse literary genres (contemporary and historical realistic fiction, poetry, and fantasy) as well as in stories that reflect the diversity found in our nation's classrooms

2. To provide opportunities for children (1) to learn to make inferences about thoughts, feelings, motives, and intentions of story characters; (2) to learn to anticipate consequences of words and actions of story characters; and (3) to make use of these understandings in their own social interactions

3. To provide opportunities for children to learn about different types of friendships; ways to establish, build, and maintain friendships; and language used in talking about social relationships

4. To provide opportunities for children to learn and practice the reading-thinking strategies that good readers use to generate meaning

---

5. To provide opportunities for children to explore the craft of authors and artists by studying their favorite books

6. To provide opportunities for children to engage in literary discussions about shared texts and to become involved in independent reading and writing experiences

Session 1

In order to introduce the focus for this literature unit in the first whole-group session, the teacher asked the children to talk about the word *friendship* and what it means to them. In response, the children shared their own experiences with best friends, their search for friends in new settings, their stories of making new friends in old settings, and problems they had encountered in social settings. Key ideas and issues that emerged out of this initial discussion about friendship were recorded on a wall chart near the story circle. The teacher introduced the tool of *semantic mapping*, to help the children organize the array of words and phrases on this chart until they had identified three central categories. A new chart was created with columns for each of these categories: "Making New Friends," "Best Friends," and "Problems." This new format was used as a work-in-progress chart throughout the unit.[1]

After writing *Circus Girl* (Bogacki, 2001) under the heading "Making New Friends," the teacher held up the front and back covers and initiated a cover-to-cover study of this book with the question: "What do you notice?" The children pointed to the girl on the front of the book and decided that she must be the main character because her picture fills up the front cover. Some children thought she was probably a performer in the circus. Others pointed to the back cover and decided this girl was called "circus girl" because she loved to watch the circus. They had noticed that on the back cover the girl from the front cover is sitting with two other children watching trapeze artists. The teacher opened the book and read the last line on the front flap: "In this lovely re-creation of an experience from his childhood, Tomek Bogacki shows that one simple act of kindness can open many doors." When asked to explain the meaning of these words, the children were able to figure out that this story is "about something that really happened when the author was a kid." However, they were puzzled by the last part and decided to come back to it after they had heard the story. When the children examined the title page, they identified the children they had seen on the back cover.

When the teacher read aloud the opening lines of the story, "It was late spring. I remember the day very well" (n.p.), several children had difficulty with the use of first person and asked about the "I" in this sentence. One child pointed to the picture of the boy looking out the window and said, "Maybe he's telling the story." Another child said, "I get it! It's the author talking! Remember it said that the story's about his childhood. Maybe that's a picture of him as a little boy!" After further examination of the multiple panels of illustrations on this page, another child pointed to the clothes on this character and recalled that this boy was also on the title page with the "circus girl." This prompted an additional discovery: "The girl on the title page is the same as the one on the first page of the story." In response to the children's discoveries, the teacher commented that they were using the kind of thinking strategies that all good readers use. She explained that good readers use all the clues they can find to help them make sense of the story by figuring out the parts of the story that the author leaves out of the text.

In this story, the narrator describes his excitement about the arrival of a traveling circus in his town and tells about the day a girl from the circus joins his class at school. The new girl is seated next to a very shy, friendless boy, Tim, and behind the desk of the narrator. The next day during a geometry lesson, Tim asks the narrator if he can borrow his eraser. The narrator's response surprised the children listening to the story unfold: "'Can't you see I'm using it,' I said abruptly" (n.p.). Then the new girl asks to borrow the eraser, and he breaks it in half and hands half to her. She thanks him and hands the eraser to Tim. After class, she returns the eraser. In response to this scene, one of the children listening to the story wondered: "Was that the act of kindness on the front flap?" A second child said, "It could be because it said it was just a little thing." At this point the teacher reread the line from the front flap. A third child asked: "But what about the part about the door?" The teacher replied: "Let's keep reading to see if we can find an answer to your question" (Strategy 8).

On the next page the narrator thinks about his behavior and decides to apologize to Tim and to give him the eraser half. Tim and Circus Girl both smile. Later, she invites the narrator and Tim to watch rehearsals, and when she asks Tim about his interests, he shares with them the remarkable model airplanes he had made. By the time they say goodbye to Circus Girl at the end of the week, Tim and the narrator have become friends. The closing line of the story is: "I often think that if it had not been for Circus Girl I would never have had this great friend, Tim." This closing line prompted a discussion about these characters.

The children noticed that Tim's classmates seemed to ignore him, but Circus Girl paid attention to him and "got the boy [the narrator] to pay attention to him, too." They found the connection between the eraser incident and the closing line of the story, and they found the answer to the question about the meaning of the words on the front flap. They understood that Circus Girl had helped the narrator appreciate the classmate he had previously ignored and had opened the door to a new friendship.

These children were invited to share their thoughts and questions in response to the text *as the story unfolded* and to practice the kinds of reading-thinking strategies good readers use to generate meaning in the course of their transaction with a literary text. The children gained confidence as active participants as they engaged in think-alouds and articulated their thinking processes in the collaborative discussion of the unfolding text (Strategy 13). This collaborative discussion began with a cover-to-cover study of each new selection (Strategy 1) introduced in this cumulative literature unit and continued as the children responded to the unfolding text and returned to relevant segments in the peritext to build understandings and generate meaning. They used visual and verbal clues to make predictions and inferences and to figure out significant ideas about establishing new friendships (Strategies 3, 4, and 5), and they generated questions that guided the meaning-making process (Strategy 8).

Session 2

In this group session, the teacher wrote a second title under the heading, Making New Friends, and showed the front and back covers of *David's Drawings* (Falwell, 2001). This is another story about a shy child. David is a young African American child who sees a "beautiful tree" on his way to school and decides to draw a picture of this leafless tree when he is in his classroom. He is alone until one of his classmates passes by, admires his picture, and suggests that it needs color. As other classmates join them, David lets them add their own details to his drawing so that it becomes a winter landscape. This informal collaborative activity enables the children to discover their shy classmate, and it opens the door to new friendships for David. When David goes home after school, he draws the leafless tree again, just as he had seen it that morning, standing alone on a snowy hill.

When the children examined the front cover, they decided that the boy drawing a line under the title was David. The back cover continues the cut-paper collages that form the background for the front cover. One child predicted: "This story is going to be about an art class." When the children looked at the two title pages, several children discovered that the second title page was a continuation of the first and that the common background was the design on a tablecloth. One child noticed the very small words, "Thanks Louise," printed on the pencil in the picture, and wondered if Louise was the author's friend. When they looked at the next large picture, they noticed that four children were walking together and wondered why David was walking alone. On the next page, the story opens with the words, "One gray winter day, David saw a beautiful tree" (n.p.). One child tried to answer their earlier question: "Maybe David just walks slower because he's looking at things in nature." As the children listened to the story unfold, they expressed their surprise that David let his classmates work on his picture:

> "He shouldn't let them mess up his picture. It's his picture!"
> "When someone tries to draw on my picture, I tell them *no*."
> "I was surprised he did that—but maybe he just wants to *share*."
> "Like when Tim [in *Circus Girl*] let his friends work on his model airplanes."
> "I liked it that David shared his picture with the other kids. Everyone had fun, and that's why the other kids wanted to be friends with him."

The ending of the story triggered more comments:

> "But that's what he wanted to draw in the first place! How come he let the kids put all that other stuff in his first picture?"
> "I think he had a good time doing a group picture with the other kids. Sometimes it's more fun doing things together—instead of just alone."
> "But sometimes you want to do things your own way—and that's why he did that *second* picture at home!"
> "But he *shared* in school—not like that boy in *Circus Girl*."
> "We should add 'sharing' to our chart—under 'making new friends.'"

At the conclusion of this discussion about the story, the teacher read aloud information about the author on the back flap: "Falwell's family moved often when she was a child, and like David, drawing was a catalyst for making new friends." The children compared this information with the note on the front flap of *Circus Girl* and were interested to discover that both authors had used childhood experiences to create their picture books.

A review of the children's responses to this story reveals some of the reading-thinking strategies they had used to generate meaning as the story unfolded. Their cover-to-cover study prompted predictions and questions that, in turn, guided their involvement in the story and helped them focus on important ideas in the text. They made connections between the events in this story and experiences in their own lives (Strategy 11). These "text-to-self connections" were based on their personal knowledge of classroom settings in which "sharing" is a major issue. They recognized another issue in this story: the conflict between enjoyment of collaborative endeavors and the need for privacy to engage in creative pursuits. The children also used intertextual links to generate meaning as they explored connections between *David's Drawings* and *Circus Girl*. In this way, they were becoming involved in a cumulative dialogue in which they initiated a comparative analysis as a natural dimension of literary study, using prior texts to understand current texts (see Strategy 11).

Session 3

In the third group session, *Amber on the Mountain* (Johnston, 1994) was introduced as another example of a story about building new friendships. Amber's isolated mountain home is a lonely place to live, but her world changes when Anna arrives from the city with her parents. Anna's father and his crew have come to build a road. A friendship grows between the girls as they share their worlds with each other. Anna joins Amber in doing the farm chores and helping Granny with her quilting; Amber joins Anna in the magical world of reading and stories. There is no school on the mountain, so Anna teaches Amber to read. When the road is finished, Anna must leave. Amber enjoys reading the letters Anna sends her, but she longs to be able to write to her friend. Amber works long and hard to teach herself to write, until the day she is able to write a letter to her friend. The children made two-way connections between the text and their own lives. The story triggered thoughts of personal experiences with new friends, and these personal experiences helped them reflect on the friendship between Amber and Anna:

> "Even though they're so different, they really enjoyed doing everything together. It's just like when we visit my grandpa's farm . . . and there's a girl that lives near his farm and we're different but also the same. We're really good friends."
>
> "You're like Amber and Anna. So this story could really happen!"
>
> "It's realism! The pictures make it *look* real, too." [The oil paintings that illustrate the story are by Robert Duncan.]
>
> "I liked how they taught each other new things. That's what real friends do."

"We should add this to our chart—that real friends help each other."

At the conclusion of the group discussion in the third session, the teacher called attention to a display of "friendship stories" and invited the children to choose titles they would like to read independently in the classroom or at home with members of their families. This text set or collection included a wide variety of books to meet the needs of children with diverse reading abilities: books for beginning readers and chapter books for transition readers or more experienced readers as well as picture books for read-aloud and independent literary experiences. The collection was divided into the three categories listed on the chart, and the teacher offered brief book talks about titles in each category to help the children select books for independent reading. The children were supplied with notebooks to be used as *literature journals* to record their responses to the stories they heard or read in the course of this literature unit.

The teacher also explained that children who would like to read their books with fifth-grade reading partners, should write their names on cards so each of the fifth-grade students who had volunteered for this reading-partner project could pick a name out of a jar. Many of the children chose to do their independent reading with a fifth grader; others chose to read with a classmate, or peer partner. These partners worked together throughout this literature unit. They read and discussed the books and worked together on the journal entries. For the most part, these partnerships enriched the children's experiences as readers and writers, and many of the partnerships evolved into special friendships that continued long after the unit was concluded.

An annotated list of the titles categorized as Making New Friends is included below:

Emma's Magic Winter (Little, 1998), part of an I Can Read Book series, is the story of shy Emma, whose new friend, the girl who moves in next door, helps Emma overcome her shyness enough to read aloud at school.

Samantha the Snob (Cristaldi, 1994, 2003), another book for beginning readers, is a first-person account of a young girl who resents a new, rich classmate who seems to be pulling her own best friends away from her. When they become better acquainted, they become friends.

Storm Cats (Doyle, 2002), a picture book with a rhymed text, is about two cats and their owners, two children who are neighbors but have never met. When the cats are lost during a storm, the children's search for their missing cats brings them together.

Leon and Bob (James, 1997) is a picture book about Leon, a young boy who is new in town and invents an imaginary friend, Bob, who is always available to play with him. When another boy moves in next door to Leon, he and Bob go to the house next door. Leon discovers that Bob is no longer with him, and he wonders if he is brave enough to make a new friend on his own. Although the text is simple and somewhat predictable, the story requires readers to "fill in the gaps" (Strategy 3).

Lizzie's Invitation (Keller, 1987) is the story of two girls who develop a new friendship after they meet and play together on the day of a birthday party to which they were not invited.

Ruby the Copycat (Rathmann, 1991). Ruby is a new student who tries to copy everything Angela does. Angela gets angry, and their teacher helps Ruby discover her own inner gifts. Eventually, the girls become friends.

Natalie Spitzer's Turtles (Willner-Pardo, 1992) is a transition chapter book about Jess, who fears that her friend Molly prefers to be with the new girl in their second-grade class.

The Best Friends Club (Winthrop, 1989) is a story of best friends Lizzie and Harold, who do everything together. Lizzie suggests they have an exclusive club, but when Harold wants to do things with Douglas, Lizzie is angry and Harold quits the club.

Junk Pile! (Borton, 1997) is the story of Jamie, a quiet young girl with a wonderful imagination, who lives in Appalachia and helps her Papa in his auto junkyard. Every day she listens to the cruel taunts of Robert, a new boy from the big house up on the ridge. When Jamie decides to make him a friend, she uses her creative imagination to reach out to him. By the end of the story, he has joined her in her magical world.

Little Dog Lost (Moore, 1991) is a picture book about Liz and her brother, Tom, who feel lonely when they move away from the city to the country with their family. However, their search for their little dog, Pip, helps them make new friends. (See *Storm Cats*.)

The Pizza Monster (Sharmat & Sharmat, 1989) is a humorous tale about secret agent Olivia Sharp, who helps gloomy Duncan find a friend.

The Scarebird (Fleischman, 1988, 1994) is about a lonely old farmer who discovers the pleasure of friendship when a young man seeking a job arrives at his farm.

Insects Are My Life (McDonald, 1995) is the story of Amanda, who has a passion for insects. Nobody seems to appreciate her passion until she meets Maggie, who explains, "Reptiles are my life." Readers know that she and Amanda will develop a very special relationship.

Anna's Secret Friend (Tsutsui, 1987). A young girl misses her friends when she moves to a new home, but she is not alone for long: a girl her age quietly reaches out to her in friendship.

Emily and Alice (Champion, 1993) is the first in a series of books about two friends who live next door to each other and become best friends (Champion, 1995, 2001a, 2001b). A note about the author explains that the story "was inspired by her childhood desire to have a next-door neighbor and best friend who was exactly like her."

Absolutely Lucy (Cooper, 2000), for transition readers, is the story of Bobby, a shy boy, who makes new friends with the help of his new beagle puppy, Lucy.

Shooting Star Summer (Ransom, 1992) and *Fourth of July Bear* (Lasky, 1991) are both about friendships that develop during summer vacations.

Dear Whiskers (Nagda, 2000), for transition readers, is the story of Jenny, who gradually develops a friendship with her second-grade pen pal, a new student from Saudi Arabia.

The Chalk Box Kid (Bulla, 1987) is a transition chapter book about Gregory, who has difficulty adjusting to his new neighborhood and school. Lonely and without friends, Gregory enjoys drawing on the walls of an abandoned chalk factory. He develops a special friendship with Ivy, a shy girl who is the one person who appreciates Gregory's artistic gifts.

The Girl Who Could Fly (Hooks, 1995) is a fantasy for transition readers about a boy who develops a friendship with a new neighbor, an extraterrestrial girl with mysterious powers.

Elaine, Mary Lewis, and the Frogs, also titled *Elaine and the Flying Frog* (Chang, 1988, 1991) another transition chapter book, is about Elaine, a Chinese American girl who feels like an outcast in her school. However, things change when she develops a friendship with her science partner.

Guinea Pigs Don't Talk (Myers, 1994) is another transition chapter book about adjusting to a new school. Lisa makes a new friend on her first day, but she also makes an enemy.

Teacher's Pet (Hurwitz, 1988) is another chapter book. Cricket competes with a new girl, Zoe, to be the teacher's pet. In the end, they become good friends.

Seeing Sugar (Brinson, 2003) is a chapter book about fourth grader, Kate, whose world is changed when her favorite teacher decides to give Kate's prized front and center seat to the new girl, Sugar Rose, and to place Kate at the back of the classroom. The title of the book refers to the turning point in the story: as Kate gets to know the new girl, they develop a friendship.

If the Shoe Fits (Mason, 2004) is a modern fantasy novel in which four princesses from four traditional fairy tales meet at a boarding school and become close friends.

The Gold-Threaded Dress (Marsden, 2002) is an early chapter book about a Thai American girl's search for friendship in her new school.

A number of the stories in this collection feature personified animal characters:

The Bear's Water Picnic (Yeoman, 1970)

Chester's Way (Henkes, 1988, 1989)

Friend or Frog (Priceman, 1989)

The Great Snake Escape (Coxe, 1994)

Lost (McPhail, 1990)

Oliver and Albert, Friends Forever (Van Leeuwen, 2000)

Orson (Rascal, 1995)

The Tale of Tawny and Dingo (Armstrong, 1979)

A Worm's Tale (Lindgren, 1988)

Session 4

In the fourth group session, the teacher entered a new title on the easel pad under the heading "Best Friends" and held up the book, *Simon and Molly plus Hester* (Jahn-Clough, 2001). Although this book is most appropriate for a younger audience, it was selected as a vehicle for studying the craft of an artist. The teacher invited the children to study the illustrations and try to figure out what choices the artist made or what the artist was thinking when she illustrated her story. When the children looked at the front cover, they identified the boy and girl dancing together as Simon and Molly and the girl walking toward them as Hester. One child predicted: "Simon and Molly were best friends first and then Hester came along and that caused a problem." He supported this prediction with observations about the way the artist positioned the three characters and the format of the title: "It looks like the words 'plus Hester' were added later." A girl who had read *Natalie Spitzer's Turtles* explained: "Jess [one of the characters in this story] was afraid her best friend wanted to be best friends with the new girl. Maybe that's the problem that happens when Hester comes!" Another child commented: "We could put that title under Best Friends, too." This observation prompted another child to suggest that the story about Natalie Spitzer could also be entered under the heading, Problems. The children were intrigued to discover this overlap in the categories they had established.

At this point the teacher commented: "You are thinking just the way good readers think as they begin to read a new book! You are using your experiences with other books and clues in the illustrations to make predictions about this story." Then she held up the back cover and front cover and asked: "What do you think the artist was thinking about as she created this whole picture?" [The background is bright yellow, and a large sun is placed in the center of the back cover.] The children used their prior knowledge to respond:

> "Yellow is a happy color. So maybe she wanted to show they're happy."
> "I think she also used the sun to show happiness."

When the children looked at the title page, they wondered why the artist put a bluebird, a bicycle, and a paper airplane in the center of the page. One child commented, "I think we'll have to get the answer from the story!" (see Strategy 8). On the next page, the dedications are written on two paper airplanes and around a plate with toast. Another child responded: "She [the artist] must be giving us clues. She drew more airplanes!" The first page of the story features the words "Simon and Molly play together every day. Just the two of them" (p. 3). The words are surrounded by pictures of these characters happily engaged in various activities. The children confirmed their classmate's initial prediction that "Simon and Molly were best friends first." The next page provides answers to questions about the bicycle and the toast: "Molly lets Simon ride her two-wheeler. Simon makes Molly toast with butter" (p. 4). When the children saw the third page of the story, one child immediately commented on the picture of a sun just above the two friends: "There it is again. She [the artist] put it there to show they're happy because they're best friends."

When Hester moves in and joins Simon and Molly, she wants to make paper airplanes instead of riding the bike. Molly joins her; Simon says, "Not me" (p. 9). The children noticed what the artist has done on this page:

> "Now Molly and Hester are on one page, and Simon is on the other page. So they're not together anymore."
> "And look what she [the artist] did! She put a cloud next to the sun!"
> "So we were right. It's a problem."
> "And now we know about the paper airplanes that she drew before. Maybe the airplanes start the problem—because Simon doesn't want to do it."

Later, when Simon makes toast with butter, Hester wants cinnamon-sugar on hers. So does Molly. "Simon ate his toast plain" (p. 10). The children noticed that the girls look happy, but Simon looks sad:

> "I think he feels left out. He wants to do it like they always did."
> "And look at the color in the back—it's orange instead of bright yellow."
> "I think the artist wants to show how Simon feels. He's not so happy."

When Simon thinks to himself, "Molly likes her better than me" (p. 14), he is sitting alone and is surrounded by a dark gray color. The children focused on the artist's craft again:

> "Now she shows how terrible he feels inside. It's like he feels dark inside."
> "I know how he feels. It's hard when things change."
> "And look—now there's only one bluebird in the picture. On the other pages there were two bluebirds. [This comment prompted the others to go back to check out this observation.]
> "Maybe the bird lost his friend, too."

As the story unfolds, the reader discovers that Hester doesn't want to ride the bike because she doesn't know how, and Simon doesn't want to make paper airplanes because he doesn't know how. When he is alone, he tries many times to make an airplane but is not successful. In frustration, he writes on one paper, "Hester, go away." When this information is revealed, the artist shows that both Hester and Simon are unhappy. The children noticed that the artist has painted a cloud that covers the sun on this page. They also notice that there are three bluebirds on this double-page spread. On the next page, Molly tells Hester that Simon can teach her to ride a bike, and then says: ". . . he is my very best friend" (p. 22). Fortunately, Simon overhears these words, and the children comment on the illustration:

> "Look how happy he is. He knows they are still best friends."
> "And now the sun is out! So it does show how he feels inside."
> "And you can see three birds again. Does that have something to do with the three friends?"

On the next page, Hester sees the crumpled paper with the angry words. The picture in which she reaches for it includes another cloud almost covering the sun. This prompts a comment about the artist's craft: "Oh no. That means trouble!! She always uses those clouds to show when there's trouble!" Fortunately, Simon is able to tear up the paper before

Hester sees the words. He agrees to teach Hester how to ride the bike, and she agrees to teach him how to make a paper airplane that flies. Again, the children commented on the artist's craft:

> "Now the cloud is gone, and the sun is shining because everyone is happy."
> "And now she painted that bright yellow—like on the front cover. And the three bluebirds are there. Maybe that shows that the three kids are friends now."

This interpretation was confirmed when the children looked at the last page: The three friends are dancing together with arms intertwined, and the three bluebirds seem to be dancing above them. Then the children returned to the back cover:

> "The artist did this to show the happy ending because the problems are solved, and they're all friends."
> "I like the way this artist shows how the characters feel inside."

At the end of this session, the children decided that this story could fit under all three headings ". . . because it's about making new friends and about best friends and about problems."

Session 5

For the fifth group session, the teacher entered another title under the heading, Best Friends, and held up the book *Matthew and Tilly* (Jones, 1991). The children used the title and pictures on the front and back covers to figure out that the setting is "a city with apartment buildings" and that Matthew and Tilly are best friends who live in the same building. They used the pictures on the title page and subsequent pages to confirm that the author used an urban setting for this story and that the central characters "were best friends who did everything together." At one point in the story a small misunderstanding escalates into name-calling and separation. The children identified and talked about the "problem in the friendship":

> "This story has a problem in the friendship, too. Maybe this should be under Problem and Best Friends." [He pointed to the headings on the easel pad.]
> "It started with such a little thing—but then they called each other names."
> "That's when Matthew went off by himself . . . he 'stomped up the stairs.'"
> "And the artist shows him sitting on the step with his head in his hands."

> "Sometimes you say stuff like that and you don't really mean it—it just sort of pops out. But words can hurt."
> "I wonder if they're going to be friends again."

This question is answered as the story continues. Matthew and Tilly engage in activities on their own, but they soon miss each other. Gradually, their anger fades, and Matthew is able to say "I'm sorry," to which Tilly responds with "So am I." At the end of the story, the children shared their thoughts:

> "I'm glad they got back together."
> "It's so easy to say mean words—and it's so hard to say 'I'm sorry.'"
> "In this story, it was the mean words that caused the problem."
> "When they are alone, the artist *shows* how lonely they feel—like in the story of Simon and Molly." [This prompted the children to examine these pictures and to practice "reading the pictures." They demonstrated their growing appreciation of artists' craft and their awareness of the power of a picture to reveal a character's inner feelings.]
> "It seemed like they both *wanted* to be friends again. But someone had to say sorry first! Matthew said it."
> "But he said it *after* he saw Tilly out the window, and she smiled at him!"

This comment prompted a return to this particular scene in the text as well as further discussion about the connections between this story and the children's personal experiences. Finally, the teacher read the note about the artist on the back flap. The children were interested to learn that the artist had used the Washington Heights neighborhood in New York City, where she used to live, as the setting for this story. One child responded: "So that's how she made the setting look so real. I like it when they tell you about the artist or the author."

At the conclusion of this session, the teacher shared a number of brief book talks about stories featuring best friends in order to help the children select a second book for independent reading. For example, she held up *Three Wishes* (Clifton, 1992) and explained that this was another book about best friends who discover the power of a few words to cause a problem in their friendship. In response to this book talk, the children decided that stories featuring problems could be integrated into the list of stories featuring best friends. An annotated list of the titles placed under the new category Best Friends/ Problems is included below:

> *Robbie and Ronnie* (Kliphuis, 2002), a book for transition readers, is about two boys who are best friends. Their problem is

Dennis, a bully who often picks on them. However, by engaging in teamwork, they manage to outsmart Dennis and his friends.

Jamaica and Brianna (Havill, 1993). When Brianna teases Jamaica, hurt feelings lead to angry words and a rift in their friendship. When Jamaica begins to understand the reasons behind Brianna's words, she is able to express her empathy. Her words, "I know how you feel," open the door for the communication that allows them to resume their friendship.

Meet Danitra Brown (Grimes, 1994). Zuri Jackson introduces the reader to her best friend, Danitra, in a collection of thirteen poems.

Together (Lyon, 1989) is an illustrated poem about friendship.

Alex Is My Friend (Russo, 1992). Ben tells about his friendship with Alex, which had begun years before when they were both toddlers. Their friendship continues and grows in spite of the fact that Alex is a dwarf and sometimes has to use a wheelchair. On the back jacket flap, a note about the author explains that this story was inspired by her own son's friendship with a boy like Alex.

Best Friends (Kellogg, 1986). Best friends Kathy and Louise do everything together until Louise goes away for the summer. Kathy feels lonely and then angry and jealous when Louise writes to her about the good time she is having with her new friends. When Louise returns, they resume their friendship, and their relationship is almost, but not quite, the same.

Shack and Back (Crowley, 1993) is about a group of friends who have formed a gang. When one boy says, "Cooking is for sissy-girls," the girls leave the gang. Only a change in attitude and an apology can settle the differences between them.

Ira Says Goodbye (Waber, 1988) and *The Best-Ever Good-Bye Party* (Hest, 1989) are both about best friends who must cope with separation because one is moving away. In both stories, the children have difficulty expressing their feelings about the anticipated move. Only when they reveal their inner thoughts are they able to repair their relationship.

Lester's Dog (Hesse, 1993) portrays a friendship between two boys who have learned to communicate with each other in spite of the fact that one of the boys is hearing-impaired and does not speak.

The Tin Heart (Ackerman, 1990) is a picture storybook intended for more mature readers. It is about two girls who live on opposite sides of the Ohio River at the onset of the Civil War. Although the girls are separated by a river and a war, their friendship continues.

Freedom Summer (Wiles, 2001). This picture book for older readers is another example of historical realism. The setting is 1964; the central characters are Joe, a white boy, and his best friend John Henry, an African American boy. Joe is pleased that a new law will allow John Henry to swim in the town pool, but they discover that prejudice still exists.

The Bracelet (Uchida, 1993) is also a picture book for more mature readers and is another example of historical realism. This story is based on the author's own experience as a young Japanese American girl during World War II. When seven-year-old Emi and her family are forced to leave their home and go to an internment camp in 1942, her best friend, Laurie Madison, gives her a gold heart bracelet.

Albertina, the Animals, and Me (Fowler, 2000), a chapter book for transition readers, is about Molly and her best friend, Albertina, who collaborate on a plan to get a pet.

Can Do, Jenny Archer (Conford, 1991) is another transition chapter book. Jenny discovers the meaning of a true friend when a can-collecting contest puts a strain on her relationship with her best friend.

Red Ribbon Rosie (Marzollo, 1988), another transition chapter book, is the story of a friendship that is almost destroyed when winning a race at school becomes more important to Rosie than her friendship with Sally, until she begins to reexamine her priorities.

The Great Fishing Contest (Kherdian, 1991), a transition chapter book, and *Addie's Bad Day* (Robins, 1993), a book for beginning readers, are both about good friends who help each other.

The Skirt (Soto, 1992), for transition readers, is about two best friends who work together to retrieve a folklorico skirt that has been left on the school bus.

Amber Brown Is Not a Crayon (Danziger, 1994) is a transition chapter book about best friends coping with separation. A sequel to this story, *Amber Brown Goes Fourth* (Danziger, 1995), is also in the collection.

Maggie and Me (Staunton, 1990), a transition chapter book, is a first-person account by Cyril about his friend, Maggie. In a series of humorous episodes, Cyril describes the challenges involved in maintaining a friendship with a dynamic, self-confident individual who will dominate him if he lets her.

Jake Drake Know-It-All (Clements, 2001). In this early chapter book, Jake's attempt to win the third-grade science fair competition threatens his relationship with his best friend, Willie.

Winnie (Dancing) on Her Own (Jacobson, 2001), an early chapter book, is the story of Winnie, who is upset when her two best friends enroll her in a ballet class with them. She would prefer to spend this time at the library with them according to their previous routine.

Truly Winnie (Jacobson, 2003), an early chapter book about Winnie and her two best friends during their first summer camp experience.

The Double-Digit Club (Bauer, 2004). In this chapter book, Sarah and Paige are best friends until Paige accepts an invitation to join a local clique of popular girls—without Sarah.

Several of the books about good friends are animal fantasies:

Jack and Rick (McPhail, 2002). For beginning readers.

Pearl and Wagner: Two Good Friends (McMullan, 2003). For beginning readers.

New Pig in Town (Wheeler, 2003). For beginning readers.

Rockin' Reptiles (Calmenson & Cole, 1997). An early chapter book.

Farfallina and Marcel (Keller, 2002). A picture book.

Why Are You Fighting, Davy? (Weninger, 1999). A picture book.

Don't Fidget a Feather (Silverman, 1994). Picture book.

George and Martha 'Round and 'Round (Marshall, 1988). A picture book.

Two of the stories included in this collection are traditional tales in which animal characters are personified but retain basic characteristics that are true to their own species. These stories represent two different literary genres and provide an opportunity for children to discover that friendship has been a topic of interest around the world for centuries!

The Ringdoves: From the Fables of Bidpai (Kamen, 1988), is an ancient tale told in 300 BCE. This Indian fable teaches the power of friendship, loyalty, and teamwork and features several animal friends who band together to help one another escape from the hunter.

Eagle Boy: A Pacific Northwest Native Tale (Vaughan, 2000). According to the author's note, "The legend of Eagle Boy has long been told along the Pacific Northwest coast . . . . Yet, no matter the source or whether the tale is written or spoken, a common thread prevails of a boy befriending the majestic eagle. Their relationship demonstrates to all people the values of friendship and trust—underscored in this version by the power of forgiveness between the boy and his people" (n.p.). Eagle Boy is an orphan boy who is protected by his friends the eagles during the harsh winter, and his friendship with the eagles eventually saves his village from starvation.

Session 6

Rosie and the Yellow Ribbon (DePaolo, 1992) introduced in this session, is a contemporary story that features the "values of friendship and trust" and the "power of forgiveness." Rosie and Lucille are best friends who like to do the same things and like to do things together. However, distrust almost shatters their friendship. An accusation leads to angry words and separation. When Rosie says, "I'm sorry, Lucille," the words and the feelings expressed in them seem to be enough to repair the rift between them and to enable them to resume their friendship.

The illustrations in this book suggest that this is an interracial friendship in an urban setting. Many of the friendships portrayed in the stories included in this text set reflect the diversity found in our nation's classrooms today. These stories were selected to help break down barriers of race and gender and to move beyond stereotypes that have been accepted in children's books in the past. For example, boy-girl friendships are featured in *The Best-Ever Good-Bye Party, Maggie and Me, The Chalk Box Kid, Addie's Bad Day, Matthew and Tilly,* and *Three Wishes.* The latter book and *Meet Danitra Brown* feature African American children. *The Skirt* features a Mexican American girl. Interracial friendships are featured in *Shack and Back, Together, Matthew and Tilly, Jamaica and Brianna, The Bracelet,* and *Freedom Summer.* In Kellogg's *Best Friends,* the two girls develop a friendship with a neighbor, a seventy-two-year-old man. Other stories introduced in subsequent sessions also feature intergenerational friendships. Stories such as *Lester's Dog* and *Alex Is My Friend* are about friendships that include children with physical handicaps. *The Tin Heart* tells the story of best friends who live on opposite sides of the Ohio River, which places their families on opposing sides during the Civil War. Children who are exposed to a wide variety of stories about friendships that cross lines of gender, age, race, culture, and ability are given the opportunity to broaden their perspective about the human experience and to learn to view diversity as a natural part of social interactions.

After *Rosie and the Yellow Ribbon* was read aloud, the children talked about the importance of trust in a friendship. The children also initiated a discussion of the intertextual links they had found as they compared this story with other stories they had heard or read independently:

> "The friends in this story and in *Three Wishes* split up because of mean words."
> "In both stories, they *wanted* to be friends, but sometimes it's too hard to say you were wrong."

> "I read *I'm Not Invited?* [Bluthenthal, 2003]. Minnie thinks her friend didn't invite her to his birthday party, and she feels terrible all week. But then she finds out it's his *sister's* party. And she's so happy. I know just how she was feeling—so left out! But she should have *trusted* him!"
>
> "I read *Eagle Boy* with my mom. It's an old story but it's also about saying you're sorry and about forgiveness."

As the children discussed other stories in which a problem causes a rift in a friendship, they identified the nature of the problems and the resolutions in each story and found interesting connections.

Session 7

When the children gathered together for Session 7, the teacher added another heading on the chart, Characters Who Change, and entered a title in this new column: *Bailey, the Big Bully* (Boyd, 1989). Bailey is a bully who needs to have his own way and threatens anyone who defies or questions his demands. He uses fear and force to get the other children to play with him. When the new boy, Max, appears on the scene, Bailey's position is challenged for the first time. Max not only refuses to go along with Bailey's demands, he actively defends victims of Bailey's physical abuse. When Max invites the children to build a tree fort with him, Bailey is left alone until he decides to join the group as a partner and a friend. After this story was read aloud, the children drew from their own personal experiences to respond to the story. In addition to making text-to-self connections, they made text-to-text connections (Strategy 11):

> "There's a big kid in my neighborhood who is just like Bailey. He always picks on the little kids, and everybody is afraid of him."
>
> "Max was the first one to stand up to Bailey."
>
> "When Max *invited* Bailey to join the group in the tree fort, that was probably the only time anyone was nice to him. Max showed him how to be friends."
>
> "I like that last part when Max said, 'Isn't it more fun to be a friend?' and they had their arms around each other. So Max really helped him change from a bully to a friend!"
>
> "So *that's* why this story is under Characters Who Change!"
>
> "In that first story we read [*Circus Girl*], the narrator changed. When he got to know that shy kid, they got to be friends."
>
> "I read a book with my dad called *Junk Pile!* There's a bully in that story, too, but the girl he's mean to gets him to change. She's like Max!"
>
> "In the book I read, there's a bully like Bailey and a new kid in school like Max. It's called *The Recess Queen* [O'Neill, 2002]. In this story, the mean girl changes, too."

"In the book I read there's a shy girl who is afraid to read out loud in school when it's her turn. Then she makes a friend, and the friend helps her change."

After the children had had time to share these and other connections triggered by the text, *Bailey, the Big Bully*, the teacher asked them to think about the way the author had portrayed this character and to focus on *how and why he changed* as well as how other characters helped him change. She clarified the notion of "inner change" by focusing on the children's own discoveries of story characters who had changed. For example, she used the narrator in *Circus Girl* as an example of a character who changed his attitude about Tim and then changed his behavior toward this boy he and his classmates had previously ignored. The teacher used Emma (in *Emma's Magic Winter*) as an example of a character who gained self-confidence and the courage to read out loud in school as a result of the encouragement and support of a new friend. At this point, the children identified Circus Girl, Max, and Emma's new friend as examples of "helper characters" who helped these characters change on the inside.

At the end of this session, the teacher introduced the children to a few new titles of stories featuring bullies as well as "characters who change inside" (or *dynamic characters*). These titles were added to the collection:

> *Bully Trouble* (Cole, 1989, 2003), written for beginning readers, is about best friends Arlo and Robby and a bully, Big Eddie, who picks on the smaller children until Arlo and Robby decide to stand up to their enemy.
>
> *Cory Coleman, Grade 2* (Brimner, 1990), another chapter book for transition readers, is about seven-year-old Cory, whose birthday skating party is ruined by Delphinius, the class bully.
>
> *Hats!* (Luthardt, 2004) is an almost wordless story that shows the power of kindness and cooperation.
>
> *King of the Playground* (Naylor, 1991, 1994). Kevin is intimidated by Sammy, a boy at the playground. Kevin discusses this with his dad, who helps him gain the confidence to stand up to Sammy.
>
> *Sycamore Street* (Christiansen, 1993), a chapter book for transition readers, is the story of best friends, Angel and Chloe, who love to engage in games of pretend. They try to avoid Rupert, who "doesn't know how to pretend" and always manages to annoy them.
>
> *Shredderman: Secret Identity* (Van Draanen, 2004), a chapter book featuring older characters, is about fifth grader Nolan Byrd,

who is tired of being a victim of the class bully and seeing him get away with his cruel treatment of other children. Nolan decides to create a secret identity for himself—on the Internet. He launches Shredderman.com as a place where he can "fight for truth and justice" (p. 138) and expose the bully. In the process, Nolan gains the self-confidence and the courage to stand up for himself as well as the other victims of this bully. By the end of the book, the bully doesn't change but his other victims begin to stand up for themselves, too.

Summer Wheels (Bunting, 1992), an illustrated transition book with six chapters, was introduced as an example of a story in which an antagonistic character changes as he encounters someone who trusts and cares about him.

Bunting's book evoked an emotional response and sparked much discussion among the children who selected it for independent reading. Because of the special appeal of this book, the teacher shared it with the whole class and invited them to try to detect how Bunting had developed the character who changed as well as the "helper character" and how this author had elicited an emotional response in her readers.

This study of authors' craft set the stage for a creative writing project in which the children composed new stories featuring characters who change inside as well as "helper characters." The children were invited to work together in small groups or with their reading partners for this project. Lucy Calkins (1994) refers to this process of learning to write by studying an author's craft as an apprenticeship in which authors of favorite books become children's mentors. Calkins used the term *touchstone* to refer to books that have the potential for teaching children about author's craft (pp. 277–78).

Session 8

When the teacher introduced *Sing to the Stars* (Barrett, 1994) in this session, she asked the children to listen to the story and then decide in which column on the chart this title should be entered. After examining the picture on the front cover [an African American boy playing a violin], the children talked about the boy and his possible role in this story:

"He looks like he really likes to play the violin."
"I think he's going to be friends with someone who likes music as much as he does."
"I think so, too . . . like my best friend likes to do the same stuff I like to do."
"A lot of the characters we've read about are like that."

These children had initiated a cover-to-cover study of this book using clues from the front cover to activate prior knowledge from stories and personal experiences to make predictions and inferences. This is the story of Ephram, a young boy who is learning to play the violin, and his friendship with Mr. Washington, who had been a famous pianist before he lost his sight in the car accident that killed his daughter. Ephram tries to convince Mr. Washington to play the piano at a neighborhood concert in the park. Only at the last minute, when the lights go out because of a power failure, does Mr. Washington agree to join Ephram on stage, where the two friends share their music with the crowd. The story concludes with the words: "and in the darkness the music sings to the stars."

The story opens with the lines: "Ephram walks sprightly down the street. Head high, he swings his black case back and forth, to and fro." One child responded to the author's craft reflected in these opening sentences: "The author tells you right away how happy he is because of his violin . . . by the way he's walking. You don't even need the picture . . . the words say it. And the way he's walking, it's like he has a song in his head."

When the teacher reached the end of the story and read the closing lines, the children were silent for a few moments . . . a silence that seemed to suggest they had entered into the story and had caught its mood. Even when they began to share their responses to the story, they seemed to sustain the mood, speaking in almost muted voices, as if they were still part of the crowd at the outdoor concert sitting in darkness, listening to the music singing to the stars.

> "That was awesome! I didn't think he would play because he stopped when his daughter got killed. Now I think he'll start playing again . . . with Ephram . . . and maybe even for audiences."
> "That's what friends do . . . they help each other do stuff they don't think they can . . . like when Emma's friend helped her to read out loud in class."
> "I liked it when everyone on stage had to stop because the microphone and speakers didn't work . . . but Ephram and his friend didn't need electricity to make music."

After the children shared their thoughts and feelings about these characters, the teacher read aloud the author's dedication, words from Ecclesiastes 4:12: "Where a lone man may be overcome, two together can resist. A three-ply cord is not easily broken." This dedication prompted a discussion of the meaning of the words as applied to the nature of friendship.

At the conclusion of this session, the children observed that this story included a character who had changed on the inside as well as a helper character. However, the children decided that they needed a new category on the chart, and they agreed to call it Friendships with Older People. In response, the teacher added to the collection several titles that would fit in this new category and talked briefly about each book to promote interest in one of these titles for additional independent reading.

John and the Fiddler (Foley, 1990) is the story of a friendship between a young boy and an old violin-maker who gives the boy his first violin and teaches him to play.

Shoeshine Girl (Bulla, 1975, 2000). The cover of this transition chapter book shows the central characters: a young girl and an elderly man who runs a shoeshine stand.

The Gift (Coutant, 1983) is a story for transition readers about the friendship between an Asian American girl and an elderly woman.

Pink Paper Swans (Kroll, 1994) is a picture book about Janetta, an eight-year-old African American girl who develops a friendship with her neighbor, Mrs. Tsujimoto, an elderly Japanese American woman.

The Storyteller (Weisman, 1993). In this picture storybook, nine-year-old Rama, a Pueblo Indian, develops a friendship with a lonely old woman, Miss Lottie. Rama shares with Miss Lottie the stories told by her grandfather and gives her a "storyteller doll" to keep her company.

Mrs. Katz and Tush (Polacco, 1992) is a picture storybook about a friendship between Larnel, a young African American boy, and his neighbor, Mrs. Katz, a lonely Jewish widow.

Camille and the Sunflowers (Anholt, 1994) is a picture storybook about Vincent van Gogh. Despite the ridicule of the neighbors, Camille, a young French boy, and his family befriend the lonely painter who comes to their town.

Elijah's Angel: A Story for Chanukah and Christmas (Rosen, 1992) is also based on a real person, Elijah Pierce (1892–1984), a black barber and woodcarver who lived in Columbus, Ohio. This is a thought-provoking story of the friendship between Michael, a nine-year-old Jewish boy, and Elijah, a Christian man in his eighties.

Loop the Loop (Dugan, 1992) follows the friendship between a quiet young girl and a lively old woman in a wheelchair. Their friendship continues even after the woman enters a nursing home.

Island Baby (Keller, 1992), set on a Caribbean island, is about a friendship between Simon, a young boy, and Pops, an elderly man who runs a bird hospital. Simon helps Pops nurse an injured baby bird back to health.

The Last Snow of Winter (Johnston, 1993) is about an elderly sculptor and his friends, the neighborhood children. The great artist creates a snow sculpture for his friends, and later he receives a similar gift from the children during the last snow of winter.

One child who had read several of these stories featuring cross-generational and cross-cultural friendships shared this insight in a group session: "Sometimes it was the old person who needed a friend and sometimes it was the young person who needed a friend. But at the end of the story, they weren't lonely anymore. And they shared things and they learned a lot from each other. That's what friendship is . . . even if you're different ages."

Session 9

In preparation for a *synthesis session*, the teacher invited the children to review the work-in-progress chart and their journal entries about the stories they had explored in this cumulative literary experience. Then they were asked to record important ideas about friendship they had discovered in the course of their growing involvement with friendship stories and poems. When the children gathered together for the ninth session, they shared their discoveries and insights about the nature of friendship. Many of the children supported their contributions with relevant stories or poems they had heard or read. For example:

> "Sometimes people say stuff before they *think* . . . like in *Matthew and Tilly*."
>
> "And when angry words come out, you can't get them back, and it can wreck a friendship . . . but you can use words to fix it [the friendship] , too . . . like in the story of Rosie and in *The Best-Ever Good-Bye Party*."
>
> "In a lot of these stories, the friends stop talking to each other, and it gets harder and harder to get back together again even when they *both* really want to."
>
> "I think that friendship means that friends should *talk* about stuff they really feel instead of hiding it or just walking away or pretending they don't care."
>
> "I think friendship also means trying to *understand* the other person. Like in my book, this girl figures out why her best friend is saying mean things to her [*Jamaica and Brianna*]."
>
> "Another thing about friends is that they really trust each other."

"In that book about the Bicycle Man—He trusted those kids . . . and they knew he was their friend because he trusted them [*Summer Wheels*]."

"Friends *help* each other . . . like in *Amber on the Mountain*."

"A friend is someone who *appreciates* you. . . like in *The Chalk Box Kid*."

"People can get to be friends . . . even if they're *different* . . . like one's old and one's young or one's a boy and one's a girl or they're from different countries or have a different religion or have to use a wheelchair like Alex or can't hear like in *Lester's Dog*."

"When you like the same things, it's like the glue in a friendship. Like in *Backyard Rescue* [Ryden, 1994] two friends rescue hurt animals and take care of them together."

"Some of the books are about *groups* of friends like in *Roxaboxen* [McLerran, 1991] or *Angela's Top-Secret Computer Club* [Keller, 1998]."

"And friends *cooperate* . . . like in that fable, *The Ringdoves*."

"I read a funny one about cooperation . . . *Fishing for Methuselah* [Roth, 1998]. They both changed after they learned how to use teamwork. A lot of the books we read have characters that change inside."

The nature of this discussion changed as the children gradually moved from a focus on the story world to a focus on their own social worlds. At this point, the children were asked to identify how they were using the insights and understandings articulated in this session to develop new friendships and to solve problems in existing relationships. Some of the children talked about making new friends as they worked together in the course of the literature unit activities. Several children shared examples of particular stories that had given them ideas for solving problems they were having with a best friend, and others talked about story characters that had helped them learn to cope with bullies.

Beyond Talk

The excerpts taken from this synthesis discussion reveal the children's ability to draw significant ideas about social interactions and the nature of friendship from their experiences with diverse selections of prose and poetry. Throughout this literary unit, the children were invited to talk about these reading experiences in the whole-group sessions, with peer partners or fifth-grade partners, in small dialogue groups, or in informal encounters at lunch or on the playground. They also responded to these literary selections by drawing and writing in their journals. Throughout the unit, the children engaged in a variety of other forms of meaning generation and exploration of ideas. For example, several children chose *Circus Girl* as a touchstone text to help them write a story with a character who "changes inside." Others used *Amber on the Mountain* as a touchstone text for their creative writing. Paint, markers, clay, etc., were available for creative responses to favorite stories or poems. Some chose to interpret stories through drama, dance, or music. Often, in the middle of listening to a story, a child would think of an idea for a play or a painting. Sometimes an impromptu dramatization of the story would emerge at the end of a read-aloud session. This usually started with one or two children expressing an interest in "doing this story." Other children had already thought about what character they wanted to be! These impromptu creative dramatizations of favorite stories generally reflected the children's ability to portray emotional responses, in words and body language, in the process of acting out the social relationships in the story. That is, they demonstrated their grasp of the consequences of words or behaviors in a social interaction and provided the teacher with evidence of what they had learned from their immersion in the friendship stories. One child used whispers to reveal the inner thoughts or motives of a character whose words expressed a different meaning. Other children began to use this dramatic technique in their informal plays. These *whispers* revealed the children's grasp of a character's motives, thoughts, and feelings and their use of clues in the text to make inferences about a character's internal responses and to create subtext (see Strategy 3). In addition to these informal, child-initiated responses to the literary experiences, the teacher offered suggestions for other ways individuals, partners, or groups could demonstrate their understandings about friendship. Examples of some of the projects the children selected are included below.

Book of "Helpful Hints"

In a whole-class session, the children generated a list of "helpful hints" for being a friend. Here are a few examples of the hints suggested by the children:

- Share things and ideas with your friend.
- Share secrets with your friend and *keep* them secret.
- Do things with your friend.
- Find out what your friend likes to do.
- Teach your friend how to play chess, and ask your friend to teach you something.
- Read together; exchange favorite books.
- Write a story together and illustrate it.

- Tell funny stories to make your friend laugh.
- Invite your friend to come over.
- Help your friend look for something that's lost.
- If you have a fight, *talk* about it.
- If your friend gets bossy, tell your friend how you feel.
- Remember: Words can hurt and help!
- Use teamwork to make a model airplane or build a snowman.
- You can play with other friends and still be a *best friend* with your special friend.
- Remember: Best friends trust each other!

After the children completed their list, they worked with partners to act out each of the hints, and the teacher took a picture of each scene with a digital camera. The children composed appropriate captions for these pictures and then entered the text into the computer. The final product was an illustrated book called *The Big Book of Helpful Hints for Being a Friend.*

Word Portraits

The children were asked to think about how one can get to know another person. In response, they generated a list of questions one could ask another person to learn about his or her special interests, hobbies, or talents; favorite books, food, or sports; what he or she likes to do and doesn't like to do; and so on. The children wrote their names on slips of paper, placed them in a jar, and then each child pulled a name from the jar. The next step was to discover what was special about the person whose name each had selected. When they had gathered enough information, they wrote "word portraits" of those individuals. One purpose of this project was to encourage the children to look outside themselves, to see another person with sharpened awareness and greater appreciation, and to learn to view the world through the eyes of another person.

When these word portraits were shared in a whole-class session, many of the children were able to guess the identity of the subject of the portrait. However, most of the children discovered new things about their classmates as well. In some cases, the discovery of common interests drew individuals together into new social interactions, and, for some, into new friendships. One child observed that the teacher in the story *Circus Girl* should have introduced this project to his students so that all the children would get to know classmates like Tim. This child added: "Tim was so shy, he seemed to be invisible to the other kids."

Secret Pen Pals

Another class project involved children in other classrooms. Two teachers paired up children in two same-grade classrooms. The children were given code names for their pen pals; only the teachers knew the names of the children in each pair. The children were asked to write to their "secret friend" or pen pal to get to know each other. They could use some of the same questions they had used to get to know a classmate for the word-portrait project. The children who had not developed adequate transcription skills for this project worked with their fifth-grade partners or with the teacher. Some of the children chose to use e-mail to communicate with their pen pals. Several pen pal partners shared their responses to the book, *Dear Whiskers,* a story about a second-grade pen pal project. The correspondence continued until the end of the semester. At this point, a lunch was arranged for the children in the two classrooms; each child wore a name tag with his or her code name so the secret friends could meet each other and have lunch together. Many of these pen pals continued to get together on their own after this initial meeting, and a number of new friendships emerged.

Retelling Favorite Stories

The children were also invited to collaborate with classmates on projects that involved retelling a favorite story through art, drama, dance, or music. For example, two children worked together on a cartoon sequence that included thought and speech bubbles and that revealed their grasp of the relationship between the inner thoughts of their characters and their verbal utterances. Others re-created key scenes through pantomime that required their audience to *read* gestures, body language, and facial expressions in order to grasp the emotional content of the retelling.

Writing Original Friendship Stories

A final project for the Friendship Literature Unit involved the creation of original friendship stories inspired by the rich literary experiences offered in this thematic unit. The children could choose to write their stories independently or with a peer partner or fifth-grade partner or they could form small groups to engage in a collaborative process. In preparation for this creative writing project, the children were introduced to questions to help them think about their story:

- Will it be a realistic story? A fantasy? A poem?
- Will the story be based on personal experiences?

- What is the setting?
- Who are the central characters?
- What is the problem or conflict? How is the problem solved?
- Do the characters change?

The stories that evolved during this final project reflected the children's growing ability to create characters with feelings, motives, and intentions and to show the consequences of words and actions in the context of the social interactions that formed the core of their stories. Many of the stories included not only an external plot or what happened but the inner lives of the characters as well. Their stories reflected their own experiences in their social worlds as well as their experiences with literature about social worlds.

After the stories had been revised, edited, and illustrated, they were bound into individual books with interesting covers, title pages, dedications, and notes about the authors. The children gave special thought to the pictures on the front and back covers and the title pages. For example, some of the children included clues about the story on the front cover and a picture representing the problem on the back cover. The stories were shared in the final whole-group session, and the children were invited to respond to these stories by student authors and illustrators with the same respect and seriousness that characterized their responses to the work of professionals. The children's responses to these original stories reflected their growing understanding of genre and narrative components as well as the ideas and insights about friendship that had been explored throughout the Friendship Literature Unit.

Assessment

At the end of this unit, the teacher and children worked together to select and review relevant material for individual portfolios: samples of students' journal entries and other written work; independent-reading records; and records of student-teacher conferences set up to discuss each student's work, his or her progress, and his or her strengths and plans to address individual learning needs. An analysis of the children's responses during the read-aloud/think-aloud sessions and their involvement in group and independent projects yielded evidence that the central objectives had been realized, pointing to the children's growth in literary/literacy learning as well as in social learning. For example, the children's journal entries over the course of the unit and their insights and understandings articulated during the synthesis session indicated the extent to which Objectives 1, 2, and 3 had been met. The records of children's responses to shared literary texts introduced in group sessions and to texts read independently and discussed during teacher-student conferences revealed that most of the reading-thinking strategies had been internalized and were used to construct and reconstruct meaning in response to unfolding texts (see Objective 4). After Session 4, in which the children studied *Simon and Molly plus Hester,* they regularly focused on the craft of artists during the read-aloud sessions, in journal entries, and in teacher-student book conferences (see Objective 5). A survey of the cumulative literary discussions, the independent reading experiences, and the writing projects that were integral to this literature unit provided evidence that each element in Objectives 5 and 6 had been met in the course of this literature unit featuring friendship in literature and life.[2]

Notes

1. For a detailed account of semantic mapping or webbing, an instructional tool used in classrooms to organize information in graphic representations or visual displays of categories and their relationships, see *Webbing with Literature: Creating Story Maps with Children's Books* by Karen D'Angelo Bromley (1996).

2. Parts of this chapter first appeared in *Teaching Literature in the Elementary School: A Thematic Approach,* by Joy F. Moss (1996). This text is no longer in print.

5 Heroes, Heroines, and Helpers

Making a Difference

The fact that a single individual can make a difference in the lives of others is a message inherent in a great many narratives written for children as well as adults. The literature unit featuring "heroes, heroines, and helpers" was structured around stories that transmit this message in diverse ways. These stories portray heroes and heroines who, in spite of limitations in size, age, physical strength, social status, and/or experience, perform deeds that profoundly affect the lives of those around them. Many of these stories include characters who help heroes or heroines in response to their humane behavior. The text set for this literature unit included traditional tales and modern fiction and nonfiction featuring human beings as well as animals who serve as models of humane behavior for young readers. Over the years, many educators and students of children's literature have articulated the value of literature in the lives of children. Charlotte Huck and Barbara Kiefer write: "Literature is concerned with feelings, the quality of life. It can educate the heart as well as the mind" (2004, p. 8). Although the literature unit described in this chapter was originally developed for students in grades 2 to 4, its central message is appropriate for students of all ages. Teachers interested in adapting this unit for their own classrooms will find a wide variety of literary selections about heroes, heroines, and helpers that will meet the needs and interests of students at all grade levels.

The Literature Unit Featuring Heroes, Heroines, and Helpers

> **Objectives for This Literature Unit**
>
> 1. To provide opportunities for children to discover qualities and inner resources of heroes and heroines and to explore the concept of heroism
>
> 2. To provide opportunities for children to develop a sense of their own potential to make a difference in the lives of others
>
> 3. To provide opportunities for children to explore diverse literary genres and to discover recurring patterns in diverse stories from around the world

Continued on next page

4. To provide opportunities for children to explore multiple meanings and perspectives by engaging in analysis of literary elements and the craft of authors and artists

5. To provide opportunities for children to move from analysis to synthesis through the formulation of theme statements that articulate the central meanings of the stories in this collection and significant truths about the human experience

6. To provide opportunities for students to learn and practice reading-thinking strategies used by proficient readers to generate meaning

7. To provide opportunities for children to respond to literature in read-aloud/think-aloud sessions, in writing, and in other forms of creative expression

8. To provide a context for independent reading and for developing new reading interests and building individual literary histories

9. To set the stage for a creative writing project in which students compose their own stories with heroes, heroines, and helpers

Session 1

The introductory session opened with a discussion of the terms *hero* and *heroine.* The children were asked to share their own understandings of these words and to define them with relevant examples. Initially, the children identified various contemporary heroes and heroines from popular television programs, movies, videos, computer games, and comics. When asked to name their favorite heroes, the children identified predominantly male superheroes. Then, the dialogue moved in the direction of definition.

> "A hero is strong and fearless and fights bad guys."
> "A hero is brave. He's the one who saves the day."
> "A hero has superpowers. He uses these powers to protect people."
> "A hero can fly—or do something we can't do."
> "Sometimes girls can be heroes. A heroine is brave and fights evil."
> "Heroes and heroines save lives—like the firemen in New York City."

After all the children had an opportunity to contribute to this dialogue and to share relevant prior knowledge and beliefs, consensus was reached regarding distinguishing characteristics of heroes and heroines, and these characteristics were recorded as a working definition on a wall chart: "A hero or heroine is someone who is strong and brave and fearless and has superpowers and helps people. The hero or heroine saves the day." The children were asked to think about this definition as they listened to the shared texts in the read-aloud/think-aloud sessions and as they independently read other selections included in the text set that served as the core of this literature unit. In addition, they were asked to identify the hero or heroine in each new story as well as the qualities and characteristics that distinguished this character. In the course of this cumulative experience with diverse literary selections, the children were invited to revise their working definition as recorded at the beginning of this first group session.

A folktale from Mali, *The Magic Gourd* (Diakité, 2003), was introduced in the first session. This story is about Rabbit, who rescues Chameleon from a thorny bush and is rewarded for his kindness. The magic gift he receives is especially appreciated in a time of drought and famine: it is a magic gourd that fills itself with anything its owner desires. The kind rabbit uses his gift to feed his hungry family as well as his neighbors. When a greedy king steals the magic gourd to make gold and riches for himself, Chameleon helps his friend recover the gourd. At the end of the story, Rabbit teaches the king an important lesson about generosity and friendship. By his own example, Rabbit inspires the greedy king to change his ways. The last three pages of the book provide extensive explanatory notes about this story, the author, and the rich culture of his native Mali. For example, he explains the meaning of each of the border designs he includes throughout the book. As the children engaged in a cover-to-cover study of this book (see Strategy 1), they were particularly interested to discover that the design used to illustrate the scene in which Rabbit defeats the king and retrieves his magic gourd is designated as "Belt of the Hero" and "signifies honor" (p. 31). This discovery triggered a dialogue about the hero in this teaching tale:

> "I don't think Rabbit was really a hero. He wasn't strong or brave."
>
> "He was too small to be a hero."
>
> "And *he* didn't have superpowers. Only the magic gourd did."
>
> "I agree. This doesn't seem like it's a hero story. It doesn't fit our definition."
>
> "But he *did* 'save the day'! It was a famine, and he gave food to everyone."
>
> "And he got the greedy king to change, so he'll be a better king!"
>
> "Maybe we should change our definition. I don't think we should say a hero *has* to be strong to help people."

"The most important thing about Rabbit was his kindness. That's how he got the magic gourd and then he decided to use it to help all the starving animals."

"Maybe he even saved their lives!"

"And that's [Rabbit's kindness] what made that king stop being greedy and selfish!"

"Maybe we could add: 'Heroes think of others and do good deeds.'"

After the children agreed that Rabbit could be identified as a hero and that this statement about the qualities of a hero should be added to their definition, the teacher invited them to return to the book to examine other interesting details in the illustrations and to talk about the author's note, in which he explained the importance of stories in his life and his special connection with Rabbit stories. The children also returned to the back cover, which has a picture of the author and his two daughters holding the magic gourd. One child commented, "So he drew a picture of a real one to illustrate this old story!" When the teacher asked the children to identify the *helper* in this story, their responses revealed their understanding that Chameleon helped Rabbit because of his kindness, and their use of prior literary experiences to interpret this tale (Strategy 2):

"A lot of stories are like this. There's an old man or lady that needs help, and the character that's kind and respectful to them gets rewarded . . . like in *Boots and His Brothers* [E. A. Kimmel, 1992a]."

"And the *helper* characters do sort of a test to see who deserves to get rewarded."

"Chameleon already had the magic gourd to give. He was probably just waiting to see who was going to be kind enough to stop and rescue him from the thorn bush. So Chameleon is the helper character in this story."

On the last page of the book, the author includes a segment about variants of this folktale that he refers to as "Folkloric Cousins" (p. 32). A number of the children were familiar with one of the stories he mentions, "The Lad Who Went to the North Wind." They were also reminded of other stories (see Strategy 11) with the literary patterns featured in *The Magic Gourd*. For example, several children identified *The Magic Cooking Pot: A Folktale of India* (Towle, 1975) and a Russian tale, *The Three Magic Gifts* (Riordan, 1980), as stories that feature the theft of magical objects.[1]

At the end of this session, the children were given *literature journals* in which to record their responses to the stories read aloud and those read independently during this literature unit. The children were invited to record their personal responses to these stories, to write about the heroes/heroines and helpers in terms of their characteristics, qualities, and deeds, and to identify and use intertextual links to engage in comparative analysis and to explore the themes in these stories. The teacher introduced the children to three other stories featuring animals by offering brief book talks to help them select one title for independent reading:

> *The Brave Little Parrot* (Martin, 1998) is a Jataka tale from India in which the valiant efforts of a little parrot result in saving the lives of the animals caught in a forest fire.

> *The Story of Jumping Mouse: A Native American Legend,* retold by John Steptoe (1984), is about a small animal with an unselfish and generous spirit and a helper character, Magic Frog, who gives special gifts to the mouse to help him on his quest-journey.

> *The Foundling Fox: How the Little Fox Got a Mother* (Korschunow, 1984) is about a courageous vixen who finds a small fox whose mother has been killed by hunters, and who risks her own life to carry him home to her den, where her own three small foxes are waiting for her. The vixen had no helper in her heroic quest; she managed to escape from a hunting dog and to fight a badger on her own in order to protect the little fox.

Session 2

When *Little Fingerling: A Japanese Folktale* (Hughes, 1992) was introduced in the second session, the children noticed the title and the picture of the tiny boy on the front and back covers and predicted that this story would be like the story of Tom Thumb. As the story unfolded, they were able to confirm their prediction (see Strategy 4) by identifying the intertextual links between this Japanese variant and the German story. In *Little Fingerling,* a childless couple prays for a child . . . "even a little child, no bigger than the tip of my finger" (n.p.). When a very tiny child is born to them, they name him Issun Boshi, Little Fingerling. At age fifteen, he is the height of his father's longest finger and decides to go out into the world to seek his fortune. His father gives him a needle for a sword and a straw for a scabbard. His mother gives him a lacquer rice bowl and a pair of chopsticks that he uses for a boat and oars. When he reaches Kyoto, he gets a job in the marketplace painting gold lacquer on combs and boxes. Eventually, he is invited to join the household of a noble family, where he and Plum Blossom, the nobleman's daughter, fall in love in spite of the obvious difference in size. One day, Little Fingerling saves Plum Blossom's life by engaging in a heroic battle with two blue giants with horns and three eyes each. After he defeats the giants through cunning and courage, they vanish but leave behind their magic mallet, which has the power to grant one wish. When Plum Blossom makes a wish for both of them, Little Fingerling is transformed into a tall, handsome samurai warrior. When the nobleman gives him permission to marry his daughter, he says: "You have always shown yourself to be brave, noble, and resourceful. Now at last you appear as you were inwardly" (n.p.).

After comparing this tale with "Tom Thumb," the children talked about the hero and helpers in this well-known Japanese tale:

> "He is awfully little for a hero, but you could tell he was brave when he went off *alone* to seek his fortune . . . like heroes in quest tales."
>
> "He's so small, but he was really brave when he fought those two monsters!"
>
> "His only weapon was his needle. But he used his *brains!*"
>
> "I think we should add something to our hero definition so Issun Boshi could be included. We could say: 'A hero doesn't have to be big and strong to save someone, but he has to be smart and brave.'"
>
> "I was thinking about the *helper character* when I listened to this story. Maybe his mom and dad were the helpers because they gave him things for his journey that really helped him on his quest."

The children were invited to return to the book to examine the illustrations and to talk about the *craft* of the artist, Brenda Clark, who portrays the interiors of the farmer's house and the nobleman's house, household items, clothing, and landscapes for outdoor scenes:

> "She must have done a lot of research about Japanese houses and clothes and stuff. On the front flap, it says it's the Edo period in Japan. I'm going to look that up on Google."
>
> "I think she [the artist] used a picture by a famous Japanese artist to make that picture of Issun Boshi paddling his rice bowl in the river . . . I have a book at home with that picture. I'll bring it." [The picture she is referring to is a wood-block print by Hokusai called "Stormy Sea off Kanagawa," which shows raging waves and boats being tossed about.]
>
> "My mom has a lacquer box like the ones he [Issun Boshi] painted. [She pointed to the illustration of the stall owner in the marketplace found on the cover and later in the text.] It's from Japan, and it has the *same* gold and red design on shiny black lacquer!"
>
> "She [the artist] has so many details, it's like you're walking into another world."

To give the children an opportunity to compare this illustrated edition with the work of other artists who have illustrated this traditional tale, the teacher showed them *The Inch-High Samurai* (McCarthy, 1993); *The Inch Boy* (Morimoto, 1986); *Little One Inch* (Brenner, 1977); and *Issun Boshi, the Inchling: An Old Tale of Japan* (Ishii, 1967). After comparing the covers, title pages, and a few illustrations in each of the texts, the children identified a number of differences in the way each artist had interpreted this tale. Later, the children who had selected to read one or more of these titles independently shared additional discoveries. For example:

> "In *The Inch Boy*, Issunboshi looks fierce from the very beginning, but in *Little Fingerling*, he seems more gentle and respectful."
>
> "*The Inch-High Samurai* is told in rhyme."
>
> "In *Little One Inch*, the ending is different. When they make a wish on the magic hammers, they become the same size, but the girl becomes the same size as Little One Inch!"
>
> "I read that, too. In that one, the parents warn him about three demons before he goes off to Kyoto . . . the *kappa*, the *tengu*, and the *oni*. The oni are wicked ogres—like the two giants in *Little Fingerling*."

At the end of this session, the teacher introduced another popular Japanese folk hero, *Momotaro, the Peach Boy: A Traditional Japanese Tale* (Shute, 1986). In this story, an old woodcutter and his wife wish for a son and discover an enormous peach that holds a baby boy. When Momotaro grows up, he goes to the island of the onis to fight these wicked demons, who have attacked and robbed the people. Momotaro's kindness to a dog, a monkey, and a pheasant prompts them to help him defeat the oni. He and his helpers return in triumph and give the people the gold and silver that had been stolen from them. This story can also be found in collections such as *The Shining Princess and Other Japanese Legends* (Quayle, 1989) and *Best-Loved Folktales of the World* (Cole, 1982). The children were invited to choose this tale or one of the other traditional folk or fairy tales featuring heroes, heroines, and helpers for independent reading:

> *The Golden Mare, the Firebird, and the Magic Ring* (Sanderson, 2001). A Russian folktale.
>
> *Sindbad's Secret* (Zeman, 2003). From the tales of *The Thousand and One Nights*.
>
> *The Water of Life: A Tale from the Brothers Grimm* (Rogasky & Grimm, 1986).

The Luminous Pearl: A Chinese Folktale (Torre, 1990).

The Fourth Question: A Chinese Tale (Wang, 1991).

The Twins and the Bird of Darkness: A Hero Tale from the Caribbean (San Souci, 2002).

A Book of Heroes and Heroines (Manning-Sanders, 1982). A collection of folk and fairy tales gathered from all over the world.

Session 3

The Hero of Bremen (Hodges, 1993) was introduced in the third session as an example of a very different kind of hero from another culture. Hodges retells the German legend of the poor shoemaker, Hans, who lives in the walled city of Bremen and goes about on knuckles and knees dragging his useless legs behind him. In spite of his infirmity, he is cheerful and friendly and loves to tell stories of great heroes of long ago. His favorite is Roland, the famous knight who led in battle the army of his uncle, the emperor Charlemagne, who made Bremen a free city. Roland was known as the hero of Bremen. When Hans undertakes an impossible challenge to help the people of Bremen, the spirit of Roland appears to him and helps him succeed in his quest. Roland says to him: "Heroes come in all shapes and sizes, and there are many kinds of battle . . . I know a hero when I see one" (n.p.). At the end of the story, the children returned to Roland's words:

> "That's what we said about heroes in our definition!"
> "Hans was such a different kind of hero! He couldn't even walk, but he had determination!"
> "Maybe we should add that to our definition. That's another quality of heroes."
> "Roland was the helper in this story. But did he really come to help Hans? That was the confusing part."
> "I think Hans *believed* he did. Remember that part in the beginning when Hans was telling stories to the children and he told them that 'Roland would come again in time of need'?" [The teacher reread the scene this child had remembered (n.p.) in order to demonstrate the way readers find answers to questions about a story as it unfolds (Strategy 8).]
> "It's like Hans felt Roland was with him and that helped him keep going even when he didn't think he could go any further."
> "Another helper was that little girl who was the only one who kept in touch with him. She offered him an apple, and she probably gave him encouragement."

At this point in the dialogue, the teacher inserted a question to call attention to the literary genre: "Why is this story called a legend?"

"It says it's *retold* by Margaret Hodges, so it's an old story that's been told by a lot of different storytellers for a long time."

"A legend is an old story—but parts of it really happened in history. I think Roland and Charlemagne were real heroes, and it says [on the last page] there's a statue of Roland in Bremen. So that part was true."

"It [the text on the last page] also said there used to be a small statue of the shoemaker at the bottom of the statue of Roland. The illustration shows the statue of Roland and modern people looking at it. You can tell it's *now*—because of their clothes, and backpacks, and hairdos . . . but the houses in the background look old. But you can't see the shoemaker."

"I think he probably was a real person because on the last page it said, 'The story of Hans Cobbler was written on a stone bench that still stands by the lake in memory of his great day' [n.p.]. That's how legends get started . . . with real people."

As part of their cover-to-cover study of this book, the children examined the shield of Roland on the title page and wondered whether the picture on the back cover could be a shield for Hans:

"The red part is the same shape as Roland's shield."

"And it has a picture of a boot in the middle because he's a cobbler."

"A shield is something for knights and soldiers. I think the artist made that shield for Hans because he was as brave as a knight."

"The title—*The Hero of Bremen*—is for *both* of them, Roland and Hans!"

"So *that's* why the artist included a shield for both of them!"

"And for the people of Bremen, they're both heroes—even though one was strong and one wasn't."

"So our definition [she pointed to the working definition of hero/heroines on the wall chart] seems to fit this story because we added that part that says heroes are brave and determined but they don't have to be big and strong."

At the end of this session, the children were introduced to several legendary heroes such as Robin Hood, King Arthur, John Henry, Finn Mac Cool, and High John. A few of the many books about these heroes were included in the collection and available for independent reading:

The Adventures of High John the Conqueror (Sanfield, 1989, 1995)

American Tall Tales (Osborne, 1991)

Cut from the Same Cloth: American Women of Myth, Legend, and Tall Tale (San Souci, 1993)

Finn Mac Cool and the Small Men of Deeds (O'Shea, 1987)

John Henry (Lester, 1994)

King Arthur and the Round Table (Talbott, 1995)

The Kitchen Knight: A Tale of King Arthur (Hodges, 1990)

Paul Bunyan, a Tall Tale (Kellogg, 1984)

Robin Hood (Hayes, 1989)

The Sword in the Stone (Talbott, 1991)

Big Jabe (Nolen, 2000). An original tall tale about baby Jabe, who appears like Moses, floating in a willow basket and found by a house slave. Jabe grows quickly until he "ha[s] the strength of fifty" (n.p.). He lightens the burdens of the slaves on Plenty Plantation and uses his mysterious gift to lead the slaves to freedom.

Swamp Angel (Isaacs, 1994). Another original tall tale about a backwoods heroine, Angelica Longrider, known as Swamp Angel for her good deeds, which helped the settlers of Tennessee.

Session 4

When the children examined the title and picture on the front cover of *The Samurai's Daughter: A Japanese Legend* (San Souci, 1992), they shared observations and questions that guided their response to this medieval legend:

> "The daughter is in the title, so she must be the main character."
>
> "Could she be the heroine? The way she's standing [she demonstrated standing with her hands on her hips], she looks confident."
>
> "Look! There's a dragon behind her! I didn't notice it at first. Maybe she got captured by the dragon and a samurai warrior rescued her."

When Tokoyo, the samurai's daughter, was a young girl, "her father schooled her in the samurai virtues of courage, discipline, and endurance; he taught her a warrior's duty to protect the weak" (n.p.). By the time she was five, she could shoot a bow and arrow and ride a horse. But when she was older, "he decided she ought to learn to be more ladylike" (n.p.). Although she was no longer allowed to practice archery and horsemanship, she did spend a great deal of time learning the skills of the women divers who used daggers to harvest shellfish from the sea. Because of a mysterious illness the ruler banishes many of his knights, including Tokoyo's father, to an island. Tokoyo is determined to join her father and sets out on a quest-journey with a dagger and a cricket in a tiny bamboo cage. She encounters many challenges along the way, but when she finally reaches the island she discovers a young girl who is about to be sacrificed to a great serpent. "The girl's tears touched Tokoyo as a woman and as a samurai who was duty-bound to help the helpless" (n.p.). Tokoyo dives into the sea, with her dagger gripped between her teeth. Using the skills she had learned from the women divers, Tokoyo fights the evil monster and, after a fierce battle, kills the serpent and is able to release the ruler from the curse of the illness that had caused his madness. Her heroic deed saves her father and all the others who had been banished during the ruler's illness, and the people who live on the island no longer have to sacrifice their children to the serpent.

As the story unfolded, the children confirmed or rejected their initial predictions and found answers to their questions. They were surprised to discover that Tokoyo was the heroine and that she acted according to the samurai virtues. Their discussion of this legend focused on the nature of her heroism as well as on the genre:

> "On the title page it says this is a legend, but it doesn't say she was a real person."
>
> "The first part of the story is realism. In olden times, girls *were* expected to learn to dance and play the lute and write poems. Her father didn't want her to be a samurai warrior!"
>
> "She was a heroine because she had courage and determination and special skills that she learned from the diving woman."
>
> "So that part is real. She didn't have any *magical* help like in the fairy tales. The fantasy part was the sea monster, the ghosts, and the curse on the ruler."
>
> "Her *helper* was the cricket. Its song kept her spirits up."
>
> "There *could* have been a samurai's daughter who did heroic deeds long ago and then storytellers started telling stories about her. That's how legends start."
>
> "I liked the part when she said her duty 'as a woman and as a samurai' was to help the weak and helpless. Maybe we should add that last part to our definition."
>
> "When we first saw the cover, most of us thought that a samurai would fight the dragon and rescue the girl. But it was the *girl* who fought the serpent in this story, and *she* freed all the samurai knights!"
>
> "But I said maybe she could be the heroine because she looked so confident, but then I changed my mind when I saw that dragon. I was really glad she was the heroine, but I think we were all thinking like Tokoyo's father—he expects boys to do certain things and girls to do certain things. So it's good to have stories about heroines like this."

At this point in the session, the children were introduced to a number of traditional tales featuring heroines that were included in the collection for independent reading:

Brave Margaret: An Irish Adventure (San Souci, 1999)

The Enchanted Book: A Tale from Krakow (Porazinska, 1987)

Fa Mulan: The Story of a Woman Warrior (San Souci, 1998a)

Finn MacCoul and His Fearless Wife: A Giant of a Tale from Ireland (Byrd, 1999)

The Four Gallant Sisters, adapted from the Brothers Grimm (E. A. Kimmel, 1992b)

The Great Deeds of Heroic Women (Saxby, 1992). This collection includes stories drawn from myth and legend, history and folklore.

Lon Po Po: A Red-Riding Hood Story from China (Young, 1989)

Mrs. McCool and the Giant Cuhullin: An Irish Tale (Souhami, 2002)

Rimonah of the Flashing Sword: A North African Tale (E. A. Kimmel, 1995)

Sense Pass King: A Story from Cameroon (Tchana 2002)

Tam Lin, retold from an old Scottish ballad (Cooper, 1991)

Tam Lin: An Old Ballad (Yolen, 1990)

Vassilisa the Wise: A Tale of Medieval Russia (Sherman, 1988)

A Weave of Words: An Armenian Tale (San Souci, 1998b)

Session 5

The first four sessions in this unit were designed to introduce traditional tales featuring heroes, heroines, and helpers. In subsequent sessions the children were introduced to other literary genres: modern fantasy and realism and biography. *Nobiah's Well: A Modern African Folktale* (Guthrie, 1993), shared in the fifth session, begins with the words: "Long ago in a far-off land where it had not rained for many years, the sun baked the earth to a crusty brown, and the wind blew dust from here to there" (n.p.). This sets the stage for the story of Nobiah, a young boy who makes the long journey to the well to fill his clay jar with water for his family. On the way home, he encounters a hedgehog, a hyena and her two cubs, and an ant bear. Nobiah has a tender heart and shares the precious water in his jar with these thirsty animals. The ant bear thanks Nobiah and says, "Your heart is as big and deep as the well that gives this water" (n.p.). When Nobiah returns home, he pours a cup of water for his sister and mother, but there is nothing left for him or for their garden. But the grateful animals come to him in the middle of the night and help him dig a well that would provide for his family and all the villagers.

When the children examined the title and the pictures on the front and back covers, they found clues that prompted them to activate their prior knowledge to make inferences and predictions and generate questions about the story (Strategies 1, 2, 3, 4, 5, and 8):

> "The boy on the front is probably the hero."
> "And the animals around him are probably the helpers, like in *Momotaro*." [He had selected *Momotaro the Peach Boy* for independent reading.]
> "The well is important because it's in the title. They must've had to use a well for water because those little huts [on the cover] wouldn't have running water."
> "It shows the moon and stars . . . so maybe the problem happens at night."
> "But I wonder why they [the boy and the animals] look so sad?"

As the story unfolded, the children confirmed their predictions about the hero and helpers and the importance of the well. When they discovered that the animals helped Nobiah in return for his compassion and kindness, they identified other stories with this recurring theme, such as *The Magic Gourd* and *Momotaro, the Peach Boy*. The children were able to answer their question about the sad expressions on the faces of the boy and the animals when they discovered how thirsty they all were in that hot, dry place and when they heard that Nobiah "was also very sad because he could hear his mother crying" (n.p.). Finally, the children returned to the moon and stars they had noticed on the covers and their initial speculation that "the problem happens at night." By the end of the story, they realized that the *problem* was that Nobiah had to spend almost the whole day walking to and from the only well, and that he had given away most of the water he had collected from the well, and that the *solution* was accomplished at night, when the animals helped Nobiah dig a well close to his house. The children concluded that the artist's portrayal of the boy and animals on the front cover was intended to show them *before* their problem was solved. They concluded their interpretive discussion with comments about heroes and helpers when one of the children pointed to the wall chart with their working definition. This story confirmed their recent ideas about the nature of heroes and helpers:

> "Nobiah was just a small boy but he helped save the whole village."

"That fits with our definition . . . like heroes think of others and do good deeds."

"The animals were the helper characters—like Chameleon."

"Maybe they were magical, too—they knew *just* where to dig that hole."

"And they gave him that special clay pot to remind everyone to be kind."

"I think they were *testing* him like when there's a beggar that asks for food and the hero gives him all he has and then the beggar gives him a magical gift."

"It says [on the cover] it's a modern *folktale* so it could have the same kinds of magical helpers."

The children's spontaneous responses to this story before, during, and after it unfolded enabled the teacher to discover the kinds of reading-thinking strategies they used in their transaction with this literary text. Their use of the cover-to-cover strategy prompted them to activate relevant prior knowledge, to make inferences and predictions, to determine importance, and to generate a central question about the characters. As the story unfolded, the children engaged in metacognition and think-alouds to confirm or revise their initial predictions and to answer their initial question. They drew from their awareness of text structure and artist's craft to talk about the *problem* in the story and the significance of the night sky as the background for the picture that extended from the front to the back cover. The children also identified intertextual links with other stories they had heard in the group sessions or read independently in the course of this cumulative literary experience, and they used their knowledge of genre to analyze the character types in this modern folktale.

A review of the dialogue that evolved in the course of this read-aloud/think-aloud session also revealed the collaborative nature of the meaning-making process. The children listened to one another and often expanded on the contributions of their classmates as they worked together to construct new interpretations about the shared text and gained new insights about the human experience as they continued to study heroes, heroines, and helpers in literature around the world.

Session 6

As soon as the children saw the cover of *To Capture the Wind* (MacGill-Callahan, 1997), they predicted that the girl with the sword would be the heroine in this story, but they wondered about the meaning of the title and the picture on the back cover. This is the story of Oonagh, who sets out on a quest to rescue Conal, her fiancé, who has been kidnapped by the warriors of Malcolm, the pirate king of the islands. When she faces Malcolm, he challenges her to solve four riddles in four weeks. During that time Oonagh enlists the help of Conal and the other prisoners to carry out her ingenious plan for all to escape. Finally she is ready to give the answer to the last riddle, "How do you capture the wind on the water?" She invites the king and his men to come to the harbor so she can reveal her answer. All the prisoners are hiding in small rowboats below the pier when Oonagh jumps into Conal's boat and they all set out, rowing for their lives, pursued by a "hail of arrows" (n.p.). When Oonagh gives a signal, "white, blue, and scarlet wings blossomed over the boats" and she calls out to Malcolm her answer to the last riddle: "They have no name, but I call them 'sails.' A new word for a new idea" (n.p.).

As they listened to the story unfold, the children confirmed their prediction about the girl on the cover, and they found answers to their questions about the title and the picture of the sailboat on the back cover when they discovered Oonagh's remarkable solution to the riddle, which enables her and her friends to escape. The children also focused on the genre of this modern tale and decided that it was a "realistic adventure."

> "There's no magic in it. She didn't have any magic objects to help her."
> "That's right. But she was very brave and smart—like the other heroes!"
> "She thought up the plan, but they [Oonagh and the prisoners] all worked together secretly for four weeks. They helped each other."
> "It was a realistic adventure because it could have happened in real life."
> "And she was a heroine because she rescued all the prisoners."

The children also identified an interesting intertextual link with an Irish folktale that was included in the collection for this unit and that most of them recalled having heard over a year earlier, during a literature unit featuring giant tales:

> "The name of this heroine is the same as Finn MacCool's wife!"
> "That was an *old* tale from Ireland, and this is a *new* Irish tale."
> "Maybe the author got her ideas from the old story."
> "You're probably right. In the old story, Oonagh saved her husband from that other giant . . . Cuhullin! He was much stronger and mean."
> "And Finn was really afraid of him, but Oonagh thought up a really good plan to trick him and save her husband—just like in this story!"

"But that old story was fantasy—with giants—and it was funny."

[According to a note about the story in Jessica Souhami's retelling: "This Irish tale makes fun of two of the greatest heroes of Celtic legend—Cuhullin and Finn McCool—who could never have met. Cuhullin's tales are told in the Ulster Cycle of the first century A.D., while Finn McCool's legends appear in the Fenian Cycle of the third century A.D. This tale possibly dates from the sixteenth century when comic parodies of heroic legends started to appear" (n.p.).]

"Both stories are about heroines who are brave and smart . . . and stand up to villains! This author must have read the old tale!"

At the end of this session, the teacher introduced additional modern tales for independent reading:

> *Beautiful Warrior: The Legend of the Nun's Kung Fu* (McCully, 1998)
>
> *The Boy Who Knew the Language of the Birds* (Wetterer, 1991)
>
> *Dove Isabeau* (Yolen, 1989)
>
> *The Mapmaker's Daughter* (Helldorfer, 1991)
>
> *Merlin and the Dragons* (Yolen, 1995)
>
> *A Ride on the Red Mare's Back* (Le Guin, 1992)
>
> *Sosu's Call* (Asare, 2002)

Session 7

In this session, the children were introduced to selected examples of *realistic fiction*, including stories based on actual people or events, and *nonfiction* accounts of heroic deeds and historic events. They were invited to choose one of these titles to read independently and to discuss in small dialogue groups formed by those who had chosen the same title or from the same group of related titles. The members of each group were asked to collaborate on a written discussion of the book(s) they had studied together. This written discussion would focus on the same patterns and themes they had identified as they explored tales of heroes and heroines and helpers in the read-aloud sessions. Their working definition of heroes and heroines was used as a frame of reference to guide their study of these stories. Brief book talks were presented about each of these stories to assist selection of books to read independently:

> *Kate Shelley and the Midnight Express* (Wetterer, 1990) is part of the "On My Own" series published by Carolrhoda Books. Kate Shelley was fifteen years old in 1881 when a railroad bridge

near her home in Iowa collapsed during a summer storm. She risked her life to get to the nearest railroad station to send a warning to an oncoming passenger train about the danger ahead. In order to reach the station, she had to crawl across a seven-hundred-foot-long railroad bridge, with a raging river beneath her. Her courageous efforts saved the lives of the two hundred passengers as well as two men who had fallen into the floodwaters.

Kate Shelley: Bound for Legend (San Souci, 1995) is a picture book about this American heroine. It is illustrated with the paintings of Max Ginsburg.

"Kate Shelley" is included in a collection of poems called *All By Herself: 14 Girls Who Made a Difference* (Paul, 1999). The children who selected these different portraits of this heroine formed a dialogue group to discuss and compare the work of three different writers and artists who had focused on a single subject.

Balto and the Great Race (E. C. Kimmel, 1999) is an early chapter book about Balto, the Siberian husky who saved the people of Nome, Alaska, from a diphtheria epidemic in 1925 by leading his team of sled dogs through a terrible snowstorm to deliver the antitoxin serum. This nonfiction book opens with a foreword that describes the statue of Balto in Central Park in New York City.

The Bravest Dog Ever: The True Story of Balto (Standiford, 1989, 2003) is a "Step into Reading" nonfiction book for beginning readers.

Togo (Blake, 2002) is a picture book based on the true story of another Siberian husky, who led one of the other dog sled teams in the serum run from Anchorage to Nome, Alaska, in 1925. Togo led his team over 350 miles on his part of the relay race to Nome. Elizabeth Kimmel included background information about Togo in her book, *Balto and the Great Race*. Togo and Balto were trained by the same man, Leonhard Seppala, but Balto often ran with another team of dogs owned by one of Seppala's friends, Gunnar Kaasen. Balto became famous for running the last lap of the serum run in a blinding blizzard, but Togo and the other dogs who participated in this heroic mission have been ignored. In an epilogue, the author notes that those who regret this lack of recognition believe "that the hero is not always the dog who crosses the finish line first, but, as in this case, the dog who made the last lap even possible" (n.p.). The children who selected these books about Balto and Togo formed a dialogue group to discuss these stories of actual canine heroes and to compare the work of the writers and artists who described their role in this historic event. One member of this group also read the book about the Iditarod Trail by Debbie Miller; others read about working and rescue dogs.

The Great Serum Race: Blazing the Iditarod Trail (Miller, 2002) is a retelling of the heroic team efforts of the humans and canines involved in the diphtheria crisis in Nome in 1925. This book provides a history of the Iditarod, and a map of the original trail is shown on the endpapers.

Hero Dogs: Courageous Canines in Action (Jackson, 2003) provides an in-depth look at working and rescue dogs and the remarkable role they play in the lives of human beings. The book includes some of the heroic moments during the September 11 World Trade Center attack.

Emma and the Night Dogs (Aller, 1997) includes a page of background information that begins with the words: "This story was inspired by a group of dogs and handlers belonging to Connecticut Canine Search and Rescue, Inc." (n.p.). It is the story of a young girl and a team of search and rescue dogs who find a small boy lost in the woods at night.

Especially Heroes (Kroll, 2003) is a picture book about the heroic deeds of individuals who translated their ideals into action during the civil rights movement in the early 1960s. It is the story of a young girl who witnessed the heroism of her father and several of his friends when they protected their neighbor from a group of racists. According to the information about the author on the front flap, this story is "based on a series of incidents, all true, that had an enormous impact on her [the author] when she was a child." The children who studied heroes, heroines, and helpers in this literature unit had been exposed to some of the issues, people, and events that were an integral part of the civil rights movement. Thus they had the prior knowledge necessary to understand the subtext of this story. The children who selected *Especially Heroes* to read independently formed a dialogue group with classmates who had selected stories of some of the other heroes and heroines who emerged during that period, including Ruby Bridges, "The Little Rock Nine," and Rosa Parks.

The Story of Ruby Bridges (Coles, 1995) is a nonfiction picture book about the courage and faith of the six-year-old girl who faced the hostility of segregationists to become the first African American child to attend an all-white school in New Orleans, Louisiana, in 1960.

Through My Eyes (Bridges, 1999) is Ruby Bridges' own story of her involvement in the integration of the William Frantz Public School in New Orleans. This autobiography includes comments and photographs of others who were part of this pivotal event in our history.

Cracking the Wall: The Struggles of the Little Rock Nine (Lucas, 1997) is part of the Carolrhoda "On My Own" series of books for young readers. This book provides an introduction to the nine African American students who integrated Central High School in Little Rock, Arkansas, in 1957.

If a Bus Could Talk: The Story of Rosa Parks (Ringgold, 1999) is a picture-book biography of the African American woman whose refusal to give up her seat to a white passenger on a bus led to her arrest and a yearlong bus boycott in Montgomery, Alabama. Rosa Parks is known as the mother of the civil rights movement for her role in precipitating this boycott.

Rosa Parks (Greenfield, 1973, 1996) is a brief biography of the woman whose simple act of protest galvanized America's civil rights revolution.

Freedom School, Yes! (Littlesugar, 2001) is based on the 1964 Mississippi Freedom School Summer Project, which involved more than six hundred courageous volunteers who risked their lives to go into the state of Mississippi to help thousands of black children and adults learn to read and write and learn about their own rich heritage. This is a story about one of the brave black families willing to take these volunteers into their homes that summer; it is the story of Jolie, whose mother takes in a young white woman who will teach in the Freedom School. The opening lines of the story reveal the hostility and danger encountered by those involved in this project: "On the first night the Freedom School teacher came to stay in Chicken Creek, a brick burst through the front room window of Jolie's house, shattering the stillness" (n.p.).

The Battle for St. Michaels, by Emily Arnold McCully (2002), an early chapter book, is historical fiction based on events that occurred during the War of 1812 in the small shipbuilding town of St. Michaels on the Maryland coast. It is the story of a nine-year-old girl, the fastest runner in town, who carries messages to the soldiers and helps the residents of St. Michaels carry out a plan to defend their town against the British.

Laura Secord: A Story of Courage (Lunn, 2001), an early chapter book, offers another perspective on the War of 1812, the war between Great Britain and the United States. American leaders intended to win the war and add British Canada to the United States. Laura Secord and her husband were living in Upper Canada (known as Ontario today) with their five children when American officers took over their home. When Laura heard them talking of a plan to defeat the British, she knew it was important to warn the British lieutenant. Since her husband had been severely injured in an earlier battle, it was up to Laura to make the grueling and dangerous journey to bring this information to the attention of the British. In Canada, Laura

Secord is celebrated as a heroine. In the epilogue, the author observes: "Neither the British nor the Americans won the war. The only people who really won were the Canadians. The boundary lines between British North America and the United States remained the same" (n.p.).

Abigail's Drum (Minahan, 1995) is an early chapter book about Rebecca Bates and her sister Abigail, daughters of the lighthouse keeper at Scituate, Massachusetts. Inspired by an actual event during the War of 1812, this is the story of two young girls who became heroines when British soldiers took their father hostage and threatened to burn their town. Rebecca and Abigail found a way to save their father and prevent the burning of Scituate.

The Ballot Box Battle (McCully, 1996) is a picture book that provides a brief biographical account of the day in 1880 when Elizabeth Cady Stanton attempted to vote in Tenafly, New Jersey, but was told, "Women don't vote." McCully introduces young readers to this remarkable woman, who fought all her life for equal opportunities for women, and describes how after Stanton's death, Susan B. Anthony and others continued her heroic battle for women's rights.

Winter Rescue (Valgardson, 1995) is a picture book about a fictional character who helps his grandfather, an ice fisherman on frigid Lake Winnipeg. Although this character, Thor, is apparently not based on an actual person, the setting portrays the traditional way of life among the Icelandic fisherfolk who live in Canada. In this story, Thor is a young boy who loves to watch television and talk about his favorite superheroes and their brave deeds. However, Thor becomes a real hero when he saves the life of a man who has fallen through the ice and is in danger of drowning.

New York's Bravest (Osborne, 2002) is a picture book that tells about the heroic deeds of the legendary New York City firefighter, Mose Humphreys, in the 1840s. Over the years many Mose legends have appeared; Osborne has created another tall tale about this folk hero. In a "historical note" opposite the dedication page, Osborne writes: "Mose was America's first urban hero. He represents the courage and strength of firefighters throughout history. Never was that courage and strength on greater display than on September 11, 2001. As workers fled the burning World Trade Center towers, New York's firefighters rushed toward the danger. Hundreds gave their lives to save others. Their extraordinary actions provide an example of all that's best in America." This story is dedicated "To the memory of the 343 New York City firefighters who gave their lives to save others on September 11, 2001."

The Lighthouse Keeper's Daughter (Olson, 1987) is based on actual people and events associated with lighthouses along the Maine coast. This is the story of a young girl who lives with her parents in a lighthouse on a rocky island outpost off the coast of Maine. When her father's return from a trip to the mainland for supplies is delayed by a violent storm, she manages to keep the lighthouse lamps burning for many days in spite of brutal weather and her own illness.

Keep the Lights Burning, Abbie (Roop & Roop, 1985), part of the Carolrhoda "On My Own" series for young readers, is a biography of Abbie Burgess, the daughter of the keeper of a lighthouse off the coast of Maine. In the winter of 1856, Abbie kept the lamps burning when a storm delayed her father's return to the island. The children who discussed the stories and poem about lighthouse keepers were excited to discover the connection between this book and Olson's story. They wondered whether Olson had used Abbie Burgess as the model for her fictional character, Miranda, in *The Lighthouse Keeper's Daughter.*

"Ida Lewis" is a poem about one of the most famous female lighthouse keepers in America. She was appointed keeper of the Lime Rock beacon near Newport, Rhode Island, in 1879 and continued at her post until her death in 1911. She is known for her remarkable rescues and is credited with saving more than twenty lives during her years at Lime Rock. This poem is included in the collection by Ann Whitford Paul, *All By Herself: 14 Girls Who Made a Difference.* The children who read this poem were inspired to use the Internet to search for more information about this remarkable woman.

Birdie's Lighthouse (Hopkinson, 1997) is the story of a fictional heroine told in diary entries dating from January 15, 1855, to January 15, 1856, the year Birdie was ten years old and managed to keep the light burning one stormy night when her father was too ill to take up his post as lighthouse keeper. An author's note at the end of the book states that this story "was inspired by many true-life lighthouse heroines" (n.p.). Two of the heroines mentioned in this note were Ida Lewis and Abigail Burgess.

Lighthouse Dog to the Rescue (Perrow, 2000, 2003) is a picture book about a springer spaniel that lived on Penobscot Bay in the 1930s and loved to ring the lighthouse bell. During a raging blizzard, he used this skill to guide a mailboat safely home. The story of the mailboat rescue is based on an actual event: "A springer spaniel named Spot really did live at Owls Head lighthouse, in Maine, in the 1930s. He was the pet of Pauline Hamor, whose father was the keeper of the lighthouse. . . . After she was grown up, Pauline described the mailboat rescue to author Edward Rowe Snow, who wrote about it in his book, *The Lighthouses of New England"* (an author's note on the final page of the book). The children who read and discussed the stories featuring lighthouse keepers were invited to use Gail Gibbons's *Beacons of Light: Lighthouses* (1990) as a resource.

The Firekeeper's Son (Park, 2003). Set in Korea in the early 1800s, this story features a young boy, Sang-hee, who faces a personal dilemma before he attempts to take over his father's task of lighting the evening fire to signal to the king that all is well in the land. A historical note is included at the end of this picture book.

The Butterfly (Polacco, 2000). This story of courage during World War II is drawn from the author's family history. Her aunt's mother was part of the French Resistance during the Nazi occupation, and she risked her own life to hide a Jewish family and help them escape to freedom. This is one of many picture books that reveal the remarkable stories of heroic deeds during the Holocaust. Several of these picture books were included in the collection for this literature unit.

The Lily Cupboard (Oppenheim, 1992) is the story of a fictional Jewish child who is hidden from the Nazis by a non-Jewish farm family in Holland. This story celebrates the heroism of the Dutch people during the Nazi occupation.

Passage to Freedom: The Sugihara Story (Mochizuki, 1997) is narrated by Hiroki Sugihara, who tells the story of his family's decision to risk their own lives to help save the lives of many Polish Jews trying to escape the Nazis in 1940. His father, as Japanese ambassador to Lithuania during World War II, defied the orders of the Japanese government and granted thousands of visas to allow Jewish refugees to exit Europe.

A Special Fate: Chiune Sugihara, Hero of the Holocaust (Gold, 2000) provides a more in-depth account than Mochizuki's picture book. Alison Gold offers an overview of Sugihara's life and his decision, with the encouragement of his wife and children, to save the lives of as many Jews as possible.

A Hero and the Holocaust: The Story of Janusz Korczak and His Children (Adler, 2002) is a brief biography of the Polish doctor and founder of orphanages who lost his own life trying to protect his orphans from the Nazis. He walked with his children to the freight car that would take them to Treblinka.

The Cats in Krasinski Square (Hesse, 2004). The central character in this story was inspired by accounts of Adina Blady Szwajger, who worked in the Jewish Resistance in Poland and risked her life to help those who were trapped behind the walls of the Warsaw Ghetto.

Rose Blanche (Innocenti & Gallaz, 1985, 1996) is a parable about a young girl, Rose Blanche, who witnesses the Nazi occupation of her small German town and becomes personally involved in helping the Jews behind barbed wire. "Rose Blanche" was the name of the group of young German university students who protested Hitler's policies and practices. All of these heroic young people were executed.

The Snow Goose (Gallico, 1992). When a shy village girl brings an injured snow goose to a lonely, crippled painter who lives in a lighthouse on the Essex coast of England, a friendship develops as they care for the bird together. Over time, both the girl and the bird grow to love the painter. During World War II, when the allied soldiers are stranded on the beaches of Dunkirk, his daring rescue saves their lives, but he is killed by machine-gun fire. When the snow goose returns to the lighthouse alone, the girl knows this courageous man will not return.

Session 8

After the members of each dialogue group had had time to read, discuss, and write about the stories they had selected from the realistic fiction and nonfiction texts introduced in Session 7, they were invited to work together to create a class mural to portray the various heroes and heroines they had discovered in their independent reading experiences. Finally, the children came together to share their discoveries about these heroes and heroines and to discuss them in terms of the definition that had evolved over the course of this literature unit.

In this "synthesis discussion" they noted that the heroes and heroines in real life had traits that were similar to those of the characters in folklore and fantasy whose inner qualities enabled them to overcome obstacles and to persevere to achieve a goal. They discovered that these individuals were ordinary people who drew from inner reservoirs of courage and moral strength to help others in time of need. For example, the children who had read *Winter Rescue* observed that Thor seemed to define "hero" in terms of the superheroes he loved to watch on television:

"Thor was always talking about Batman and those cartoon heroes."

"Remember when we first wrote our definition of heroes on the chart? It was sort of like what Thor thought about heroes!"

"But then we figured out a hero or heroine could be just ordinary—like Thor."

"And he didn't have to be strong or big or have superpowers. Issun Boshi and that poor shoemaker and the samurai's daughter weren't big and powerful!"

"Neither was Kate Shelley!"

"Maybe we should change that part in our definition [he pointed to the working definition on the wall chart] that says heroes are brave and fearless. A lot of the ones we read about were brave—but they were also *afraid*. Thor was afraid, and he really just wanted to be home, but he kept going anyway to save that man in the water."

"I agree. If you *know* what the danger is, I think it's normal to be scared. But it takes courage to do a thing you're scared of."

"Like if you're just learning how to swim and you can *imagine* what it would be like to drown, it's brave to get into the water anyway. But sometimes little kids just jump in because they don't *know* enough to be afraid! So that isn't brave!"

"So you mean if you're really not scared to do something, then you're not really brave to do it?"

"Yes! That's important! I agree with K. We should definitely fix our definition!"

"I thought of another thing. Thor could *choose* between doing the easy thing—going back—or doing the hard thing—keep on going to help that man. A lot of the heroes in the other stories had the same dilemma. We should add that, too." [At this point, several children explained the meaning of dilemma by using examples in their own lives.]

The children who discussed the stories about Balto and Togo suggested another change in the definition:

"Animals can be heroes, too! Those sled dogs kept going and going even though it was so freezing and they were so tired."

"And they knew things that the drivers [mushers] didn't know. Like when Balto knew the way and Gunnar didn't and like when Balto stopped the whole team so they wouldn't break through the thin ice."

"I read a book that we could add to our collection. It's called *Stone Fox* [Gardiner, 1980, 2003], and it's also about a dog sled race, and the dog is a hero, too."

"I saw that movie!"

"I like that one about the Saint Bernard dog that saves people who are lost in the snow" [*Barry the Bravest Saint Bernard* (Hall, 1973, 1992)].

"I know another one about an animal hero. It's called *Dolores and the Big Fire* [Clements, 2002]. It's a true story about a cat that risked her life to save her owner from a terrible fire."

"We read a really good book in our group. It's called *Hero Dogs: Courageous Canines in Action* [Jackson, 2003], and it tells about bomb-sniffing dogs and guide dogs and search and rescue dogs and therapy dogs and it tells about the dogs that helped out on 9/11."

The children were also able to identify "helpers" in the stories of real-life heroes and heroines. For example, Elizabeth Stanton's "helper" was identified as Pastor Hosack, who was willing to help her become a scholar at a time when most people "believed that girls' brains were not capable of absorbing anything but simple reading, writing, and arithmetic" (n.p.). The children who read about heroes and heroines of the civil rights movement identified Ruby Bridges' "helper" as the white teacher who was willing to teach a black child to read and write and add. Ruby and her teacher, Barbara Henry, spent a year together in an empty classroom, and, for Ruby, her teacher was her only friend in a world of prejudice, hatred, and racial turmoil.

Throughout this session, the children explored the concept of heroism by reading intertextually. By thinking in terms of multiple texts, the children built an increasingly rich and complex understanding of the qualities and characteristics of heroes and heroines and the dilemmas they confronted. The children used their working definition as the framework for this cumulative process, and they moved from analysis to synthesis as they brought together the diverse genres introduced in this unit to study the meaning of heroism. In the course of this literature unit, they gained new insights about their own potential to draw from inner qualities associated with heroism in order to engage in heroic behavior to help others.

Session 9

In the previous session, the children engaged in a review of the qualities and characteristics of heroes and heroines and the role of "helpers" in their lives. This review prepared them for a narrative writing project involving the production of original hero/heroine/helper tales. Their first step was to discuss the kinds of decisions they had to make in order to write a new tale of heroism. A brainstorming session produced the following list of questions that could be used to guide the writing process:

- What kind of story is it? (Fantasy? Realism? Autobiographical?)
- Who are the central characters? (Hero? Heroine? Helper?)
- What special qualities and inner strengths do these characters have?
- What is the setting?
- What is the problem in the story? How is it solved?
- What is the dilemma for the hero or heroine?

■ What obstacles does the hero or heroine have to overcome to save the day or make a difference?

The children composed stories that reflected their grasp of the literary concepts explored in the group read-aloud/think-aloud sessions as well as their insights about heroes, heroines, and helpers. A few children, who had been involved in actual situations requiring heroic actions, built their stories around eyewitness or personal accounts of these events to create an autobiographical narrative. Most of the children used their imaginations and their knowledge of genre to create realistic narratives, fantasies, or humorous tales. For the children who created first-person fictional narratives with themselves as hero or heroine, the creative process proved to be especially pleasing as it afforded them opportunities to use their inner resources to overcome obstacles and perform brave deeds to help others in hypothetical situations within the protective walls of the imagination. After completing the first drafts of their stories, the children revised and edited these drafts and then illustrated and bound their final drafts into books. These books were read aloud during the final group session and placed on display along with the other books selected for the classroom collection.

After listening to each of the hero/heroine/helper tales written by their classmates, the children discussed them in terms of the definition they had formulated and compared them with other stories they had heard or read in the course of this literature unit. They were especially interested in the autobiographical accounts and the first-person narratives of hypothetical events. These stories triggered a lively dialogue in which classmates imagined other hypothetical situations in which they could play heroic parts. These stories reflected their growing sense of their own potential to make a difference in the lives of others. At the end of this sharing and imagining session, the children identified several of these student-authored stories they thought would be especially suitable for dramatization—stories with a great deal of action, interesting and realistic dialogue, and believable characters. Small drama groups were organized to plan ways to present these stories. For example, the children in one group chose to interpret their story through mime; another group created finger puppets for their presentation; and a third group translated their story into a dance-drama. The final productions, presented to the class and invited guests, evolved out of the collaborative efforts of children working together to solve problems as they experimented with various dramatic forms. In the process, they learned more about character and plot development, and they experienced the pleasures of sharing their own interpretations of stories written by their classmates.

Assessment

Evaluation of the children's understanding and growth is an ongoing process throughout each of the literature units described in this book. The objectives used to guide the planning and implementation of each unit also serve as the criteria for assessment. An overview of the children's involvement in the unit featuring heroes, heroines, and helpers suggests the extent to which the objectives were met in the course of this cumulative literary/literacy experience.

As the children explored diverse stories about heroes and heroines and examined these characters in terms of the definition of heroism they were formulating, they discovered new ways to think about heroism (see Objective 1). For example, the children discovered that the heroes and heroines they encountered in fantasy, in realistic narratives, and in nonfiction were ordinary people without superpowers or extraordinary physical strength and size. The children found that they could identify with these individuals and realized that they, too, could make a difference in the lives of others. At one point in this unit, when the children were asked to write in their journals about heroes or heroines in their own lives, they used their group-constructed definition of heroism to identify such individuals. Some wrote about individuals in the news such as the firemen in New York City or soldiers in Iraq or a very small child who had called 911 to get help for his mother who had collapsed in their home. One wrote about the doctor who took care of his sister when she was severely injured in an accident. Another wrote about a teacher who helped him discover that he was a writer. These children had identified individuals who had inspired them with their deeds and their willingness to do something for others (see Objective 2).

The stories introduced in this unit were carefully selected to expose the children to diverse literary genres featuring a wide variety of heroes and heroines and to enable them to discover intertextual links that would help them to expand their understanding of heroism. Their contributions to comparative analyses of multiple texts revealed their discoveries of recurring patterns in stories from around the world (see Objective 3). The children's oral and written responses to the shared texts and to stories selected for independent reading demonstrated their ability to think about stories in terms of narrative elements and the craft of authors and artists (see Objective 4). Throughout this literary experience, the children explored multiple texts in terms of a central question about human experience: what is the meaning of heroism? The children engaged in the process of refining their definition of heroism from one session to the next. For example, they discovered that the heroic deeds featured in the stories in this literary unit required inner strength rather than physical strength. By Session 8, the children had moved from analysis to synthesis (see Objective 5). Their contributions to the literary discussions revealed the children's growing awareness of the reading-thinking strategies good readers use to generate meaning (see Objective 6). For example, by the third group session the children began to initiate a cover-to-cover study of each new text. This strategy set the stage for activating relevant prior knowledge, making predictions and inferences based on clues in the peritext, asking questions, identifying genre, determining importance, and learning something about the story or author that would enrich the reading transaction. As the children monitored their comprehension, they revised or confirmed predictions in response to new information in the unfolding text or they found answers to their questions in this new information or they identified an intertextual link with a prior story that enabled them to make an inference about a current text. They drew from their knowledge of text structure to understand character and plot development as well as the *subtext* of a narrative. That is, they entered into the story and imagined the thoughts and feelings of characters, interpreted their motives, and explored the "why" behind the story events. Throughout the literary/literacy experiences in this unit, the children responded to literature in discussions, in writing, and in art and drama (see Objective 7).

The series of group sessions was designed to introduce the children to carefully selected literary texts and to invite them to engage in interpretive discussions about these texts. These read-aloud/think-aloud sessions set the stage for further independent reading. In the process of exploring diverse texts selected for this unit, the children were building their literary histories and developing new reading interests (see Objective 8). For example, after reading about Balto and Togo, several children began looking for other books about animal heroes and heroines in the library. One child developed a special interest in the Iditarod and began to read books about participants in this grueling race such as *Racing the Iditarod Trail* (Crisman, 1993); *Adventure in Alaska: An Amazing True Story of the World's Longest, Toughest Dog Sled Race* (Kramer, 1993); *Iditarod Dream: Dusty and His Sled Dogs Compete in Alaska's Jr. Iditarod* (Wood, 1996); and *Big-Enough Anna: The Little Sled Dog Who Braved the Arctic* (Flowers & Dixon, 2003). This literature unit concluded with a creative-writing project that provided the children with an opportunity to compose their own stories about heroines, heroes, and helpers (see Objective 9) and to demonstrate their growing understanding of heroic behavior that reflects the human experience.

Note

1. These children had become acquainted with literary patterns such as "the theft of magical objects" and "quests" found in texts suggested for independent reading in the context of a previous literature unit, and thus were able to draw from their prior reading experiences to read intertextually in response to the stories selected for the unit featured in this chapter. An extensive study of these and other patterns in traditional literature is the focus of the literature unit described in Chapter 6.

6 Patterns in Traditional Literature

The Value of Traditional Literature

The literature program described in this book provides elementary school children with opportunities to enjoy and study a wide variety of literature: traditional and modern, prose and poetry, realism and fantasy, contemporary and historical fiction, and nonfiction. The literature unit introduced in this chapter features traditional literature and highlights the connections among traditional tales told in diverse cultures as well as the connections between the oral tradition and modern literature.

Charlotte Huck and Barbara Ziefer's observations (2004) about the value of folk literature for young children were mentioned in an earlier chapter. They call attention to the role of the oral tradition in the lives of children:

> Traditional literature is a rightful part of a child's literary heritage and lays the groundwork for understanding all literature . . . Northrop Frye maintains that "all themes and characters and stories that you encounter in literature belong to one big interlocking family" [1964, p. 48]. As you meet recurring patterns or symbols in mythlike floods, savior heroes, cruel stepmothers, the seasonal cycle of the year, the cycle of a human life, you begin to build a framework for literature. Poetry, prose, and drama become more emotionally significant as you respond to these recurring archetypes. (p. 238)

By studying traditional tales that originate from cultures in all parts of the world, children learn about the never-ending process of transformation of stories that are passed on from storyteller to storyteller, across centuries and continents. Jane Yolen (2000) explains this process of continuous transformation:

> Thus the oldest stories were transmitted and transmuted, the kaleidoscope patterns of motifs changed by time and by the times, by the tellers and by the listeners, by the country in which they arose and the countries to which they were carried. The old oral tales were changed the way culture itself changes, the way traditions change, by an erosion/eruption as powerful in its way as any geological force. Follow a story through its variants and you

are following the trade routes, the slave routes, the route of a conquering army, or that of a restless people on the move. (p. 23)

Patterns in Traditional Literature

In the literature unit described in this chapter, third- , fourth- , and fifth-grade children were invited to search for recurring patterns among diverse tales from around the world. They were invited to engage in a comparative study of traditional tales to discover *similarities* that point to clues about universal human experiences and *differences* that point to clues about individual cultures. After exploring recurring patterns in stories from the oral tradition, the children were introduced to stories written by modern writers who drew from traditional literature to create new stories. These experiences provided a context in which children could discover the relationships between traditional and modern literature. According to Yolen: "Stories lean on stories, art on art. This familiarity with the treasure-house of ancient story is necessary for any true appreciation of today's literature" (p. 15).

To facilitate a comparative study of traditional literature, the teacher selected four groups of tales to represent different folktale patterns: *the theft of magical objects, opposing characters, quest tales,* and *transformation tales.* At least two examples of each of these patterns were introduced in the group read-aloud sessions to enable the children to discover and discuss these patterns along with other recurring story elements. A central characteristic of the literature units presented in this text is the use of *book selection* as a teaching tool. Each story is selected to enable students to make discoveries and gain insights about literature. Each sequence of stories introduced in the group read-aloud sessions is intended to promote comparative analysis and the use of intertextual links to generate meaning. The children's grasp of each folktale pattern featured in the literature unit presented in this chapter was reinforced through their independent reading and their responses in literature journals and in small dialogue groups. This cumulative experience with traditional tales was designed to open the door to "the treasure-house of ancient story" and to unlock the meaning of Yolen's words: "Stories lean on stories . . . ."

This literature unit was designed as a flexible framework for developing a long-term experience with traditional literature. The unit as a whole consisted of four segments to focus on each of four different folktale patterns. As described in this chapter, the stories were introduced in consecutive group sessions and followed by independent reading and writing experiences and small-group work. The four segments were woven into a single unit that evolved in a single time period. However, each segment could also be developed as a discrete unit, or the four segments could be introduced during four different time periods over the course of the school year. Regardless of how these literary experiences are incorporated into the overall curriculum, the goal is to help children learn to view the study of traditional literature as a cumulative process in which the discovery of recurring patterns lays "the groundwork for understanding all literature" (Huck and Ziefer, 2004, p. 238).

Objectives for This Literature Unit

1. To introduce students to traditional literature from around the world and to some of the literary patterns found in these diverse tales

2. To invite students to engage in a comparative study of these diverse tales in order to discover *similarities* that reflect universal human experiences and *differences* that define specific cultural or historical contexts of storytellers

3. To provide opportunities for students to learn about the nature of the oral tradition

4. To provide opportunities for students to discover relationships between traditional and modern literature and modern writers' use of recurring patterns found in traditional tales to create new stories

5. To provide opportunities for students to use think-aloud strategies to respond to literature in group discussions and to engage in collaborative construction of meaning in the social context of literary discussion

6. To provide opportunities for students to practice other reading-thinking strategies that good readers use in their transactions with texts

7. To provide opportunities for students to respond to literature by writing in their journals, composing original narratives, and interpreting literature through other forms of creative expression

8. To provide opportunities for students to engage in independent reading and writing and to expand their interests as readers and writers

Introducing the First Pattern: The Theft of Magical Objects

Session 1

Stolen Thunder: A Norse Myth, retold by Shirley Climo (1994), was introduced with a brief discussion of the nature of myth as one of the genres in traditional literature and the nature of Norse mythology, in particular. According to Rebecca Lukens (2003): "Myths are stories that originate in the beliefs of nations and races and present episodes in which supernatural forces operate" (p. 26). Like all oral tales, myths were handed down by word of mouth from anonymous storytellers; they existed orally until they were recorded in written form. Many of the children were familiar with some of the gods and goddesses, heroes and heroines, and monsters in Greek and Norse mythology. Children whose exposure to these mythical characters was through electronic games were surprised to discover their origins in ancient myths. *Stolen Thunder* is a retelling of a Norse myth about Thor, the god of thunder; Thrym, the king of the Frost Giants who steals Thor's magic hammer, Mjolnir; and Loki, the trickster god who helps Thor retrieve this magical object.

The children were asked to search for clues about this story by examining the front and back covers and the pictures on the pages leading up to the beginning of the narrative. The children who were familiar with Thor and his magic hammer were able to respond to the questions of classmates:

> "The title tells you that something is stolen, so that's the problem in the story. But I don't get how *thunder* can be stolen!"
>
> "I think that guy on the front is Thor. He's the god of thunder."
>
> "He's the one with the hammer. When he throws the hammer, it sounds like thunder. Maybe that's what was stolen."
>
> "It [the picture that extends from the front to the back cover] shows him in his chariot. He flies across the sky in it."
>
> "You can also see a huge bird with a face flying next to him. What is that?"

As they listened to the first three pages of text, the children were asked to confirm or revise their initial comments and to search for answers to their questions (Strategy 8). These pages provide an introduction to Norse mythology and set the stage for the theft of Thor's hammer. Later in the text, when Loki begins to implement his plan to retrieve the hammer, he borrows the goddess Freya's falcon cloak. This scene triggered these comments:

"So it was *Loki* on the front cover. He was wearing the falcon cloak!"

"I think Loki is like a trickster character. But in this story, maybe he's a *helper!*"

"Maybe he'll use his tricks to get the hammer back."

The boys who offered these predictions were able to confirm them as the story unfolded: Loki flies to Jotunheim, the land of the giants, to meet with Thrym, who demands Freya, the goddess of love and beauty, in exchange for the hammer. When Freya refuses to be the giant's bride, Loki's plan is for Thor to appear dressed up as the bride and Loki as the bridesmaid. When Thrym expresses his surprise at "Freya's appetite," Loki has an explanation. When Thrym asks, "Why are your eyes so red and angry, Freya?" Loki, again, provides an explanation (p. 28). This interchange in the text prompted several children to compare this myth with "Little Red Riding Hood":

"It's the same pattern! It's just like when the wolf dressed up like the grandmother and Little Red Riding Hood said 'Grandma, what big eyes you have!'"

"Maybe the storyteller knew that story and decided to use the disguise part for this one."

After hearing Thor's triumphant declaration following the defeat of Thrym, the children's eyes again lit up with recognition as they made another connection. One child articulated their discovery: "In his last line he says it's 'Thor's-Day'! That must be how we got the word for *Thursday!*"

At the end of the story, Loki promises Thor that he will not tell anyone "about Thor the beautiful bride" (p. 32). This promise triggered an immediate response:

"We *know* he's not going to keep that promise! He's a trickster!"

"It's like at the end of the Anansi stories. He *never* learns his lesson."

The final lines of the story confirmed this prediction drawn from their prior experiences with trickster characters.

At the conclusion of this first session, the children were invited to select a book for independent reading from a group of traditional tales featuring the pattern of the theft of magical objects:

Aladdin and the Wonderful Lamp (Lang, 1981). A tale from "The Arabian Nights."

"The Chuang Brocade" in *Treasure Mountain: Folktales from Southern China* (Sadler, 1982, pp.16–29).

The Crystal Mountain (Sanderson, 1999), retold from the Chinese story "The Magic Brocade."

The Enchanted Tapestry—A Chinese Tale (San Souci, 1987).

Liang and the Magic Paintbrush (Demi, 1980). A folktale from China.

The Magic Boat (Demi, 1990). A folktale from China.

The Magic Cooking Pot: A Folktale of India (Towle, 1975).

The Magic Gourd (Diakité, 2003). A teaching tale from Mali.

The Magic Horse (Scott, 1985). A Persian folktale.

"The Magic Mortar," in *The Magic Listening Cap: More Folk Tales from Japan* (Uchida, 1955).

The Magic Stove (Ginsburg, 1983). A folktale from Russia.

The Nose Tree (Hutton, 1981). A folktale from Germany.

Palmiero and the Ogre (Domanska, 1967). A folktale from Italy.

Peter and the North Wind (Littledale, 1988). A folktale from Norway.

The Silver Charm: A Folktale from Japan (San Souci, 2002a).

The Three Magic Gifts (Riordan, 1980). A folktale from Russia.

"Treasure Mountain," in *Treasure Mountain: Folktales from Southern China* (Sadler, 1982).

Tye May and the Magic Brush (Bang, 1981). A version of this tale for beginning readers.

The Weaving of a Dream: A Chinese Folktale (Heyer, 1986).

"The Wonderful Pumpkin" in *A Treasury of Turkish Folktales for Children* (Walker, 1988).

After selecting at least one of these titles to read independently, the children recorded their personal responses as readers, the story patterns they identified, and the differences between the stories they had selected and the stories shared in the group sessions. These children had learned to create story maps to guide their written analyses. Their maps included such items as title, country of origin, central characters (including heroes or heroines, villains, and helper characters), problems and solutions, secondary patterns, viewpoint, and themes. The children were invited to bring their literature journals to small dialogue groups or to whole-group read-aloud sessions in order to share relevant journal entries during these discussions. They also placed markers on a wall map of the world to indicate the origins of the stories they heard in the group sessions or read independently. As each country of origin was located, a small marker with the story title was affixed on the map. This experience provided a graphic reminder that these recurring folktale patterns are found around the world.

Session 2

Iduna and the Magic Apples (Mayer, 1988), another story from Norse mythology, was introduced in the second session featuring the pattern of the theft of magical objects. Iduna was the keeper of a golden chest of magic apples that gave immortality to the great god Odin, his brother Loki, and all the other gods in Asgard. This is the story of the wicked giant Thiassi, who envied the gods and vowed to capture Iduna and her magic apples. Since Loki was the one who helped Thiassi steal Iduna and her apples, he was the only one who could rescue her and undo the evil he had caused. The gods forced him to put on a mantle of falcon feathers, and he was transformed into a bird so he could fly to Thiassi's castle to rescue Iduna.

When the children examined the front cover of this beautifully illustrated picture book, they identified the woman holding the apples as Iduna, and they wondered if the large black bird with the human face was Loki. As the story unfolded they discovered that this bird was actually Thiassi, who had disguised himself as a bird of prey, and that, later in the story, Loki is transformed into a bird. The children's comments about these discoveries reflected their use of intertextual links with other stories and their metacognitive response to this literary experience:

> "When Loki had to put on the falcon feathers—it said it was a 'mantle.' I think that's like a cloak. So maybe that was Freya's falcon cloak."
> "It made me so mad when Loki tricked Iduna so Thiassi could catch her."
> "And the only reason he began to worry about Iduna was when he realized *he* would grow old without the apples, too! He was so selfish!"
> "I liked that part when Thiassi tried to take the apples out of the chest, and they changed into tiny seeds and he couldn't pick them up."
> "I read a story like that—about a mean brother who stole a magic thing from his good brother. But the mean brother didn't know how to work it because he wasn't the true owner—and in the end he got punished for stealing it!"
> "Thiassi got punished for stealing Iduna's apples, too."
> "And Thrym got punished for stealing the hammer."
> "It's like in "The Magic Brush" [Sadler, 1982]. The emperor tried to steal a magic paintbrush from a boy, but it only worked

for the boy, and in the end, the emperor got punished for his greed. It's a good story."

"Maybe it's the same pattern in all of them—the greedy characters get punished for stealing the magic things, and the true owners *deserved* the magic things because they were good to others."

"And all the stories have helpers. In my story ['The Magic Mortar' (Uchida, 1955)] an old man helped the good brother get the magic mortar. In *Stolen Thunder,* Loki was the helper! In this one, the sisters of fortune helped Odin."

"Loki is like that trickster Anansi. Sometimes he's mean, but sometimes he's helpful."

Session 3

The teacher read aloud "The Magic Brush" in response to the children's requests, and then asked them to speculate about those who told and listened to this tale in ancient China:

"I think those people must have hated the emperor because he was so cruel."

"They probably wanted to get rid of him but they couldn't because he had all those soldiers. So maybe they told stories about what they *wished* for."

"I think this story is sort of like those protest marches where people have signs about what they're *against*—like the war. But this is a free country so you can say it out loud. But *then* [in ancient China] the people couldn't say what they really thought or they'd get thrown in the dungeon . . . or worse!"

"So maybe they [the ancient Chinese storytellers] told protest stories in secret instead of having marches. It probably made them feel better . . . even though they couldn't change anything."

Following this discussion, the teacher introduced two examples of modern picture-book versions of this ancient story: *The Magic Paintbrush* (Muller, 1990) and *Cabbage Rose* (Helldorfer, 1993), as well as a novel based on this ancient Chinese tale: *A Brush with Magic* (Brooke, 1993). This is the story of Liang, a boy in ancient China, who is found as a baby in a basket by a poor farmer named Li. The only thing in the basket with the baby is a brush that can give life to drawings. This is a complex tale about the nature of magic and Liang's quest, which takes him to the court of the emperor. The teacher also introduced two modern short stories featuring the "theft of magical objects" pattern: "A Necklace of Raindrops" in *A Necklace of Raindrops and Other Stories* (Aiken, 1968, 2001) and "Bridget's Hat" in *Tale of a One-Way Street and Other Stories* (Aiken, 1978).

The children were asked to choose one of these stories to read independently and to record in their journals their own thoughts about the story as well as responses to questions such as: How is this modern story similar to particular traditional tales? What changes did the author and/or artist make? What patterns can you identify? What theme or message is developed in the story? This assignment was intended to provide an opportunity for the children to discover relationships between traditional and modern literature and the way modern writers use the oral tradition to create new stories.

This comparative analysis of traditional and modern tales featuring a common pattern set the stage for a creative-writing project in which the children used the pattern of the theft of magical objects, to create a new tale. These original narratives were shared in a whole-group session where they were discussed in terms of the traditional patterns and themes used by these young writers to compose their own modern tales.

Introducing the Second Pattern: Opposing Characters

Session 1

The Stone Lion (Schroeder, 1994) is a traditional tale of Tibet about two brothers. Jarlo, the elder, is a greedy, dishonest merchant; Drashi is a good-hearted boy who helps his mother and their neighbors. A stone lion at the top of a mountain rewards Drashi for his kindness and his respect for all living things; the lion punishes Jarlo for his greed and cruelty. This pattern is found in oral tales in all parts of the world: the tale of kind and unkind brothers or sisters or neighbors who are rewarded or punished appropriately (see *The Tale of the Kind and the Unkind Girls: AA-TH 480 and Related Titles* [Roberts, 1994]). Lukens, in *A Critical Handbook of Children's Literature* (2003) defines a *character foil* as a "character whose contrasting traits point up those of the central character" (p. 344). After the children listened to *The Stone Lion*, they compared it with other tales featuring characters with contrasting traits:

> "It's like 'The Magic Brush.' The boy and the emperor are just the opposite. One is kind and the other is cruel and greedy . . . just like these two brothers."
>
> "It's also like *The Three Magic Gifts*. One brother is nice and the other one was mean. Maybe that's the pattern here. . . . These three stories have *opposite* characters."
>
> "But this one [*The Stone Lion*] didn't have the theft in it. Jarlo goes to the stone lion to get more gold for himself. He thought he would get a lot more than his brother. But he didn't steal magic objects like in the other ones."

> "So *The Three Magic Gifts* has *two* patterns in it—the two op-
> posite brothers *and* the theft of magical objects."

At this point in the dialogue, the teacher introduced the term *opposing characters* to use in referring to characters with contrasting traits.

Session 2

When the children were introduced to *The Language of Birds* (Martin, 2000) in the second session featuring stories with "opposing characters," they recognized the reteller as a well-known storyteller in Rochester, New York. Most of them had participated in one or more of his storytelling presentations and were delighted to discover that he was the reteller of this old Russian fairy tale. In this story, a wealthy merchant sends his two sons out into the world to prove themselves. The older brother, Vasilii, is clever, selfish, and a realist; the younger brother, Ivan, is wise, generous, and a dreamer. A mother bird rewards Ivan for his kindness to her baby bird; she grants his wish to understand the language of birds. His father and brother do not appreciate the worth of Ivan's gift until he is able to use it to solve a problem for the czar, to save Vasilii's life, and to marry the czar's daughter.

After the children examined the illustration for the opening lines of the story, they explained the clues they used to make predictions that the boys in the picture were probably the opposing characters (Strategy 12):

> "One boy is looking at the gold . . . he must be the greedy
> brother."
> "And the other one doesn't seem to care about the gold, so
> he's probably *not* greedy . . . like the younger brother in *The Stone
> Lion.*"

As the story unfolded, the children were able to confirm and expand on their initial predictions. One student provided textual support for his discovery of an interesting difference between Jarlo, the older brother in *The Stone Lion,* and Vasilii, the older brother in *The Language of Birds:*

> "Jarlo was cruel to his mother and brother, but Vasilii wasn't
> cruel to Ivan. Vasilii was selfish and greedy like Jarlo, but he tried
> to help Ivan by teaching him how to be tricky to get what you
> want."
> "But Ivan and Vasilii *were* opposing characters. . . . Ivan was
> kind and cared for living things. Vasilii was greedy and dishon-
> est."

At the end of this session, the children were introduced to a second text set made up of examples of tales featuring *opposing characters,* and they were invited to choose at least one of these titles for independent reading and writing and to engage in comparative analysis in small dialogue groups:

Angkat: The Cambodian Cinderella (Coburn, 1998).

Baba Yaga: A Russian Folktale (Kimmel, 1991).

Boots and His Brothers: A Norwegian Tale (Kimmel, 1992a).

Chen Ping and His Magic Axe (Demi, 1987). A Chinese tale.

The Five Sparrows: A Japanese Folktale (Newton, 1982).

The Goose Girl: A Story from the Brothers Grimm (Kimmel, J. Grimm, & W. Grimm, 1994).

Jouanah: A Hmong Cinderella (Coburn & Lee, 1996).

Just Rewards, or, Who Is That Man in the Moon and What's He Doing Up There Anyway? (Sanfield, 1996). An adaptation of a Chinese folktale.

The Luminous Pearl: A Chinese Folktale (Torre, 1990). A Chinese tale.

"The Man Who Made the Trees Blossom," in *Japanese Fairy Tales* (Marmur, 1960).

The Month-Brothers: A Slavic Tale (Marshak, 1983).

Moss Gown (Hooks, 1987). A tale from North Carolina.

Mother Holly: A Retelling from the Brothers Grimm (Stewig, J. Grimm, & W. Grimm, 2001).

Mufaro's Beautiful Daughters: An African Tale (Steptoe, 1987).

Papa Gatto: An Italian Fairy Tale (Sanderson, 1995).

The Perfect Orange: A Tale from Ethiopia (Araujo, 1994).

The Rich Man and the Shoemaker: A Fable (Watts & La Fontaine, 2002).

The Rumor of Pavel and Paali: A Ukrainian Folktale (Kismaric, 1988).

Sitti and the Cats: A Tale of Friendship (Bahous, 1993). A Palestinian tale.

The Talking Eggs: A Folktale from the American South (San Souci, 1989).

Toads and Diamonds (Bender & Perrault, 1995). A French folktale.

Toads and Diamonds (Huck, 1995).

The Tongue-Cut Sparrow (Ishii, 1987). A Japanese tale.

The Treasure Chest: A Chinese Tale (Wang, 1995).

The Twins and the Bird of Darkness: A Hero Tale from the Caribbean (San Souci, 2002b).

Session 3

During this whole-group session, scribes from each small dialogue group shared the results of their comparative analyses. They identified recurring patterns in the stories they had selected as well as different settings associated with individual tales. Finally, the whole group collaborated to summarize the patterns they had found:

> "The opposing characters get what they deserve. The greedy or mean ones are punished and the kind and generous ones are rewarded."
>
> "There are villain characters and helper characters."
>
> "There are patterns of three . . . like three tests or three magic objects."
>
> "When heroes or heroines go on a quest journey, they meet someone that needs help. The kind ones are polite and helpful, and the other ones are rude and don't help. The kind ones get helped in return."
>
> "Sometimes they have to *choose* something, and the greedy and selfish ones choose wrong . . . like in *The Luminous Pearl*."
>
> "Sometimes they're told *not* to do something and you *know* who's going to do it anyway . . . like in *The Talking Eggs* and in *Mufaro's Beautiful Daughters*."
>
> "In some stories, like *Chen Ping and His Axe*, there's a test for honesty."
>
> "Another test is for *courage*—like in *The Twins and the Bird of Darkness*."
>
> "In some stories the tasks are impossible. In *The Month-Brothers* the task was to get strawberries in winter!"
>
> "We found a lot of story patterns that are the *same*, but when you look at the pictures you see a lot of *differences*. I especially liked all the colorful birds and flowers in *Mufaro's Beautiful Daughters*." [This comment prompted a closer look at the work of the artists who portrayed the different types of landscapes, houses, clothing, occupations, and festivities that reflected the diverse settings and cultures in these stories from around the world.]

At the conclusion of this session, the teacher introduced modern writers who had created new stories or new versions of old stories by using the "opposing character" pattern found in traditional literature:

Cinder Edna (Jackson, 1994). A picture book.

Ella's Big Chance: A Jazz-Age Cinderella (Hughes, 2004). A picture book.

Jennifer Murdley's Toad (Coville, 1992, 2002). A novel.

Prince Nautilus (Melmed, 1994). A picture book.

The Snow Rose (Laroche & Laroche, 1986). A picture book.

Again, the children were invited to select one of these titles to read independently and to record their responses in their journals. A number of children were inspired by these traditional and modern tales to write their own stories using the opposing characters pattern as a starting point.

Introducing the Third Pattern: Quest Tales

Session 1

A quest or journey tale is an almost universal story pattern, according to Joseph Campbell, who describes in *The Hero with a Thousand Faces* (1968) the initiation journey of departure; adventure, trials, and tests; and return:

> A hero ventures forth from the world of common day into a region of supernatural wonder: fabulous forces are there encountered and a decisive victory is won; the hero comes back from this mysterious adventure with the power to bestow boons on his fellow man. (p. 30)

Whether the story is about Peter Rabbit's quest for adventure, Max's quest for inner control (in Maurice Sendak's *Where the Wild Things Are* [1963, 1988]), Theseus' journey to Crete to slay the Minotaur, Leje's quest for his mother's stolen brocade (in *The Weaving of a Dream* [Heyer, 1986]), or the quest of the young girl who seeks her beloved in the castle that lies east of the sun and west of the moon, the heroes and heroines leave home, set out on a journey, survive a series of trials and ordeals, and return home triumphant. Those who encounter supernatural helpers earn magical assistance through humane behavior. At the end of their journeys, these heroes and heroines have gained significant insights about themselves as individuals and, in fulfilling their quests, they have gained the power to make a difference in the lives of others. The reader who lives through the experiences of these heroes and heroines discovers what it means to widen one's horizons and confront challenges with courage, determination, and wit. These stories are especially meaningful to young readers searching for their own identity as individuals and as members of the larger community.

Before reading the first example of a quest tale, the teacher invited the children to share their understandings of the meaning of the word *quest* and to predict what elements they would find in a *quest tale*. Some of the children recalled the quest in *The Luminous Pearl*, one of the opposing-character stories they had read earlier. The children shared what they knew about quests, and the teacher recorded their comments on a wall chart. Then the teacher introduced *Oom Razoom, or, Go I Know Not Where, Bring Back I Know Not What: A Russian Tale* (Wolkstein, 1991). When Alexis, the king's archer, allows a blue pigeon to go free, it changes into a wise and beautiful young woman whose name is Olga. They marry and live happily together until the king decides to claim Olga for himself. To get rid of Alexis, the King sends him on an impossible quest. With the help of Olga, her mother and sisters, and a magical frog, Alexis travels to the end of the world and discovers Oom Razoom, an invisible genie who becomes his companion and takes him back to Olga. At the end of his successful quest, Alexis is able to defeat the evil king, and he and his beloved Olga rule the kingdom together . . . "very wisely."

The children's study of the front and back covers triggered several questions. They wondered about the meaning of the unusual title; they wondered what the young man was carrying; they wondered about the identity of the "lady in blue"; and they wondered about the "strange-looking man" featured on the back cover. As they listened to the story, they found answers to each of their questions. That is, by initiating a cover-to-cover study of this new tale, they generated questions that guided and deepened their involvement in the reading-thinking process (Strategies 1 and 8). As they continued their study of the peritext, the children found a familiar quotation in a yellow box opposite the first page of the story text: "'The morning is wiser than the evening.' That's what the archer's wife says. Alexis met his wife in the woods. I'll tell you how" (n.p.). They used another reading-thinking strategy (Strategy 11) to make a connection between this text and other texts:

> "That's like that story about the frog princess that we read last year. She kept saying to Ivan—'Go to sleep, the morning brings more wisdom than the evening.'" [*The Frog Princess* (Isele, 1984).]
>
> "They're both Russian tales!" [He pointed to the full title on the front cover.]
>
> "We read another Russian tale like this . . . about Vasilisa's doll that always said, 'Go to sleep, things look brighter in the morning.'" [*Vasilisa the Beautiful* (Whitney, 1970)]
>
> "The storyteller who told *this* story must've known those other old stories, too!"
>
> "The title seems like the opposite of a quest. I thought someone who goes on a quest knows *where* he's going and *what* he's looking for."

As soon as the story came to an end, the children talked about the characters and patterns they had identified as the story unfolded. The patterns associated specifically with quest tales were added to the elements of quest tales recorded on the wall chart during the introductory discussion about the quest as a literary pattern.

> "The king is the villain; he tried to get rid of the archer and steal his wife."
>
> "And he sent Alexis on an *impossible quest* to get rid of him . . . like when the girl in *The Month-Brothers* was sent to get strawberries in winter."
>
> "Vasilisa's stepmother wanted to get rid of her and sent her to get a light from Baba Yaga—that was an impossible quest."
>
> "This could be a pattern in quest tales. We should add this to the chart."
>
> "Another pattern is when Alexis was nice to the genie [Oom Razoom] and he [the genie] helped him get home and defeat the king. There's usually a reward for being kind. That's the theme."
>
> "Another pattern was the transformation. The bird changed into Olga."
>
> "Another pattern was the magic objects that helped Alexis."
>
> "I liked the ending when the people asked Alexis to rule their kingdom and he said he would let them know in the morning and he said, 'The morning is wiser than the evening.'"
>
> "It's a good ending because the people will be much better off with Olga and Alexis ruling the kingdom instead of that mean king!"
>
> "So it was good for *everybody* when he came back from that impossible quest! I wonder if that's part of the pattern."

At the conclusion of this session, the teacher showed them a longer version of this tale, *I-Know-Not-What, I-Know-Not-Where: A Russian Tale*, adapted by Eric Kimmel (1994). Several children chose to read this story in eight chapters on their own. During a later group session, they shared some of the differences between the retellings by Wolkstein and Kimmel. They were especially intrigued to discover that Baba Yaga helped the archer in Kimmel's story and that she was the grandmother of the archer's wife. One boy found the familiar phrase: "Morning is wiser than evening" (1994, p. 27).

Session 2

The Samurai's Daughter: A Japanese Legend (San Souci, 1992), introduced in the second session as another example of a quest tale, is the story of Tokoyo, the daughter of a samurai nobleman, who sets out on a dangerous journey to join her exiled father. She encounters bandits, a ghost ship, and a monstrous sea serpent, but her quest is successful because of her loyalty, her courage, and her skills as a deep-sea diver. She saves the life of a young girl who would have been sacrificed to the serpent;

she rescues her father and others who had been banished to this island; and she breaks the spell that had caused the ruler's strange behavior. At the end of the story, she and her father return home to enjoy "peace and prosperity for the rest of their lives."

In the discussion that followed this story, the children immediately identified the elements that distinguished it as a quest tale: the heroine leaves home, encounters dangers, passes the tests of her courage and skill, defeats those who threaten to destroy her, and returns home in triumph, bringing honor to her family and peace to the kingdom. The children were especially impressed that Tokoyo was able to kill the evil sea-demon without magical help. She had used her own skills as a deep-sea diver that she had learned from the women divers who harvested abalone and pearl oysters. Several children noted that at the end of the quests in the stories shared in these two sessions, not only had the hero and heroine proved their courage and love and achieved their personal goals, but they had also improved the lives of the people in their respective kingdoms. The student who had raised the question about this in the previous session added this element to the wall chart with their working definition of the quest tale. The elements the children had recorded on this chart were remarkably similar to those included in Campbell's discussion of this literary pattern.

At the end of this session, the teacher called attention to a third text set featuring *quest tales:*

The Black Bull of Norroway: A Scottish Tale (Huck, 2001).

The Devil with the Three Golden Hairs: A Tale from the Brothers Grimm (Hogrogian, 1983).

Dragon Feathers (Dugin, 1993). An Austrian tale.

East o' the Sun and West o' the Moon (Dasent, 1992). A Norwegian tale.

The Four Gallant Sisters (Kimmel, 1992b). A German tale.

The Fourth Question: A Chinese Tale (Wang, 1991).

The Frog Princess (Isele, 1984). A Russian tale.

Gilly Martin the Fox (Hunter, 1994). A Celtic folktale.

The Girl, the Fish, and the Crown: A Spanish Folktale (Heyer, 1995).

The Gorgon's Head: A Myth from the Isles of Greece (Hodges, 1972).

The Khan's Daughter: A Mongolian Folktale (Yep, 1997b).

The Luminous Pearl: A Chinese Folktale (Torre, 1990).

On Cat Mountain (Richard & Levine, 1994). A Japanese folktale.

Ouch! A Tale from Grimm (Babbitt, 1998).

Pegasus (Mayer, 1997). A Greek myth.

Perseus (Mayer, 2002). A Greek myth.

Perseus (Hutton, 1993).

Princess Florecita and the Iron Shoes: A Spanish Fairy Tale (Stewig, 1995).

"The Princess and the Goatherd" in *A Treasury of Turkish Folktales for Children* (Walker, 1988).

The Rose's Smile: Farizad of the Arabian Nights (Kherdian, 1997b).

The Singing Ringing Tree (Hastings, 1988). A German tale.

Sir Gawain and the Green Knight (Hieatt, 1967). From the tales of King Arthur.

The Spirit of the Blue Light (Mayer, 1990). A German tale.

The Story of Jumping Mouse: A Native American Legend (Steptoe, 1984).

The Tale of the Firebird (Spirin, 2002). A Russian tale.

The Talking Tree: An Old Italian Tale (Rayevsky, 1990).

The Three Wonderful Beggars (Scott, 1987). A Serbian tale.

Vasilissa the Beautiful: A Russian Folktale (Winthrop, 1991).

Vasily and the Dragon: An Epic Russian Fairy Tale (Stern, 1982).

The Water of Life: A Tale from the Brothers Grimm (Rogasky & J. Grimm, 1986).

The Weaving of the Dream: A Chinese Folktale (Heyer, 1986).

After the children selected one or more of these illustrated editions of traditional tales for independent reading, the teacher helped them form small dialogue groups to share their responses to these stories and to record the patterns they discovered. They used their journal entries to inform their contributions to these dialogues. Eventually, they recorded additional elements on the wall chart that had been started in the first session featuring quest tales. For example, some of the children had identified the *reason* for the quest in the story they selected and discovered that some quests were initiated as a way "to get rid of the hero." The children who read *Vasilissa the Beautiful* noted that Vasilissa was sent on a quest to get a light from the witch, Baba Yaga, who was rumored to eat people "as one eats chickens" (Winthrop, 1991, p. 11). Her stepsisters push her out of the house and tell her: "You cannot come back until you bring us light" (p. 14). One child commented: "It's obvious they just wanted to get rid of Vasilissa, and they thought Baba Yaga would eat her. But they didn't know Vasilissa had that magic doll to help her!" The children who read *The Devil with the Three Golden Hairs* found that this story started with a prophecy that a baby boy born to a poor couple would marry a king's daughter. The king tries to get rid of the boy but is unsuccessful, and eventually, the prophecy is fulfilled, in spite of his efforts. So the king sends the boy on a dangerous quest to obtain "three golden hairs from the head of the devil" (n.p.). The children inferred that the king's intention was to get rid of the boy. Natalie Babbitt's lively retelling of this story, *Ouch! A Tale from Grimm*, is illustrated with marvelous, humorous pictures by Fred Marcellino. Babbitt's title is derived from the devil's response when his grandmother pulls three golden hairs from his head to give to Marco, the boy who was born with a birthmark shaped like a crown and a prophecy that he would marry a princess. Similar patterns were found in *Vasily and the Dragon* and *The Three Wonderful Beggars*. In *Vasily and the Dragon* the prophecy is that a baby boy born to a poor couple would possess all of the wealth of Marko the Rich. Although Marko tries to get rid of the baby, he, too, is unsuccessful. When the boy grows up and marries Marko's daughter, Marko sends him to the Heathen Dragon whose palace is at the world's end. Again, the children inferred that Marko sent Vasily on this dangerous quest to get rid of him. *The Three Wonderful Beggars* is another version of this Russian tale. It begins with the same prophecy that Vassili will get all of the merchant's wealth. When Vassili marries the merchant's daughter, Mark the Rich sends him on a dangerous quest— to the Serpent King. A similar tale, "The Princess and the Goatherd" is included in *A Treasury of Turkish Folktales for Children*. A king learns from a teller of fortunes that his only daughter is destined to be the bride of a goatherd. The king sends the goatherd on a long journey to deliver a letter that says, "Kill the bearer of this letter . . ." (p. 119). Fortunately, the words in the letter are changed before the goatherd arrives at his destination, and the prophecy is fulfilled at the end of the story. A child who read *The Khan's Daughter* identified the "prophecy pattern" in this story but noted a difference: "In this one, a poor man's son goes on a quest to try to make his father's prophecy come true. The prophecy was that the son would be rich and would marry the Khan's daughter!"

The children who read the retellings of the Greek myth about Perseus identified the "prophecy pattern": *The Gorgon's Head* tells the story of the Greek hero, Perseus, who, like Vasily, "lived in danger from the day of his birth" (p. 9). Perseus' grandfather "had dreamed that someday the boy would kill him. The old man locked the baby and its mother, Danae, into a wooden chest and cast the chest into the sea" (p.

9). The gods send winds to bring the chest to an island, where they lived in the king's palace for fifteen years. At this point in the story, the king wants to get rid of Perseus and sends him on a quest to obtain the head of Medusa. In Warwick Hutton's retelling of *Perseus* (1993), a prophecy foretells that the grandfather will be killed by his grandson. When Perseus is sent on the terrible quest to "fetch Medusa's head," the gods Athena and Hermes help him.

Students who selected *Pegasus* from this text set identified this myth as another example of a hero sent on a quest "to get rid of him." In this myth, a young hero named Bellerophon is sent by King Proetus to the king of Lycia with a sealed letter with these words: "Put to death the bearer of this message" (n.p.). This king is unwilling to "bring about the youth's death by his own hand" (n.p.), so he sends him on a quest to kill the monster known as the Chimera that has terrorized the people of Lycia. Although the purpose of this quest is to send Bellerophon to certain death, Pegasus, the winged stallion, helps Bellerophon defeat the monster.

The members of each dialogue group were able to examine more closely the work of the artists than was possible in the whole-group sessions. They discovered that many of the pictures supplemented information given in the verbal text and that some of the pictures included details that prompted questions and multiple interpretations. The children discovered the significance of body language and facial expressions in the portrayal of inner motives and personal qualities. They noticed that the frames around the pictures in some books were more than merely decorative. They found that small scenes were often embedded into larger ones and that small details hidden on the page sometimes foreshadowed subsequent events in the story. One group contrasted the portrayals of Baba Yaga in the two versions of the story about the archer who had to travel to "I-Know-Not-Where." In the school library, they found other Russian tales featuring Baba Yaga, and they enjoyed comparing the work of the artists who had envisioned this remarkable Russian witch and her hut on chicken legs. Their study of the visual images created by diverse artists fostered lively discussions and active participation as the children searched for hidden meanings, explored possibilities, and constructed interpretations. Many of the children were motivated to examine other works by their favorite artists, and some were inspired to incorporate the artist's techniques into their own artwork. The collaborative study of single illustrated editions of quest tales in these small dialogue groups provided opportunities for the children to discover connections between the craft of writers and the craft of artists.

Session 3

The Enchanted Wood: An Original Fairy Tale (Sanderson, 1991) was introduced as an example of a modern quest tale. In this story, three princes go on a quest to the Heart of the World to try to end the terrible drought that has ravaged their father's kingdom. Each prince encounters the wise woman who warns them to "be true to the quest" and not to stray from the path. The two older brothers ignore the warning, and they stray from the path when they are "tempted by what they love most, hunting and fighting" (n.p.). Galen, the youngest brother, is tempted to stray from the path to help his brothers, but he chooses "to stay on the path and remain true to [his] purpose to help all the people of the kingdom" (n.p.).

Before the story was read aloud, the children talked about the front and back covers and the oil paintings on the two pages prior to the first page of story text:

> "The title is a clue that this is a fantasy. The stag on the back cover could be a magical creature. It's probably important in the story, because it's right in the middle of the back cover."
> "The person riding the horse could be the one who's going on a quest, because it looks like he's going into a dark forest."
> "On the title page it shows the trees sort of lost in fog. It looks sort of mysterious."

After listening to the opening lines of the story and learning of the queen's death and the terrible drought, the children examined the landscapes of the kingdom on the facing pages above the text. They noticed that these two paintings show the contrast between the kingdom as it looked *before* the death of the beloved queen and the kingdom as it looked *after* this tragedy and the drought that followed. As the story of the quest unfolded, the children confirmed or revised some of their initial predictions and drew from their literary experiences with traditional tales to predict their way through the narrative. As soon as they heard about the drought, they identified this as the *problem* in the story and predicted that the goal of the quest would be to save the kingdom. They predicted that the two older sons would be unkind to the wise woman and would ignore her warning. As the story unfolded, they learned that Edmund, the hunter, couldn't resist pursuing the beautiful stag that led him off the path and that Owen, the warrior, was tempted to leave the path to duel with the knight in black armor who appeared in the forest and seemed to mock him with "stony silence." The children decided that the stag and knight were used to test the resolve of the two older brothers to remain true to the quest. They decided that Galen's test was seeing his beloved older brothers in trouble, ". . . but [knowing that] he had to stay on the path to stay true to the quest." Several children confirmed their earlier predictions that the stag on the back cover was a magical creature that would play an important role in the story.

At the end of the story, the children used the list of elements on the wall chart to analyze it as a quest tale:

> "Owen and Edmund were punished because they only thought of themselves instead of the purpose of the quest, but Galen thought of all the people of the kingdom."
>
> "And Galen was kind to the wise woman and her daughter, so they helped him."
>
> "Part of a quest is passing tests. Owen and Edmund failed the tests, but Galen didn't and that's why he finished the quest."
>
> "That's when the forest changed from dark to sunny, and wildflowers sprouted up." [This student pointed out relevant scenes in the book.]
>
> "Also, his brothers and all the other knights who went into the enchanted wood were freed . . . Part of a successful quest is to help others."
>
> "The *purpose* of the quest was to get rid of the drought. Galen had a pure heart, so his wish for rain and a good harvest came true."
>
> "So Galen returned from the quest, and the kingdom was saved, and he became king, and it was a happy ending for everyone!"

Session 4

Fortune (Stanley, 1990) was introduced as another example of a modern quest tale. Set in Persia, this complex tale is the story of Omar, a farmer's son, who sets out on a quest to seek his fortune. His quest leads him to a dancing tiger that he names Fortune. Through a series of magical twists revealed through a *story-within-a-story* device, Omar becomes a *hero by mistake* when he finds a princess and brings about her reunion with her long-lost prince, who had been transformed into a dancing tiger. By the end of his quest, Omar has gained a life-companion as well as wisdom, self-knowledge, and wealth. The lovely Persian miniatures that illustrate this story are rich in details that invite close inspection. The children identified the literary patterns used by this modern writer:

> "Omar goes off to seek his fortune, and he gets Fortune, the tiger. It has a double meaning! Fortune helps him get his fortune!"
>
> "It also has opposing characters . . . Jahnah, the wicked princess, and Shirin, the kind princess."
>
> "Another pattern is *deception.* The lady wrapped in scarves who sold the tiger was really the wicked princess."
>
> "Another pattern is love breaks a spell . . . like in 'Beauty and the Beast.'"

> "I liked the way she [Stanley] made it like two stories in one. The story of the prince and the two princesses was inside the story about Omar and Sunny . . . but they were really connected."
>
> "We read stories like that last semester . . . the ones with the *story-in-a-story* pattern like *The Changing Maze* (Snyder, 1992)."

At the end of this analysis, the children were invited to choose another modern quest tale from the collection to read independently, to record their responses in their journals, and to include in their entries comments about the quest and other patterns in the stories as well as similarities and differences between traditional and modern tales. A text set of modern quest tales included

Bearskin (Pyle, 1997)

A Frog Prince (Berenzy, 1989)

The Golden Heart of Winter (Singer, 1991)

The King's Equal (Paterson, 1992, 1999)

The Magic Nesting Doll (Ogburn, 2000)

The Mapmaker's Daughter (Helldorfer, 1991)

Prince Nautilus (Melmed, 1994)

To Capture the Wind (MacGill-Callahan, 1997)

The Well at the End of the World (San Souci, 2004)

The children's comments about these tales reflected their understanding of the quest tale and their ability to identify the craft of modern writers and the literary devices and traditional patterns they used to create these original tales. Several excerpts from their written responses to these tales were shared with the group and are included here.

The King's Equal begins with a king's deathbed blessing given to his only son, Prince Raphael. In order to wear the crown after his father's death, Prince Raphael must marry a woman who is his equal in beauty, intelligence, and wealth. He sends his councilors on a quest for such a bride. After an extensive, but unsuccessful, search, Rosamund, a wise and kind shepherdess, proves that she is not only the prince's equal but is *more than equal* to him. Now, the arrogant and foolish prince must prove that he is worthy to have Rosamund for his wife. At the end of his quest, the prince gains the self-knowledge, humility, and wisdom that enable him to win Rosamund's heart and to serve as a good king. Here are some of the children's responses to this story:

> "The author had *two* stories. One was about the prince and one was about Rosamund and the magical wolf. They were side-by-side stories and in the end they get connected."

"This is *different* from the old stories because Rosamund isn't a wimp like a lot of the girls who marry a prince. It's the *same* because he has to find a bride, but it's *different* because she makes *him* prove that he is good enough for *her!*"

"At the end of his quest, the prince was really different. Like he learned to be kind and to do things for himself and not to think he was so great."

"At the end of his quest, the prince would be a better king because he learned that you should treat people like *you* want to be treated. So he would treat the people better and they'll have better lives."

"The prince learned that love is more important than gold. He learned what love *felt* like. He learned what it was like to *care* about other people. This is the theme in this story."

"This author didn't use stereotypes about men and women. Rosamund was intelligent and independent and gentle and kind, and the prince *learned* how to be gentle and kind and independent."

"The wolf taught the prince that someone with friends is richer than someone with gold. So now he could be a good husband and a good king and the people will be happier. So his quest helped him and all the people!"

Several children focused on the endings in *Prince Nautilus* and *The Mapmaker's Daughter*. *Prince Nautilus* is the story of a fisherman's two daughters: Columbine, who is beautiful but vain, cold-hearted, and lazy, and Fiona, who is generous, kind, and courageous. Their quest is to break the spell that has kept Prince Nautilus imprisoned in a seashell. *The Mapmaker's Daughter* is the story of Suchen, the mapmaker's daughter, who sets out alone on a dangerous journey into an enchanted land to rescue the king's son from an evil witch.

"The ending of *Prince Nautilus* was different from the old fairy tales. When the prince asked Fiona to marry him, she said she couldn't until after she had some adventures out in the wide world! And you never find out if they get married!"

"*Prince Nautilus* starts out like 'Cinderella' and has opposing characters, but it's a quest tale and the girl rescues the prince, and it doesn't end with a wedding at the palace!"

"Fiona proves how kind and smart and brave she is. I think the guy who wants to marry her has to prove that he respects what is important to *her!*"

"The ending in *The Mapmaker's Daughter* is really different. Suchen is a brave heroine, but after she rescues the prince, he rewards her with a horse and a red cape for her next adventure, and that's how it ends!"

"In the old fairy tales, the only thing in life for girls was to get married. But Suchen wants to have an interesting life!"

> "Suchen is like Tokoyo [in *The Samurai's Daughter*] because both are brave, and they rescue guys instead of waiting for guys to rescue *them!* I was surprised that the story about Tokoyo was an *old* tale!"

Students who read *A Frog Prince* focused on the craft of the author/artist who created this modern revision of the familiar Grimm brothers' tale, "The Frog Prince." According to a note on the jacket flap about the author, Alix Berenzy, her sympathies were with the frog instead of the spoiled princess featured in the Grimms' tale. Berenzy notes, "I couldn't help but wonder what the ideal story would be from the frog's point of view." In response to this beautifully illustrated modern revision, the students identified the choices Berenzy made as she created her "ideal story," and they compared it with a retelling of the Grimms' tale illustrated by Binette Schroeder (J. Grimm, W. Grimm, 1989):

> "From the very first lines of the story, she [the author] lets you know the story is told from the viewpoint of the frog instead of the princess."
>
> "In Berenzy's book the frog is large all the way through the story. It shows how important he is. In the other book, the artist made him small because it's really the princess's story."
>
> "The first part of the story is the same as in the old story, but then she [Berenzy] adds a whole new part—a quest!"
>
> "In the old story, when the princess threw the frog against the wall, it turned into a prince. In this new story, when the princess showed how disgusted she was, she threw the frog against the wall, but *that's* where the story changes."
>
> "When that spoiled princess rejected the frog, he went on a quest for 'a true princess, of a different mind'" [This student used actual words from the text.]
>
> "On the quest journey he proves how brave and kind he is."
>
> "One of the tests on his quest journey was when everyone called him a prince, and he always said, 'I'm not a prince—just a dressed-up frog.' That's how he proves he's modest and honest."
>
> "The surprise at the end was that he really *was* a frog!"
>
> "I read another modern revision of 'The Frog Prince' that was sort of like this one. It's called *The Horned Toad Prince* [Hopkins, 2000]. It's about a spoiled cowgirl who made a bargain with a horned toad to get her new hat out of the well. In the end, the toad changed into a prince like the old story. But he *left* her . . . just like the frog in *this* story. But the last picture shows a lasso coming toward the prince as he's stepping out of the picture. So maybe she caught him after all!"

The children's analyses of Berenzy's story revealed their use of intertextual links and their knowledge of literary patterns and genres as well as the craft of the author/artist.

Session 5

The purpose of the fifth whole-group session was to provide an opportunity for the children to share their experiences with the traditional and modern quest tales they had selected for independent reading and to engage in a comparative analysis of all the stories they had read on their own and had heard in the group sessions in this segment of the Traditional Literature Unit. As they reviewed these stories together, they looked for evidence of the distinguishing features of quest tales they had listed on the wall chart; they searched for other intertextual links among these diverse tales; and they explored the similarities and differences between traditional and modern quest tales. By this time, all the children had internalized most of the literary concepts introduced during their study of these tales, and were ready to contribute thoughtful comments to this final group session in this segment of the literature unit. A few examples of their observations are included below:

> *"Bearskin* starts out with a prophecy like in the story *Vasily and the Dragon."*
>
> "When Bearskin goes on a quest to slay the dragon and save the princess and all the people, the mother bear is the *helper character.* She gets him the armor and horse and sword he needs."
>
> "I heard a story like *Bearskin.* A mother bear took care of him, and in the story about Romulus and Remus, wolves took care of them."
>
> "There's another one like that. Remember when we read about Atalanta? [*Atalanta's Race: A Greek Myth* (Climo, 1995).] The king wanted a boy but they had a girl, so the king told the soldier to leave the baby on the mountain and a mother bear took care of it, and the baby grew up to be a heroine!"
>
> "A lot more of the modern stories have brave *heroines* who go on quests."
>
> "I think it's because they were written *after* women got more rights and could be doctors or truck drivers like men. Like Suchen and Fiona go on adventures."
>
> "In *The King's Equal,* Rosamund sent the *prince* on a quest to prove himself! And the quest caused him to *change*—like on our chart about quest tales."
>
> "There was a prophecy in that story, too! Before she died, Rosamund's mom said that Rosamund would be a king's equal!"
>
> "I read *The Magic Nesting Doll.* It's about a girl who rescues a prince. I chose that book because I have a nesting doll from Russia just like that."
>
> "In the one I read, Oonagh goes on a *really* dangerous quest to rescue the man she plans to marry [*To Capture the Wind*]. Conal was captured by an evil pirate king and all his warriors. At the

end of that quest, Oonagh helped save Conal *and* all the other captives, too." [She pointed to the item on the wall chart highlighting the benefits of successful quests for many people.]

Introducing the Fourth Pattern: Transformation Tales

In the fourth segment of this literature unit, the children were introduced to stories featuring the literary motif of *transformation.* Lukens (2003) defines the term *motif* as a "recurring element in literary work, often found in traditional literature" (p. 345). Magical objects, long sleeps, supernatural beings, three wishes, and transformation are typical motifs in folk tales. In the group sessions in this segment, the children were introduced to *external transformation* as a common motif in traditional as well as modern fantasy. They were also exposed to *internal transformation* or the *dynamic character* in more complex tales. A *dynamic character* is a literary term defined by Lukens as "one who changes in the course of the action" (p. 84). According to Lukens, the dynamic character may "change from being shy to being poised or even domineering; or from cowardly to brave, from selfless to selfish. The character may demonstrate a new realization about himself or herself, or about his or her personal values" (p. 84).

Session 1

Greyling: A Picture Story from the Islands of Shetland (Yolen, 1968) was selected for the first session to introduce the *selchies*, seals who take on human form on land. Selchies are featured in the seal legends told in the Scottish Islands of Shetland and Orkney. When the students examined the cover, many of them recognized the author and mentioned some of her other stories they had heard or read. They also made predictions based on the picture of the boy and the seal on the cover. Most of them predicted that the story would be about a friendship between the boy and the seal. A few observed that the boy and the seal had similar eyes and wondered why the illustrator created this connection. The teacher pointed to the subtitle and explained that this story is rooted in the ancient legends told by fisherfolk who lived on these islands. After a brief focus on the nature of the legend as a literary genre, she began to read this tale of a fisherman and his wife who long for a child of their own. One day the fisherman finds a small grey seal pup stranded on a sand bar. When he brings it home, it becomes a human child. They love him as a son, but they know he is one of the selchies, "men upon the land and seals in the sea" (n.p.). They try to keep him away from the sea, but when the fisherman is in danger of drowning during a terrible storm, Greyling dives into the sea to save his father and is transformed into a great grey seal.

After listening to this story, the students shared their own thoughts and feelings and then returned to the initial predictions and questions that had been prompted by the book cover. For example, "Oh . . . now I see why the artist made them [the boy and the seal] look alike. The boy is the seal!" At the end of their discussion of this transformation tale, the teacher invited the students to compare the original 1968 edition of *Greyling*, illustrated by William Stobbs, with the 1991 edition illustrated by David Ray (Yolen, 1991).

At the end of this read-aloud/think-aloud session, the children were invited to select a book for independent reading and to respond to these selections in their journals and in small dialogue groups. Three of the books in the text set were retellings of a Japanese tale featuring a white crane that transforms itself into a beautiful woman in response to a kind deed. Like *Greyling*, these crane tales feature *shapeshifters,* who can change their form as a voluntary act: *The Crane Wife*, retold by Sumiko Yagawa (1981); *The Crane Wife*, retold by Odds Bodkin (1998); and *The Crane's Gift*, retold by Steve Biddle and Megumi Biddle (1994). Another Japanese tale in this text set is also an example of shapeshifting as a voluntary act: *On Cat Mountain* (Richard & Levine, 1994).

Session 2

Robert D. San Souci's *The Six Swans* (1988) was introduced in this session to call attention to *spell-induced transformations.* This old tale by the Grimm brothers is about a princess who rescues her six brothers, who have been transformed into swans by their evil stepmother because of her jealousy of their close relationship with their father, the king. The students initiated a cover-to-cover study of this illustrated text by attempting to identify the characters on the front and back covers and the two title pages. The picture on the first title page, which shows a boy transforming into a swan, prompted predictions:

> "The six swans on the cover probably all used to be boys."
> "I think that witch on the back cover transforms them."
> "But maybe they were swans to begin with like in the selchie story."

As they listened to the story unfold, the children returned to the covers and the portraits of the central characters on the major title page to confirm or revise their initial speculations and predictions. By the end of the story they were able to identify three different transformations:

"The evil stepmother was the witch's daughter, so she had the power to change the king's sons into swans."

"She *caused* the transformation with a spell because she hated the children because the king loved them more than her."

"After the sister broke the spell, the witch tried to escape by changing into a blackbird. But the king shot her."

"There's a blackbird on another page. I wonder if that witch sometimes transformed herself into that bird to spy on people."

"Another transformation was when the evil stepmother found out that the spell was broken, and she was so mad she changed back into an ogress and ran away."

"So the witch and her daughter were shapeshifters like Greyling, but they also had the power to transform others as well as themselves. The six brothers were *victims* of a transformation spell."

Session 3

The Glass Mountain, another Grimm brothers' tale, retold and illustrated by Nonny Hogrogian (1985), is the story of a princess who has been transformed into a raven and the young man who manages to release her from this enchantment. The students examined the front and back covers and predicted that the "sad-looking man" on the front cover would be transformed into the raven featured on the back cover. They revised this initial prediction when the teacher read aloud the first page of the story, which reveals that the queen's new baby is restless, and

> . . .the Queen grew very impatient . . . She looked at her daughter and cried, 'If only you were a raven, you could fly away, and I would have some peace!' As these words came out of the Queen's mouth, the child turned into a raven . . . and flew from the arms of her mother. (n.p.)

In response to this scene, the students made literature-life connections as they tried to explain the Queen's behavior. They shared examples of personal moments in which they had felt so frustrated or angry that they had spoken words they didn't really mean. Although they seemed to understand *why* the Queen uttered these terrible words, they wondered, "Who *caused* the words to come true?"

As the students listened to the rest of the story, they learned that, years later, a young man managed to break the spell and free the raven-princess from her enchantment. By the end of the story, the students had found answers to some of their earlier questions, but they had to construct their own interpretations to figure out "who had caused the words to come true." Their unanswered question initiated the concluding dialogue, in which they tried to fill in gaps in the text about the "transformer" who caused the transformation and the motive for casting the spell:

> "I think that old woman in the woods was really a witch who heard the queen's words and made them come true. That's why she kept trying to get the man to take the food or drink so he wouldn't be able to break the spell."
>
> "I agree! The witch put something in the drink to make him sleep. But she didn't *know* that he could also break the spell by going on a quest to the golden castle."
>
> "I was glad he got a second chance. In *The Six Swans,* it was *much* harder to break the spell. It took the sister six years, and she had to risk her life."
>
> "*The Six Swans* was different in another way. The queen in that story was the stepmother and an ogress. She *wanted* to get rid of the children. But I think the queen in *The Glass Mountain* loved her baby and didn't really want her to change into a raven."
>
> "Maybe that witch—the old woman—was jealous of the queen and didn't want her to be happy with her baby. Maybe she was like the stepmother in the other story and didn't want anyone else to be happy."
>
> "I didn't like the ending because it doesn't tell if the queen and her daughter ever got together again. Maybe we just have to imagine that it'll be a fairy-tale ending with a grand reunion and a wedding."
>
> "But her mom *got* her changed into a raven! Wouldn't the girl be angry about that? And wouldn't the queen feel awfully guilty about what she did? Maybe the storyteller decided *not* to have a reunion at the end!"
>
> "I think we have to decide for ourselves if they have a happy reunion or not!"

At the end of this session, the children were introduced to other transformation tales they could select for independent reading. They were invited to write about their reading experiences in their journals and to form small dialogue groups to discuss these selections with students who had read the same titles.

> *Beauty and the Beast* (Willard, 1992) is an unusual retelling of this traditional tale set in the early 1900s in New York City.
>
> *Birdwing* (Martin, 2005). In the Grimm Brothers' *The Six Swans,* six brothers are transformed into swans, and when they finally return to their human form, the youngest has a swan's wing instead of a left arm. *Birdwing* is a novel that tells the story of what happens to the boy with a swan's wing growing from his shoulder.
>
> *The Boy Who Knew the Language of the Birds* (Wetterer, 1991). In this story, the transformation is caused by the careless wish of a spoiled princess.

The Brave Little Parrot (Martin, 1998) is a Jataka tale from India about a small gray-white parrot who risks her life to try to save the small animals who are trapped in a forest fire and who is transformed into a beautiful bird with colorful feathers as a reward for her courage and selflessness.

The Canary Prince (Nones, 1991) is an old Turinese tale about a princess in a tower and a prince who manages to reach her when a good witch provides a magical book that transforms him into a canary whenever he wishes to fly up to her room.

The Children of Lir (MacGill-Callahan, 1993), based on an Irish legend, is the story of the king's four children, two boys and two girls, who are transformed into swans by their evil step-mother. Jasconius, a whale, and some wild swans work to-gether to break the spell and save the children. An author's note tells about a stone slab on Inniskeel Island on which are carved four swans and two men and two women.

The Donkey Prince (Craig, 1977), adapted from the Grimms' tale, is the story of a vain queen and a greedy king who wish for a child. A wizard agrees to help them in exchange for gold. When the greedy king gives the wizard lead pieces dipped in gold paint, the wizard punishes him by casting a spell on the baby so it is shaped like a donkey.

The Dragon Prince: A Chinese Beauty and the Beast (Yep, 1997a) is the story of Seven, the youngest daughter of a poor farmer, who agrees to marry a dragon to save her father's life. In this story, the dragon is a shapeshifter who transforms itself into a handsome prince when Seven responds to his inner self instead of his terrifying outward appearance. The students who read this story identified Seven and her sister, Three, as "opposing characters" and the prince's search for his lost wife as a "quest." They also compared the snake/king in *Mufaro's Beautiful Daughters* with the snake/prince in this tale. Both characters use their shapeshifting powers to discover the inner qualities of potential brides.

The Frog Prince, or Iron Henry (J. Grimm & W. Grimm, 1989), is one of many illustrated editions of the old tale about the prince who was transformed into a frog by a wicked witch. The students who selected this one were surprised that the spell in this traditional retelling was broken when the princess threw the frog against the wall instead of with a kiss, as in the Disney version.

The Frog Princess (Isele, 1984) is a Russian tale about Ivan, the youngest son of a czar, who marries a frog and then learns that his wife is a beautiful princess named Vasilisa the Wise whose father, in a jealous rage, had transformed her into a frog because "she was born wiser than her own father" (p. 22).

The Hedgehog Boy: A Latvian Folktale (Langton, 1985) is the story of a hedgehog boy who marries a princess whose true remorse over a thoughtless act leads to his transformation into a handsome young man.

Little Brother and Little Sister: A Fairy Tale (J. Grimm & W. Grimm, 1996) is the story of a brother and sister who try to escape from their wicked stepmother. But she manages to transform the boy into a deer and continues to use her evil powers to control their lives until the king who marries the sister gets rid of the witch and breaks the spell.

The Loathsome Dragon (Wiesner & Kahng, 1987, 2005), an old English tale, is about a wicked queen who is jealous of her gracious and beautiful stepdaughter, Margaret, and transforms her into a "loathsome dragon." It is her brother, Childe Wynd, who breaks the spell and punishes the queen.

The Scarlet Flower: A Russian Folk Tale (Aksakov, 1989) is a Russian variant of the "Beauty and the Beast" tale in which a young woman's love transforms a monster into a handsome prince.

The Seven Ravens (Bass, J. Grimm & W. Grimm, 1994). In this story, seven brothers have been transformed into ravens because of their father's thoughtless wish. The children who read this story found a link with *The Glass Mountain:* "In this story it's the father who makes the wish that causes the transformation. But it wasn't for a selfish reason. He wanted quiet for their sick baby; the queen wanted quiet for herself."

The Silver Charm: A Folktale from Japan (San Souci, 2002a) is the story of a boy who is captured by an ogre and gives him his good-luck charm in exchange for his freedom. When the boy falls deathly ill, his pets and a mouse manage to steal the charm from the ogre in order to restore the boy's health.

Snowbear Whittington: An Appalachian Beauty and the Beast (Hooks, 1994) is the story of Nell, whose true love enables her to break the spell cast by the Winter Witch to punish a young man for gathering snow roses she claimed were hers. Her spell transformed him into a great white bear.

The Talking Tree: An Old Italian Tale (Rayevsky, 1990) is the story of a king whose quest for the Talking Tree to add to his collection of fabulous objects leads him to risk his life to release the princess who has been transformed into a tree by a wicked witch.

The White Cat: An Old French Fairy Tale (San Souci & Aulnoy, 1990) is the story of a prince who encounters the White Cat during his quest to carry out his father's three requests. The cat helps the prince fulfill the requests, and he manages to defeat the evil shapeshifting wizard who had cast the spell that transformed a beautiful queen into the White Cat because she refused to marry him.

Session 4

The Dog Prince: An Original Fairy Tale (Mills, 2001) is a modern fairy tale about an arrogant prince whose rude behavior to a fairy woman prompts her to transform him into a hound dog. The only one to treat the dog with kindness is Eliza, the goat girl, who gives him the name Prince and teaches him humility and patience. He proves his love for her and his courage when he risks his life to save Eliza from the chimera, a legendary lion-headed beast. When Eliza expresses her love for the hound, the spell is broken.

When this book was introduced in the fourth read-aloud session in this segment, the students initiated a cover-to-cover study. They used the picture of a young girl and a dog on the front cover, the picture of a young man in fancy clothes on the back cover, and the title to predict that the young man is a prince who would be transformed into a dog. The pictures also triggered questions: Who caused the transformation? Why was the prince transformed? How was the spell broken? As the story unfolded, the students were able to confirm their predictions and to answer their questions about the transformation of the prince into a dog. However, they found another kind of transformation in this story:

> "When the prince was a dog, he felt ashamed of the way he used to treat people, and he learned to care for someone else besides himself."
>
> "He used to be so spoiled and mean, and then he changed . . . inside!"
>
> "When he changed back to a human, he also changed *inside!*"
>
> "Yes. Remember when he said to Eliza, 'I've changed. I'm not the same person I was'?"
>
> "This story was different from the other ones. At first I thought it was a realism story, but then the gardener talked about the mythical beast, the chimera."
>
> "So it was fantasy because of the chimera, the fairy woman, and the transformation. But the big difference was that he changed on the inside, too."
>
> "He wasn't spoiled anymore. The transformation was inside *and* outside."
>
> "You knew he had changed inside when he was willing to fight the chimera to save Eliza. I think that was the *turning point* in the story." [This literary concept had been introduced in an earlier study of author's craft.]

At the end of this session, the students were introduced to another group of stories for independent reading. These stories featured *dynamic characters,* a literary term for characters who experience "inner transformation":

> *Beauty and the Beast,* retold and illustrated by Jan Brett (1989), is an unusual retelling of this old French fairy tale. The artist includes details on the covers, endpapers, title page, and throughout the text that invite readers to engage in a cover-to-cover study of the book and to discover that Brett offers a new interpretation of this old tale. For instance, on a tapestry included in the scene in which Beauty first encounters the Beast is printed the message "Do not trust to appearances" (p. 16). At the end of the story, when Beauty breaks the spell that had transformed a young prince into a beast, he explains that a fairy, "displeased with people for trusting too much in appearances, has cast a spell over the palace and everything in it. . . . The spell would only be broken when a beautiful woman forsook all others and promised to marry the Beast in spite of his appearance" (p. 31). The students who discussed this book used this textual clue to unlock the significance of the tapestry message. One student inferred: "The fairy must have caused the transformation to teach them *all* a lesson and to help them change *inside* so they wouldn't be so vain and just judge people by their appearances!"
>
> *The Fisherman and the Bird* (Levitin, 1982) is a modern realistic picture book about Rico, a lonely fisherman who has rejected the friendship of the other fishermen and villagers. However, he experiences an inner transformation when he reluctantly becomes the guardian of the two eggs in a nest built by a beautiful large bird.
>
> *The Gold Coin* (Ada, 1991, 1994), an original tale set in Central America, is about a young thief who attempts to steal a gold coin from an old woman but experiences an inner transformation and learns to give instead of steal.
>
> *King Midas: A Golden Tale* (Stewig, 1999) is a retelling of the ancient myth about the king who wishes for the power to turn into gold everything he touches. When the miser's wish is granted, he deeply regrets the consequences and changes the priorities in his life. Other illustrated retellings included in this text set were *King Midas and the Golden Touch* (Craft, 1999) and *King Midas and the Golden Touch* (Hewitt & Hawthorne, 1987).
>
> *The King's Equal,* by Katherine Paterson (1992, 1999), was included in the text set of modern quest tales. Because Raphael, an arrogant and vain young prince, experiences an inner

transformation, this title is also included in this text set featuring dynamic characters.

Lady Lollipop (King-Smith, 2001) is a chapter book about a spoiled, selfish princess who learns to think more about others and less about herself when a pig named Lollipop comes into her life.

Mother Holly: A Retelling from the Brothers Grimm (Stewig, J. Grimm & W. Grimm, 2001) features opposing characters: an industrious sister and a lazy sister. In the end, the lazy sister learns to lead an industrious life.

The Narwhal's Tusk (Heymsfeld, 2001) is the story of a dishonest sea captain who cuts the ivory tusks off three narwhals to sell to a rich nobleman who believes the tusks are the powerful horns of unicorns. By the end of the story, the sea captain deeply regrets his dishonesty and cruelty after he sees the terrible consequences of his deeds, and he changes his ways for the rest of his life.

Prince Sparrow (Gerstein, 1984) is the story of a spoiled and selfish princess whose tantrums intimidate her servants and tutor. A little sparrow is responsible for her inner transformation. The children who read this picture book compared it with *The Dog Prince* and *Lady Lollipop* in terms of the helper characters who were responsible for the inner transformation in each story: "The sparrow helped the spoiled princess change; the goat girl helped the spoiled prince change; and the pig, Lollipop, helped the spoiled princess change."

Sparrow's Song (Wallace, 1986), set in Niagara Falls, opens when Katie finds an orphan bird and learns that her brother, Charles, had killed the bird's mother with his slingshot. Eventually, Charles joins her in caring for the sparrow, and, in the process, he experiences an inner transformation and hurls his slingshot into the river, a turning point in the story.

Stone Soup (Muth, 2003) is the story of three wise monks who help the self-centered members of a poor community learn the magic of generosity.

A Toad for Tuesday (Erickson, 1998). In this early chapter book, a toad is captured on Thursday by an owl who saves him to eat on Tuesday, the owl's birthday. However, in the intervening five days, the toad manages to engender in the owl a remarkable inner transformation.

A Weave of Words: An Armenian Tale (San Souci, 1998) features a prince whose only interest is hunting until an independent young woman helps him learn to value reading and writing and artistic endeavors. Another version of this tale, *The Golden Bracelet* (Kherdian, 1997a) was also included in this text set featuring dynamic characters.

Session 5

At the conclusion of this segment, the children were invited to review the shared texts and those they had read independently and to pay particular attention to the illustrations in these texts. This review session served as a preparation for a writing/art project in which they would each create an original, illustrated transformation tale. According to Frank Smith (1984), one learns to write by reading like a writer and discovering the knowledge writers require. Throughout this literature unit, the students explored the craft of storytellers, writers, and artists and what they do to create illustrated literary texts. As they studied the illustrations in this group of stories, the students discovered the great diversity of artistic styles and media used by the artists in their *visual retellings.* They noted that characters and settings were often more richly developed in the illustrations than in the texts and discovered that the artist's interpretation played a significant role in the story as a whole. This project provided them with another opportunity to make use of their growing knowledge of literature and literary craft.

After reviewing the transformation tales included in this segment in terms of genre, narrative elements, literary techniques, and artists' craft, students focused on the nature and cause of external transformations, the motives behind them, and the conditions for reversing them, as well as on the nature and cause of inner transformations including turning points. The next phase of the preparation process was to reflect on the choices they would make to create their own texts and illustrations. That is, students were asked to make decisions about genre, setting, viewpoint, characters, conflicts, and the nature and cause of the transformation as well as the artistic style and media they would use. After writing and illustrating their stories, the children shared them in a group session intended to bring to completion this segment of the literature unit.

Concluding Session: Moving from Analysis to Synthesis

The four segments in this literature unit provided opportunities for students to become immersed in the world of folklore. The whole-group read-aloud/think-aloud sessions set in motion a cumulative study of traditional literature that extended into the small dialogue groups, the informal conversations, the teacher-student conferences, and the solitary interactions between reader and text during independent reading and writing. Through oral and written responses, students engaged in an ongoing comparative analysis of the diverse stories read together or alone in the course of this extensive literature-study experience.

Prior to this "synthesis session," the students were asked to work with partners and to select one of the titles from a group of traditional and modern tales that had not yet been classified in terms of particular patterns. Their challenge was to draw from their growing knowledge of traditional literature to identify patterns as well as clues that pointed to cultural, geographical, and historical contexts of ancient storytellers or the context or agenda of modern writers. This assignment served as a preparation for the concluding whole-group discussion, in which students were invited to move from analysis of single tales with a common pattern toward a synthesis of ideas about traditional literature as a whole. The markers on the wall map triggered an initial focus on the travels of traditional tales across time and space:

> "In the olden days, people didn't have TV so at night they'd tell stories around the fire, and if a traveler was staying with them, they'd probably exchange stories. Then the traveler would carry the new stories to all the places he'd stop overnight—they didn't have airplanes."
>
> "Right! And when the children grew up, they told *their* children the same stories they heard when they were sitting with the grownups."
>
> "Or sometimes there was a traveling storyteller who came to the village square to tell stories . . ."
>
> "So that's probably how the stories traveled across the map—and across time!"
>
> "And a lot of stories have the same patterns but they get changed because the storyteller lives in a different place. Like in India a magic pot has *rice* in it and in Italy the magic pot has *pasta* but the magic object gets stolen—so it's the same pattern."
>
> "And some of the words are from different languages because the stories that were told in different countries had to be translated into English so we can understand them."
>
> "It's really good that all those old stories got written down in books so they wouldn't get lost and we can read them!"

At this point in the synthesis session, the students were asked to turn their attention to a comparison chart some of the students had been developing. Their chart highlighted the remarkable number of recurring patterns and themes that can be found in stories all over the world.

> "It seems like most stories are about good and evil or about good people and bad people. I guess people everywhere can understand a story with opposing characters."

"I think the stories are about *life*—about ways to treat other people, and about getting to be independent, and finding out if you can do hard stuff and solve problems like all those tests in the quest tales."

"I like it when you find patterns from other stories—like opposing characters and kindness rewarded, or when someone says 'The morning is wiser than the evening' or 'One good turn deserves another'!"

"Me too. I like it when you meet Baba Yaga again in a new story or an old man who asks for food . . . or a husband and wife who wish for a child . . . It sort of connects you to all the stories . . . from around the world!"

"It's fun to meet characters you know in a new story. I read *Alice Nizzy Nazzy: The Witch of Santa Fe* (Johnston, 1995), and the author made one character like Baba Yaga and one character like Little Bo Peep!"

"When we put all those patterns on the chart, it reminded me of this collage game I have. It has different shapes, and you can arrange them into a million different designs! Those old storytellers sort of did that. They kept arranging the story patterns in different ways and making new stories."

In response to this comment, the teacher told the children about the image of the kaleidoscope Yolen used to describe the "patterns of motifs changed by time and by the times . . ." (2000, p. 23). The next day, several children brought kaleidoscopes to school. After everyone had had a chance to enjoy the endless variety of forms created by the bits of glass in these instruments, one child connected this experience to her own concerns as a young author: "So we should never run out of ideas for new stories! There are so many patterns in these old stories and there're so many different kinds of characters . . . and so many different problems . . . We can just keep on making new stories!" This comment triggered thoughts about the writers of modern tales introduced in this literature unit:

"The author of that new story about the frog prince [Berenzy, 1989] did that. She started with the old story but she told it from the frog's point of view."

"Another way that author changed the old story was she added a new pattern—the quest! So she made a whole *new* story out of the old one."

"I read *Rumpelstiltskin's Daughter* [Stanley, 1997], and that's another one that starts out like the old story, but the author changes it when the girl decides *not* to marry that king who likes gold more than he cares about *her!*"

"I read that, too. The author made it into a sequel, and in the end the daughter tells the king she doesn't want to marry him either, but she'd rather be prime minister!"

"That ending sounds like in *Prince Nautilus* when Fiona tells the prince she doesn't want to get married until she goes out into the world to have adventures!"

"I read *O'Sullivan Stew* [Talbott, 1999]. It's about an Irish girl who's sort of like Scheherazade because she tells stories to escape death. She saves her whole family. At the end, when the king asks Kate to marry him, she says no because she wants to go off on some adventures of her own."

"I think these authors made up these new stories to show that girls can be independent and brave and smart."

"It's like real life today—like *now* girls can be soldiers or astronauts or the Secretary of State or a judge . . . So the modern stories have a lot of the same patterns like in the old stories but they're different because *life* is different now!"

"I found a really different kind of sequel—it's about what happened to the rat that was changed to a coachman by Cinderella's fairy godmother. The story is told from the viewpoint of the rat *after* he's been changed to a human." [*Cinderella's Rat* (Meddaugh, 1997)]

"That's just what we were talking about before . . . We can use patterns from old stories to make new stories, and we can take an old story and tell it in a different way to make it funny or to send a message like in *Rumpelstiltskin's Daughter*."

"So we can all keep on making up new stories!"

With this observation, the discussion drew to a close, ending on a note of hope (like all good fairy tales) for the future of the storytelling tradition.

Assessment

Throughout this extensive study of traditional literature, the teacher evaluated the quality of the children's involvement and understanding. She observed their participation in the ongoing dialogue in the cumulative read-aloud/think-aloud sessions, and she observed their participation in the diverse small-group or individual activities in which the children responded to the literary selections in this unit through conversation, drama, art, and written work. The teacher read the children's literature-journal entries, their creative writing, their written responses to questions introduced to foster reader response and reflection, and their preparation for the synthesis session.

An overview of this cumulative study of traditional literature sheds light on the extent to which the objectives for this experience were realized. Throughout this unit the children were exposed to a wide variety of traditional literature from around the world, and they talked and wrote about their discoveries of similarities and differences in these diverse tales as they engaged in comparative analysis. The introduction of carefully selected tales in a carefully selected sequence in these cumulative group sessions created a learning environment that fostered this comparative study of diverse tales (see Objectives 1 and 2). For example, the comparative analysis of "opposing characters" reflected the children's growing understanding of the recurring patterns in traditional literature. The discussion of the "travels" of traditional tales in the concluding synthesis session demonstrated their understanding of the nature of the oral tradition (see Objective 3). The children's review of the work of modern writers revealed their understanding of the way these writers draw from traditional tales to create new ones (see Objective 4).

From the very first group session in this four-part unit, the children were encouraged to use a "cover-to-cover" strategy to study each new text. This approach set the stage for engaging in other reading-thinking strategies such as activating and using relevant prior knowledge, drawing inferences, making predictions, generating questions, identifying and using text structure to analyze stories, engaging in metacognition to take control of the comprehension process, analyzing the craft of authors and artists, and making connections between the text and other texts, oneself, and the world (see Objective 6). The cumulative dialogue about the literary texts introduced in the read-aloud/think-aloud group sessions provided opportunities for the children to talk about thinking processes used in response to an unfolding text and to enter into a collaborative construction of meaning in the social context of these group discussions (see Objective 5). Opportunities for independent reading were provided throughout the unit to enable children to discover new stories to read and enjoy on their own. They responded to these literary experiences in their literature journals, in narrative writing projects, and in other forms of creative expression (see Objectives 7 and 8).

The children's contributions to the synthesis discussion in the concluding session suggested that by the end of this exploration of traditional literature and the work of modern writers who have been inspired by the oral tradition the children had begun to discover for themselves that "all themes and characters and stories that you encounter in literature belong to one big interlocking family" (Frye, 1964, p. 48).

7 Breaking Barriers, Building Bridges

Critical Literacy and the Transformative Power of Literature

Critical literacy "encourages readers to adopt a questioning stance and to work toward changing themselves and their worlds" (McDaniel, 2004, p. 472). Critical discussion of complex issues of race, class, and gender in intermediate classrooms can have a powerful effect on understanding, attitudes, and actions. In the literature unit described in this chapter fiction and nonfiction texts are used to introduce these issues, to generate critical discussion, to provide a context for independent reading and writing experiences, to foster compassionate concern for others' welfare, and to inspire students to take action against social injustice and inequities. The read-aloud/think-aloud sessions that are the core of the literature units featured in this book sometimes elicit initial resistance from older students who believe that reading aloud is "for little kids." It is important to explain to these students that reading aloud enables everyone to respond to an unfolding text together and to engage in a collaborative interpretive dialogue about this shared text. In *The Power of Reading: Insights from the Research,* Stephen Krashen (2004) calls attention to the academic benefits of read-aloud programs for older students. Researchers have found that reading aloud to older students can help them build their comprehension skills, increase their vocabularies, and motivate them to read independently.

Many of the texts selected for this literature unit are picture books. In recent years numerous educators have written about the wonderful possibilities of the picture book for older students (Benedict & Carlisle, 1992; Kiefer, 1995; Saunders, 1999; Serafini & Giorgis, 2003; Tiedt, 2000). According to Steven Wolk, "Picture books can be a forceful resource for exploring issues of democracy. . . . Engaging children of all ages with picture books that promote democratic ideals can nurture public involvement and civic courage, and arouse students to become active participants and healers of our democracy" (2004, pp. 27–28).

The picture books selected for the read-aloud sessions in this literature unit present provocative topics that inspire students to open their hearts and minds, stimulate critical thinking, prepare them for reading longer and more complex texts, and prompt socially conscious inquiry. The authors and illustrators of these picture books explore issues such as prejudice and discrimination and "show how people can begin to take action on important social issues . . . and help us question why certain groups are positioned as 'others'" (Harste, 1999, p. 507). These books challenge students to confront the injustice of social barriers that separate human beings from one another, to examine the role of stereotypes and prejudice in sustaining these barriers, and to become aware of their own prejudices based on stereotypes. As each book is read aloud in the cumulative group sessions, students are invited to consider the narratives in terms of historical contexts, the nature of the barriers, and how individuals can take action to promote social justice and equity. The ultimate goal of this literature unit is to enable students to envision the possibility of transforming themselves and their world by becoming "social activists who are challenging the status quo and asking for change" (Leland & Harste, 2000, p. 6). The literature unit described in this chapter was originally designed for students in grades 4 to 6; however, it has also been adapted for use with older students.[1]

The "Barriers and Bridges" Unit

Objectives for This Literature Unit

1. To introduce students to fiction (picture books, chapter books, and novels) and nonfiction texts that present complex social issues of race, class, and gender and to expose them to diverse voices in a collection of socially conscious literature

2. To provide opportunities for students to confront injustices in the past and present as they discover the realities of social barriers then and now and to open their hearts and minds to these realities

3. To provide opportunities for students to engage in informed and critical discussion concerning these complex ideas about the human experience and to explore ways to translate insight into social action: breaking barriers and building bridges

4. To provide opportunities for students to analyze and compare the shared texts and self-selected texts in terms of genre, viewpoint, social and historical settings, conflicts, character development and growth, and themes

5. To provide opportunities for students to explore the craft of authors and artists and to discover their use of symbol and metaphor to focus on issues of race, class, and gender

6. To provide opportunities for students to discover and use the reading-thinking strategies used by proficient readers in their transactions with literary texts

7. To provide opportunities for students to engage in independent reading and writing to prepare for and extend the literary experiences in the read-aloud sessions

8. To encourage students to ask and pursue their own questions as they listen to, discuss, read, and write about the diverse texts selected for this unit. By returning again and again to the human experiences and issues in this series of texts and engaging in inquiry and reflection, students are provided with opportunities to accumulate the emotional connections, understandings, and insights necessary to build a social conscience and to challenge social injustice.

Session 1

In preparation for the read-aloud sessions in this literature unit, students read the autobiography of Ruby Bridges, *Through My Eyes* (1999), as well as *The Story of Ruby Bridges* (Coles, 1995), a picture storybook about the African American girl who, as a six-year-old child, became a pioneer in school integration. In 1960, Bridges broke a racial barrier to enter the William Frantz Public School, an all-white school in New Orleans. This picture-book biography was written by Robert Coles, a child psychiatrist, who had met with Ruby during that stressful year and saw her as an inspirational model of courage and faith. Students' personal responses to these two books recorded in their response journals ranged from expressions of disbelief to shock and anger to compassion and concern. Journal entries also included questions about the people and events in American history described in these books.

In the first read-aloud session, students were introduced to *Cracking the Wall: The Struggles of the Little Rock Nine* (Lucas, 1997), a nonfiction text that offers a brief portrait of the first African American students to attend all-white Central High School in Little Rock, Arkansas, in 1957. After reading the title, the teacher invited students to examine the picture that spreads from the front to the back cover and to share what they noticed. This picture reveals a group of African American boys and girls holding books in their arms; a school bus is parked behind them; and four soldiers are facing the children, pointing rifles at them. Some of the students' questions triggered by this powerful scene were answered as they listened to the author's note that provides some background information about this historic event. This note begins with the words: "Not so long ago, laws kept black and white Americans apart in many places. This was called segregation . . . . There were separate schools for white children and for black children" (p. 5). The dedication begins with the words: "To the Little Rock Nine, and the children of all races in schools across America, who prove that the walls that keep people apart are wrong . . ."

By this time, most of the students were able to identify the connection between this introductory material in Lucas's brief illustrated text and the two books about Ruby Bridges. After listening to this story, the students shared their emotional responses to the realities of segregation revealed in these three introductory selections. Students also searched the library and the Internet for more information about these individuals and others associated with school integration and the civil rights movement.

Session 2

The discussion about Ruby Bridges and the Little Rock Nine continued in the second whole-group session. Students were asked to explain the meaning of the title, *Cracking the Wall,* and to focus on the use of the word *wall* as a symbol. Referring back to the dedication in Lucas's book, one student noted that the word was used to mean "something that keeps people apart." In response, the teacher offered a definition of the literary term *symbol* as "a person, object, situation, or action that operates on two levels of meaning: the literal and the figurative" (Lukens, 2003, p. 192). That is, a symbol has a meaning that goes beyond itself to stand for a more abstract idea. As the students explored the notion of the word "wall" as a symbol, several pointed to the picture of a woman holding a sign on the back cover of *Through My Eyes;* the sign reads: "We Want Segragation [*sic*]." One student noted: "The wall is like segregation; it keeps people apart. Cracking the wall could mean integration." Another student responded: "But a crack is like a dent. The wall didn't fall down. Maybe the title means it was a first step to get integration." This picture also triggered questions such as: "Who *wanted* segregation?" "*Why* did they want segregation?" "Why were innocent people attacked?" This was the beginning of an ongoing inquiry-based discussion about racism, discrimination, fear, ignorance, injustice, inequality, and civil rights, as well as the heroism of individuals such as Ruby Bridges and the Little Rock Nine. At one point in this continuing dialogue, a student explained the significance of the cover of *Cracking the Wall:* "At first the governor sent soldiers to keep those nine kids *out* of the white school. Later, the president of the United States sent U.S. army troops to protect them and to escort them *into* the school! So he was trying to break down the wall!"

At this point, the teacher introduced a picture book, *The Other Side* (Woodson, 2001), and invited the students to begin a cover-to-cover study of this book by talking about the cover, which portrays an African American girl on one side of a fence and a white girl on the other side. One student wondered whether the fence was like the wall in *Cracking the Wall.* As the story unfolded, this student was able to confirm her conjecture. This story is told from the viewpoint of Clover, an African American girl who lives in a town with a fence that separates the black side of town from the white side. Clover tells the story of the summer she becomes friends with Annie, a white girl who lives on the other side of the fence. Clover's mother has warned her not to climb over the fence. Annie's mother has also warned her daughter not to cross the fence.

Woodson provides no historical context for this story. She challenges her readers to fill in the gaps by using clues about the setting such as the racial separation and the clothing worn by the characters. As the story unfolded, students agreed that the fence was being used as a symbol for segregation in this story. They inferred that both mothers must have known about the laws and that's why they warn their children about the fence. One student added, "But the children didn't understand. They just did what their mothers said." Another student referred to a segment in *Through My Eyes* to add: "It's like when Ruby found out at the end of first grade that the reason people didn't want her to go to their school was because she was black. She didn't know this until a boy refused to play with her because his mother told him not to because she's black. Ruby wasn't angry at the boy because she knew he had to obey his mom. But it didn't seem like she really understood racism." Another student returned to the scene in which Clover and Annie work out a way to be together without disobeying their mothers: Annie says, "But she never said nothing about sitting on it" (n.p.). The picture shows Annie sitting on the fence and reaching down to take Clover's hand to pull her up to sit with her. The students talked about the picture and text on the last page of the story. This picture shows Clover and Annie sitting together on top of the fence. Several of Clover's friends have joined them. Annie says: "Someday somebody's going to come along and knock this old fence down." Clover nodded and said, "Yeah . . . Someday" (n.p.). One student commented: "They didn't know it would really happen one day! People like Ruby Bridges and Rosa Parks *did* knock down the fences!" Another student observed that the fence could be a symbol for the laws that kept people apart. This triggered another insight: "So *that's* what the civil rights movement was—to get rid of those Jim Crow laws—to knock down the fences!" The teacher concluded this discussion with a question: "Why do you think Jacqueline Woodson wrote this story?" This question prompted a number of students to compare this fictional story with the biographical and autobiographical stories they had read earlier. They decided that the author wanted to tell the story from the viewpoint of children who saw the fence as a fence and did not understand that it was a symbol of prejudice and segregation. One student added: "This story is almost like a fable: It teaches that a friendship between a white girl and a black girl could 'knock down fences.'" At this point, a few students asked for clarification about figurative language to help them understand the use of "wall" and "fence" as symbols and the use of the phrase "knock down fences" in a metaphorical sense (see Strategies 5 and 6). Other students made connections between this story and their own lives, using the word "wall" to talk about conflicts in their own neighborhoods.

At the end of this session, the teacher introduced other titles about the civil rights movement as well as individual African Americans who challenged racism or broke racial barriers before and after this movement. Students were invited to select one or more of the titles from this collection for independent reading and to record personal responses in their response journals:

> *Alec's Primer* (Walter, 2004). This picture storybook is based on the childhood of Alec Turner (1845–1923), a young slave whose journey to freedom begins when the granddaughter of a plantation owner teaches him how to read.

> *Almost to Freedom* (Nelson, 2003) is a picture book that tells the story of a young girl's escape from slavery through the Underground Railroad as witnessed by her beloved rag doll.

> *The Bat Boy and His Violin* (G. Curtis, 1998). In this picture book a special period in history provides the backdrop for a story of family ties and team spirit. It is 1948, and the manager of one of the teams in the Negro National League explains to his son why they are having such a tough season: ". . . all the best hitters and fielders are going over to play for white teams, the way Jackie Robinson did last year" (n.p.).

> *The Civil Rights Movement* (Ritchie, 2003). This volume covers the segregation and racism that African Americans endured before and during the 1950s and 1960s, as well as the impact of nonviolent protest on existing laws.

The Daring Escape of Ellen Craft (Moore, 2002). Based on the actual life of a fugitive slave, this biographical text for transition readers tells how Ellen Craft and her husband William escaped from their slave owners and reached Philadelphia in December 1848.

A Dream of Freedom: The Civil Rights Movement from 1954 to 1968 (McWhorter, 2004). The author fuses memoir with a chronology of this historical period.

Going North (Harrington, 2004). This autobiographical story follows an African American family during their difficult journey from their home in Alabama to Nebraska to escape segregation in the 1960s.

A Good Night for Freedom (Morrow, 2004) is a picture book about a young girl, Hallie, who discovers two runaway slaves hiding in Levi Coffin's home in Fountain City, Indiana, in 1839. Hallie must decide whether to turn them in according to the law or to let them escape to freedom. After Hallie has an opportunity to meet the two girls who are hiding from the slave catchers, she decides to defy the law and ignore her father's warning about "meddlin'" in order to help them escape. A historical note about the Underground Railroad and abolitionists Levi and Catherine Coffin is included.

Freedom Roads: Searching for the Underground Railroad (Hansen & McGowan, 2003). The authors use such sources as archaeological evidence, firsthand accounts, and historical court records to reconstruct the past and document the history of the Underground Railroad.

Free at Last! Stories and Songs of Emancipation (Rappaport, 2004). This text describes the experiences of African Americans in the South from the Emancipation Proclamation of 1863 to the 1954 Supreme Court decision that mandated the end to school segregation.

Especially Heroes (Kroll, 2003) is a picture book featuring the author's childhood memories of personal experiences during the civil rights movement in the early 1960s.

Fishing Day (Pinkney, 2003). This is a picture storybook about Reenie, a black child, and her mama, who enjoy fishing for carp together on the shores of what is locally known as the "Jim Crow River." Mama tells Reenie how the river got its nickname. "Jim Crow is the law of the land," she explains. "The law that says black people have a place, white people have a place, and the two should steer clear of each other. . . . We and white folks have kept our distance here, for as long as memory serves" (n.p.). Not far from them, Peter and his daddy are also fishing. They are white and keep their distance from Reenie and her mama. However, when Reenie reaches out in kindness to Peter, we see the beginnings of a friendship that breaks through the boundaries of prejudice and fear as in *The Other Side*. The author's note at the back of the book provides background information about Jim Crow and the author's own experience with the realities of prejudice and discrimination. The author concludes her note with these words: "I wrote *Fishing Day* in an effort to recast some of the painful times of my childhood. To show that children, if given the chance to formulate their own ideas about differences and tolerance, will often do what is right. *Fishing Day* comes from the belief that generosity and kindness reach beyond all boundaries."

Freedom like Sunlight: Praisesongs for Black Americans (Lewis, 2000) is a collection of poetry that celebrates the inspirational lives of thirteen African Americans, such as Harriet Tubman and Rosa Parks.

Freedom on the Menu: The Greensboro Sit-Ins (Weatherford, 2005). An eight-year-old African American girl describes the sit-in protest at Woolworth's lunch counter in Greensboro, North Carolina, on February 1, 1960.

Freedom School, Yes! (Littlesugar, 2001) is a picture storybook based on the 1964 Mississippi Freedom School Summer Project.

Freedom Summer (Wiles, 2001). This picture storybook is about a white boy and his best friend, an African American boy, who decide to go to the town pool together for the first time after the passage of a new law that forbids segregation, the Civil Rights Act of 1964. The title of this book is derived from the work of "the civil rights workers in Mississippi [who] organized 'Freedom Summer,' a movement to register black Americans to vote" (in "A Note about the Text").

The Friendship (Taylor, 1987). A novella set in Mississippi in the days of Jim Crow, this is the story of Mr. Tom Bee, an elderly black man, who dares to call a white storekeeper by his first name.

I Am Rosa Parks (Parks & Haskins, 1997). Rosa Parks was the African American woman and civil rights worker whose refusal to give up her seat on a bus led to a yearlong boycott in Montgomery, Alabama, and to the 1956 Supreme Court order to desegregate buses in Montgomery. Her acts of civil disobedience helped to establish the civil rights movement. In this text, Rosa Parks explains what she did and why.

I Have a Dream: The Life and Words of Martin Luther King, Jr. (Haskins & King, 1992). This text includes an introduction by Rosa Parks.

If a Bus Could Talk: The Story of Rosa Parks (Ringgold, 1999). A picture storybook.

Jackie Robinson (Scott, 1987). This text includes an introductory essay by Coretta Scott King.

Jackie Robinson and the Integration of Baseball (S. Simon, 2002).

Juneteenth: A Day to Celebrate Freedom from Slavery (Leeper, 2003).

Kira Kira (Kadohata, 2004), a Newbery Medal winner, portrays the close relationship between two Japanese American sisters growing up in rural Georgia during the late 1950s and the early 1960s. The strong love within their family enables them to cope with personal challenges, one sister's terminal illness, and the prejudice and discrimination against all those who were not white in the oppressive social climate of the South prior to the civil rights movement.

Let It Shine: Stories of Black Women Freedom Fighters (Pinkney, 2000). This collection features ten women freedom fighters from the eighteenth century to the present. In her prologue, the author characterizes the women as "sheroes" who stood up to oppression and injustice and who "let their light shine on in the darkness of inequality" (p. xi).

Liberty Street (Ransom, 2003). Set in nineteenth-century Fredericksburg, Virginia, this is the story of Kezia, a young slave whose mother helps her escape to freedom.

Linda Brown, You Are Not Alone: The Brown v. Board of Education Decision (Thomas, 2004), includes recollections and reactions to the *Brown v. Board of Education* decision by both black and white authors.

Lizzie Bright and the Buckminster Boy (Schmidt, 2004), is a Newbery Honor novel based on an actual event in 1911, when the town elders and the minister of a Congregational church in a small town in Maine planned to change a nearby island into a tourist spot. The inhabitants of this century-old island community, founded by former slaves, were forced to flee before the destruction of their homes so that prospective tourists would not be repelled by the sight of "colored people" on the island.

Major Taylor, Champion Cyclist (Cline-Ransome, 2004). This biography introduces a lesser-known African American cyclist who won the 1899 world championship title. Taylor battled racism to become a true American hero. Although he died a pauper at age fifty-three, he paved the way for other African American athletes such as Jackie Robinson, Satchel Paige, Jessie Owens, and Josh Gibson.

Many Thousand Gone: African Americans from Slavery to Freedom (Hamilton, 1993) provides personal accounts of individuals who were part of the history of slavery in America from the earliest slave trading through the growth of the Underground Railroad to the Emancipation Proclamation.

Martin's Big Words: The Life of Dr. Martin Luther King, Jr.
(Rappaport, 2001), a picture storybook.

Martin Luther King (Shuker, 1985). This text includes an introductory essay on leadership by Arthur M. Schlesinger, Jr.

Martin Luther King, Jr., and the Freedom Movement (Patterson,
1989).

Mississippi Morning (Vander Zee, 2004). Set in the Jim Crow
South in 1933, this is the story of a young white boy who learns
from his fishing buddy, a black boy, the terrible reality of the
"hanging tree" and the Ku Klux Klan.

Papa's Mark (Battle-Lavert, 2003), is a picture book about a boy
who helps his father learn to write his name and then accompa-
nies him to the courthouse, where he casts his ballot on the first
election day ever on which African Americans were allowed to
vote.

The Patchwork Path: A Quilt Map to Freedom (Stroud, 2005). This
picture book features a young girl and her father who use a
quilt map to find their way from their Georgia plantation to
freedom in Canada.

A Picture Book of Rosa Parks (Adler, 1993).

Portraits of African-American Heroes (Bolden, 2003) provides
twenty biographical sketches of well-known and not-so-well-
known heroes and heroines over the past 150 years such as
Frederick Douglass, Thurgood Marshall, and Ruth Simmons,
who became the first African American president of an Ivy
League school.

*Powerful Words: More than 200 Years of Extraordinary Writing by
African Americans* (Hudson, 2004). This text is a collection of
writings and speeches by more than thirty African Americans
such as Frederick Douglass and Langston Hughes. This text
begins with a foreword by Marian Wright Edelman and includes notes about the time period in which each individual
lived, information about each writer/speaker, and the public
response to the words.

Promises to Keep: How Jackie Robinson Changed America
(Robinson, 2004). The author, Sharon Robinson, is the only
daughter of the man who broke the color barrier in baseball.

Remember: The Journey to School Integration (Morrison, 2004)
features photographs and narrative that chronicle the events
that followed the *Brown v. Board of Education* decision and that
reveal the impact of this landmark Supreme Court case on the
American school system.

Remember the Bridge: Poems of a People (Weatherford, 2002)
features poems about the lives of African Americans from

slavery to the present time. This final poem in the collection begins with the words: "The bridge is men and women, famous and unknown, leaving paths of memories, timeless stepping stones" (p. 50).

Richard Wright and the Library Card (Miller, 1997). Based on a scene from Wright's autobiography, *Black Boy,* this picture book features a turning point in the life of this African American author. In the segregated South of the 1920s, Richard is not allowed to borrow books from the library, but he finds a white co-worker who is willing to loan him his library card, which becomes his ticket to freedom.

Roll of Thunder, Hear My Cry (Taylor, 1976), set in rural Mississippi during the Depression of the 1930s, is told by eight-year-old Cassie Logan, an African American girl and a naïve narrator, who experiences racial discrimination and struggles to understand the rationale for racist behavior. Cassie and her brothers manage to protest blatant acts of racism, although they are unable to alter the tradition of institutionalized racism in the world in which they live. Other books by Mildred Taylor about the Logan family are included in the collection for this unit.

Rosa Parks (Greenfield, 1996). A student who read this book found a connection between Rosa Parks's act of civil disobedience and the action of Clover and Annie in *The Other Side.*

Rosetta, Rosetta, Sit by Me! (Walvoord, 2004). This early chapter book tells the story of Rosetta, the daughter of Frederick Douglass. Rosetta was nine years old in 1848 when she entered a Quaker school in Rochester, New York, as the only black student. Although the other children and all but one parent accepted her, she was forced to leave because of the objections of the principal and one powerful parent. Her father spent nine years protesting the inequities in the school system before the city of Rochester integrated its schools. At the end of the book, there is more information about Frederick and Rosetta Douglass.

Run Away Home (McKissack, 1997). Set in Alabama in 1888, this novel is about an African American girl and her family who befriend and give refuge to a runaway Apache boy. This story, inspired by the author's African American and Native American ancestors, provides a historical perspective on the terrible challenges facing Native Americans as well as African Americans, including the Jim Crow laws passed in the South in the late 1800s and the ongoing threats of white supremacist groups.

Sky (Porter, 2004). This story is based on the experiences of an eleven-year-old Native American girl who survived the historic flood of 1964 in Montana. As Georgia Salois describes the impact of this flood on her family and her people, she reveals her courage as she confronts the discrimination against Indians in her community and the cruelty of her white classmates at school.

The Story of Jackie Robinson, Bravest Man in Baseball (Davidson, 1988).

Teammates (Golenbock, 1990). This picture storybook features Jackie Robinson who, in 1947, became the first African American to play on a major-league baseball team.

The Tin Heart (Ackerman, 1990). This picture storybook is about two friends who are separated by the Ohio River at the onset of the Civil War. The river also separates the Southern and Northern states, so their families find themselves on opposing sides of the war. However, like the characters in *The Other Side,* Mahaley and Flora manage to cross this barrier to maintain their friendship.

Under the Quilt of Night (Hopkinson, 2002). A young slave girl uses the Underground Railroad to escape to freedom in the North.

Up the Learning Tree (Vaughan, 2003) is a picture book about a young slave boy, Henry Bell, who lives in the pre–Civil War South and knows that "book learning is not allowed for slaves." However, Henry is willing to risk his life to learn to read. He hides in a sycamore tree next to the schoolhouse and listens to the lessons that are taught outside in the shade of this tree. When the teacher discovers his determination to learn, she offers to help him. An author's note at the end of the book closes with the words of Frederick Douglass, "Once you learn to read you will be forever free."

A Voice of Her Own: The Story of Phillis Wheatley, Slave Poet (Lasky, 2003) This is a picture-book biography of Phillis Wheatley, who was brought to New England as a slave in 1761. Her owners allowed her to break the unwritten rule that kept slaves illiterate, and she became the first black woman poet in America.

The Voice That Challenged a Nation: Marian Anderson and the Struggle for Equal Rights (Freedman, 2004). The story of Anderson's life is set against the backdrop of the civil rights movement.

Walking to the Bus-Rider Blues (Robinet, 2000). A young African American boy describes the realities of life for African Americans during the 1950s Montgomery, Alabama, bus boycott.

The Watsons Go to Birmingham—1963 (C. P. Curtis, 1995). The Watsons, an African American family, leave their ordinary routines in Flint, Michigan, to drive to Alabama to visit Grandma in the summer of 1963. There they confront the racial hatred in Birmingham—hatred strong enough that white men would blow up a black church.

When Marian Sang: The True Recital of Marian Anderson, the Voice of a Century (Ryan, 2002) a picture storybook about Marian Anderson's historic concert on the steps of the Lincoln Memorial in 1939, which drew an integrated crowd of seventy-five thousand people. Anderson was the first African American to perform with the Metropolitan Opera, in 1955.

Witnesses to Freedom: Young People Who Fought for Civil Rights (Rochelle, 1993). The girl in the white dress on the front cover of this text is Elizabeth Eckford, whose picture was included in *Cracking the Wall*. The chapter about the Little Rock Nine begins with introductory lines by Martin Luther King, Jr.: "It was the high school, college, and elementary school children who were in the front line of the school desegregation struggle. Lest it be forgotten, the opening of hundreds of schools to Negroes for the first time in history required that there be young Negroes with the moral and physical courage to face the challenges and, all too frequently, the mortal danger presented by mob resistance" (p. 18).

A Wreath for Emmett Till (Nelson, 2005).

Yankee Girl (Rodman, 2004) is a novel about eleven-year-old Alice, who moves from Chicago to Jackson, Mississippi, in 1964 and confronts the reality of the Jim Crow South for the first time. The reader sees the civil rights movement through the eyes of a young white girl who longs to be part of the popular group in her new school but learns that Yankees are not welcome in this Confederate state. She struggles with the racism of her classmates and her own desire to reach out in friendship to the one black girl in her class in this newly integrated school. Based on Rodman's own childhood, this novel presents the harsh realities of the racial turmoil surrounding the mandatory integration of a white school and explores the moral choices faced by the students and teachers and the price of courage in this setting.

After reading one or more of these selections, the students recorded their personal responses in their response journals. Sample "prompts" were provided to help them get started. For example, "I think the author . . . ," "I never thought about . . . ," "I wonder why . . . ," "I was puzzled about . . . ," "What if . . . ," "This story reminds me of . . . ," "I was surprised that . . . ," "The barrier in this story was . . . ," or "I need to find out about . . ." (Brooks and Hampton, 2005, p. 85).

Session 3

In this read-aloud/think-aloud session, the students were introduced to another picture book, *The Royal Bee* (Park & Park, 2000). This is the story of Song-ho, a poor peasant boy who is determined to learn how to read and write. However, he lives in the Korea of a century ago, in which only the sons of wealthy families are allowed to go to school. Song-ho begins to eavesdrop outside the classroom and listens to the lessons day by day. When winter comes, the teacher invites him to come inside and join the class if he can answer all their questions. He passes this test and earns the respect of the students and their teacher. Later, his classmates choose him to represent the school in the Royal Bee.

 A cover-to-cover study of this book began with speculation about the title and the pictures on the front and back covers, the page opposite the title page, and the next two pages, as well as the dedications and an authors' note. This note reveals that the central character is based on the authors' grandfather, who, as an illiterate boy in late-nineteenth-century Korea, "would eavesdrop at the door of the rich children's schoolhouse . . ." (n.p.). As the story unfolded, students discovered that the "bee" refers to a national academic contest, and they were able to identify the schoolhouse door as a symbol of segregation, similar to the fence or wall in the other stories. They also discovered that instead of racial segregation, this story is about the "separation between rich kids and poor kids" and that the "wall" metaphor could be used to address the complex issues of economic privilege and power. The students compared Song-ho with Ruby Bridges and the Little Rock Nine, who took action to get the education that had been denied them. One student used metaphorical language to describe Song-ho's actions: "He tried to break through the wall when he first asked the teacher to let him in. He didn't give up. He listened to the lessons at the door." Another student added, "When he listened to the lessons through the door, it was sort of like when Annie and Clover sat on *top* of the fence. No one said *that* wasn't allowed." Several students compared the teacher in this story with Rosa Parks: "What he did was like civil disobedience. He was very brave to let Song-ho come into his classroom." Others compared the teacher with Mrs. Henry, the white teacher who worked with Ruby Bridges in an empty classroom and tried to create an island of normalcy for her in the midst of the hatred and turmoil in the world around them. A student who had read *Up the Learning Tree,* by Marcia Vaughan, identified a connection between Song-ho in *The Royal Bee* and Henry Bell in Vaughan's story of a young slave boy who hides in a tree in order to listen to the lessons taught to the white children. The teachers in these two stories are also similar: one teacher breaks through a social class barrier to invite Song-ho into the school for the children of the wealthy; the other teacher breaks through a racial barrier to invite Henry Bell into the school for white children to offer him secret lessons after the other children have left for the day.

At this point in the study of *The Royal Bee,* the teacher inserted a question that incorporates a metaphor she wants to introduce: "How did the teacher help Song-ho 'build a bridge' out of poverty?" This question called attention to Song-ho's teacher, who gave Song-ho an opportunity to get an education that would be such a bridge. The poem Song-ho composed to recite at the Royal Bee focused on his mother and the teacher who had allowed him to attend school. "Then Master Min took me in and broke the honored rule . . . . The gift of hope has now been won for my poor mother and me" (n.p.). At the end of this session, the teacher returned to the note written by Ruby's mother and included at the beginning of *The Story of Ruby Bridges.* Her note opens with these words: "Our Ruby taught us all a lot . . ." After inviting students to talk about this note, the teacher asked them to consider what Song-ho taught *us.*

After a discussion of social class barriers prompted by this question and the story as a whole, the students were invited to read a modern fairy tale, *The Malachite Palace,* written by a well-known storyteller and social activist, Alma Flor Ada, translated by Rosa Zubiarreta and illustrated by Leonid Gore (1998). Ada's commitment to social issues is reflected in the stories she writes for children. However, students who were unfamiliar with this author asked: "What's the connection between a *true* story, *The Royal Bee,* and a *fairy tale?*" They were able to answer this question when they read this picture book as well as information about the author. Later, these students discussed the intertextual link that connects these very different genres. *The Malachite Palace* is the story of a princess who lives behind ornate iron gates to keep her from the children who play in the fields beyond the palace. She is told that these children are "rude, ignorant, and common" and that she cannot play with "those children." With the help of a tiny yellow bird, the princess discovers for herself the truth about these children as opposed to the stereotypes she had been given. The princess decides to open the ornate gates so she can join them in their play. A student explained the connection between *The Royal Bee* and Ada's tale: "The palace gate is like a police barrier that says Do Not Cross! The gate is a *barrier* that keeps out the poor children like the school door kept Song-ho out because he was poor. But in this fairy tale, the princess opens the gate to be with the children." Another student added: "The queen and the governess had a prejudice against those children just because they were poor! But the princess got to *know* them and found out she really liked them." A third student noted: "It's like the rich kids in *The Royal Bee* got to know Song-Ho and found out they really liked him! This author used a fairy tale to send a message about social barriers."

The teacher offered book talks about another set of titles in the collection of books for independent reading. These books feature characters who confront walls or barriers in their lives because of differences associated with social class, language, or literacy learning. The students were invited to select one or more titles for independent reading and to record in their response journals their personal responses, questions triggered by the text, the nature of the barrier in the story, connections with other texts, and connections between the author and his or her work. Throughout this unit, the response journals were used as "dialogue journals" in which the teacher responded to student entries and entered into an ongoing written conversation with each student (Atwell, 1987; Bode, 1989; Staton, 1988). An annotated list of these titles is included below:

> *Amelia's Road* (Altman, 1993a, 1993b), a picture storybook, is available in a Spanish-language edition. The story opens with the words: "Amelia Luisa Martinez hated roads" (n.p.). To her, roads went to "farms where workers labored in sunstruck fields"; roads were a symbol of her transient life as a migrant worker. When she attended school, she felt the wall that separated her from the other children: ". . . not even the teacher had bothered to learn her name" (n.p.). When a new teacher reaches past this "wall" to create a classroom community in which *all* her students are appreciated and respected as individuals, Amelia begins to build a sense of stability and hope.

> *Esperanza Rising* (Ryan, 2000, 2001). This novel is the story of Esperanza Ortega, who, until she was thirteen years old, had enjoyed a sheltered life of wealth and privilege in Mexico. She understood that her childhood friend, Miguel, "was the housekeeper's son and she was the ranch owner's daughter and between them ran a deep river" (p. 18). When a sudden tragedy forces Esperanza and her mother to flee to California and to work in the farm labor camps, she learns the realities of hard labor and poverty in her new life on the other side of the "deep river." According to the author's note at the end of the book (pp. 255–62), this story is based on the experiences of the author's grandmother, who had to make a similar transition from "a fairy-tale existence with servants, wealth, and grandeur" (p. 255) in Mexico to a company farm labor camp in

California. Students who read this novel compared it with other stories drawn from the author's personal experiences, as in *La Mariposa,* or from the experiences of family members, as in *The Friendship* and *The Royal Bee.*

Fly Away Home (Bunting, 1991). In this picture storybook, Andrew and his father are homeless; they live in an airport instead of on the streets. In order to stay there, they must build a wall around themselves so they won't "get noticed." From Andrew's perspective, "Not to be noticed is to look like nobody at all" (p. 8).

Gathering the Sun: An ABC in Spanish and English (Ada, 1997) is a bilingual alphabet book of poems that celebrate the lives of migrant farm workers.

Harvesting Hope: The Story of Cesar Chavez (Krull, 2003). This picture-book biography of Cesar Chavez includes an account of the peaceful protest he led against the terrible working conditions of California migrant workers.

Just Juice (Hesse & Parker, 1998). This chapter book features illiteracy as a barrier. The central character discovers that she and her father will always have difficulty being accepted by society because of their status as illiterates.

La Mariposa (Jiménez, 1998). This picture storybook is about Francisco, who lives in Tent City with his brothers, his mother, and his father, who is a migrant worker in California. Because he can only speak Spanish, Francisco has difficulty adjusting to first grade. However, his intense interest in the caterpillar in the classroom and in the art lessons helps him cope with the frustrations and isolation he experiences in this new school in which everyone else speaks English. According to a note about the author at the end of the book, this story is largely autobiographical. Spanish words are woven into the text, and a glossary is provided.

Monkey Island (Fox, 1991). This novel takes the reader into the world of the homeless. It is the story of an eleven-year-old boy who lives on the streets of New York City and feels isolated from ordinary people. ". . . out of ordinary life, out of the time that ruled the lives of people hurrying past the park on their way to work or home" (p. 61). He is told by another homeless person, ". . . people begin to think of us as nasty stains on the sidewalk, nasty things in their way" (p. 61).

Moses Sees a Play (Millman, 2004). In this picture storybook, Moses, a hearing-impaired child, develops a special bond with Manuel, a new immigrant who does not yet speak English. Both boys face language barriers, and Moses knows how lonely it can be "when no one understands you."

Once Upon a Time (Daly, 2003) is a fictional story that features illiteracy as a barrier. Set in South Africa, this story is about a young girl who feels the cruelty of her classmates, who laugh at her and tease her because of her inability to read.

Randall's Wall (Fenner, 1991) is a novel about a socioeconomically underprivileged fifth-grade boy who has built an invisible wall around himself as a defense against the pain of human relationships. Under the title on the front cover of the paperback edition is a question: "Can anyone help Randall break down the barrier between him and the world?" On the front cover a wire fence separates the boy from the other children on the playground.

Seedfolks (Fleischman, 1997). This short novel is about thirteen individuals of varying ages and backgrounds who live separate lives in an inner-city neighborhood, until they work together to transform a trash-filled empty lot into a lovely garden. In the process, they break through the barriers that separate them to form a community.

Sophie and the Sidewalk Man (Tolan, 1992). In the first chapter of this early chapter book, Sophie almost bumps into a man with two plastic garbage bags. Her friend uses the words "filthy" and "bum" to describe him; Sophie says she "didn't notice" him; Sophie's mother warns her not to go near him. Later, Sophie begins to look beyond the wall of prejudice and sees him as a human being, cold and hungry. She imagines what it would be like to be homeless, without a bed or bathroom or a place to keep his things. In the end, she gives him money she has been saving to buy a special toy.

Thank You, Mr. Falker (Polacco, 1998). This is an autobiographical tale in which the author tells of her struggle to learn to read and the cruelty of her peers, who called her "stupid" or "dumbbell" and forced her to feel alone and afraid. Mr. Falker, her fifth-grade teacher, helped her learn to read. According to Polacco, "he unlocked the door and pulled [her] into the light" (note about the author on the back flap of this picture book).

Tomás and the Library Lady (Mora, 1997). This picture book is based on the life of Tomás Rivera, a migrant farm worker who became a national education leader. The books in the local public library helped him break through the barriers of poverty, and it was the librarian who opened the library door and invited him into this world of books. At the end of the book, an author's note about Rivera concludes with these words: "When Dr. Rivera died in 1984, he was the chancellor of the University of California at Riverside. The campus library now bears the name of the boy who was encouraged to read by a librarian in Iowa."

Session 4

In this session, students listened to and discussed *Virgie Goes to School with Us Boys,* a picture book by Elizabeth Fitzgerald Howard (1999) who was inspired by the stories of her grandfather's childhood to write this book. Set in the post–Civil War South, *Virgie Goes to School with Us Boys* is the story of a young girl who is determined to go to school with her brothers, who attend a Quaker school for freed slaves. Although Virgie's brother tells her "girls don't need school," Virgie is a strong-willed, independent girl who argues for her right to attend school along with the boys. The narrator, one of Virgie's brothers, expresses similar thoughts: "What about Virgie? She was free, too. Couldn't she go to school with us boys?" Finally, her parents decide to allow Virgie to go to school with her brothers. Her father tells his children, "All free people need learning—old folk, young folk . . . small girls, too" (n.p.). The author includes a note at the back of the book to provide information about the Reconstruction period, the setting for this story, and she shares the identity of the narrator, her grandfather. The students identified a gender stereotype as the barrier in this story and noted that the barrier is broken by Virgie's determination and her father's words: "All free people need learning."

Toward the end of the discussion of this story, the teacher inserted a question: "Why do you think the author described the long walk to the school in such great detail?" This question called attention to the obstacles the children encountered to attend the Quaker school and their willingness to meet these challenges in order to get an education as "the first step in 'learning to be free'" (author's note). Finally, the teacher invited students to compare this story with the others introduced in this unit. In particular, she invited them to compare Virgie's father with the teacher in *The Royal Bee* and to compare Virgie and Song-ho. Students noted that the attitudes and beliefs of Virgie's father and those of the teacher and the determination and courage of Virgie and Song-ho made it possible to knock down fences or break through barriers. After this comparative analysis, students were invited to review the fiction and nonfiction titles selected for this unit to enable them to collaboratively construct a time line showing important historical events that occurred between the post–Civil War period and the civil rights movement many decades later.

At the conclusion of this session, the teacher introduced another set of titles in the collection for this unit and invited students to select one or more to read independently and to write about in their journals. Brief book talks were designed to pique students' interest and to assist them in the selection process. The books in this set featured gender barriers and individuals who succeeded in breaking through these barriers and building bridges for others:

Babe Didrikson Zaharias: All-Around Athlete (Sutcliffe, 2000), is a biography for beginning readers that portrays the early life of the woman who was named Outstanding Woman Athlete of the Half Century in 1950.

The Ballot Box Battle (McCully, 1996) is a picture-book biography about Elizabeth Cady Stanton, who "first called for the vote for women at the women's rights convention she organized in Seneca Falls, New York, in 1848" (author's note).

Dirt on Their Skirts: The Story of the Young Women Who Won the World Championship (Rappaport & Callan, 2000) is a picture storybook based on the 1946 championship game of the All-American Girls Professional Baseball League.

Elizabeth Cady Stanton: Leader of the Fight for Women's Rights (Salisbury, 2002).

The Girl Who Struck Out Babe Ruth (Patrick, 2000) is a nonfiction account of the day a seventeen-year-old female professional baseball player, Jackie Mitchell, struck out the New York Yankees' best hitters, Babe Ruth and Lou Gehrig, in an exhibition game in 1931.

Girl Wonder: A Baseball Story in Nine Innings (Hopkinson, 2003) is a story about Alta Weiss (1890–1964), who finds a way to show that she can play baseball in spite of her gender.

Go Free or Die: A Story about Harriet Tubman (Ferris, 1988). After her own escape from slavery, Harriet Tubman led more than three hundred people through the Underground Railroad over a ten-year period.

Harriet Tubman: Call to Freedom (Carlson, 1989). This biography traces Harriet Tubman's life and her efforts to help other slaves find their way to freedom in the North.

Lynette Woodard: The First Female Globetrotter (Rosenthal, 1986) is an account of the life and career of the first woman to play basketball for the Harlem Globetrotters.

Madeleine Albright (M. Howard, 1998) is the story of the first female secretary of state and the highest-ranking woman in the history of the U.S. government.

Mighty Jackie: The Strike-Out Queen (M. Moss, 2004) is another book about Jackie Mitchell, who became the first professional female pitcher in baseball history.

Minty: A Story of Young Harriet Tubman (Schroeder, 1996). This picture book provides a fictional account of Harriet Tubman's childhood based on the known facts of her life as a slave on the Brodas plantation in the 1820s.

Only Passing Through: The Story of Sojourner Truth (Rockwell, 2000). This picture book introduces readers to the early years of Sojourner Truth, a former slave who, along with Frederick Douglass and Harriet Tubman, helped to bring about the end of slavery and who fought for the rights of women.

Princess of the Press: The Story of Ida B. Wells-Barnett (Medearis, 1997). Ida B. Wells was the daughter of freed, educated slaves and became a journalist, a newspaper owner, a civil rights activist, one of the founders of the NAACP, and a suffragette who fought for the right of women to vote.

Ruby's Wish (S. Y. Bridges, 2002). This picture book provides a fictional account of the experiences of the author's grandmother. The story is set in China, at a time when few girls were taught to read and write. It is the story of Ruby, who dreams of going to university with her brothers and male cousins. It is interesting to read this along with *The Royal Bee.*

Sally Ride, Astronaut: An American First (Behrens, 1984). This is a brief biography of the first American woman astronaut to orbit the earth, with the second mission of the Challenger spacecraft in June 1983.

Sally Ride: Shooting for the Stars (Hurwitz & Hurwitz, 1989). This is a longer biography about Sally Ride.

Sandra Day O'Connor: First Woman on the Supreme Court (Greene, 1982).

Susan B. Anthony: And Justice for All (Gehret, 1994) is a biography of an early leader in the campaign for women's rights, particularly in getting women the right to vote.

Talkin' about Bessie: The Story of Aviator Elizabeth Coleman by Nikki Grimes (2002). This is a picture-book biography of the first African American woman to become a licensed pilot.

You Want Women to Vote, Lizzie Stanton? (Fritz, 1995). The first chapter in this biography of Elizabeth Cady Stanton and story of her fight for women's rights reveals the impact of her father's words. When her only brother died, her father said to her: "I wish you were a boy!" (p. 6). When Lizzie won a prize in Greek at the Johnstown Academy, where she was the only girl in the class, her father said: "If only you'd been a boy" (p. 7).

Zora Hurston and the Chinaberry Tree (Miller, 1994). This picture-book biography reveals African American Zora's strong bond with her mother and the trauma of her mother's death when Zora was nine. It is her mother's inspiration that enables her to become a famous writer and folklorist in spite of her father's attempt to subdue her spirit and to confine her to traditional gender roles.

Zora Neale Hurston: Writer and Storyteller (McKissack & McKissack, 1992, 2002).

Challenging Gender Stereotypes

For generations gender stereotypes have been embedded in the literature available to children. According to Linda Parsons (2004):

> Fairy tales in the patriarchal tradition portray women as weak, submissive, dependent, and self-sacrificing, while men are powerful, active, and dominant. . . . Feminist re-visions of fairy tales, however, can be one forum through which patriarchal structures are critiqued and alternatives to gendered subject positions are envisioned. (pp. 137–39)

To encourage students to question patriarchal values and to challenge gender stereotypes, the teacher invited them to read examples of "feminist re-visions of fairy tales" that were included in the collection for this unit along with other examples of texts that feature characters, both male and female, who struggle to break through gender barriers that constrain them. Roberta Trites (1997) points out that "traditional gender roles have been as limiting for boys as they have for girls" (p. 5), and she defines a *feminist text* as one in which the main character is empowered regardless of gender. "A major criterion of the feminist children's novels, then, is the protagonist's capacity for assuming and retaining the subject position within the competing voices of the narrative" (p. 29).

In the feminist novel the protagonist moves from object to subject as she or he begins to understand the "primacy of voice" (Trites, p. 7) and becomes "more aware of her ability to assert her own personality and to enact her own decisions" (p. 6). For example, *Rumpelstiltskin's Daughter* (Stanley, 1997) offers an alternative to the traditional *Rumpelstiltskin* (J. Grimm & W. Grimm, 1993) in which the miller's daughter passively accepts her fate and meekly submits to the cruelty of her father and the king, who treat her as an object. Although the king marries her, she continues to see herself as object and is dependent on others to solve her problems. The reader wonders if she does, indeed, live "happily ever after." In Stanley's revision, both male and female characters are empowered to control their own destinies when the miller's daughter chooses to marry the hardworking, sensitive, and supportive Rumpelstiltskin instead of submitting to the greedy, self-centered king. Their daughter is also an independent young woman who uses her voice and inner resources to control her own destiny when she is faced with the same greedy king sixteen years later. She manages to trick him out of his selfish and patriarchal ways, and she rejects his marriage proposal, choosing to become prime minister instead. Through brief book talks, the teacher introduced this feminist text as well as others in the collection listed below and invited students to select one or more to read independently and to discuss in small dialogue groups:

Picture Books

The Mapmaker's Daughter (Helldorfer, 1991) is a modern fairy tale about Suchen, who sets out alone on a dangerous journey to rescue the king's son from an evil witch. He rewards her with a horse and a red cape for her next adventure. There is no wedding at the end of this tale of a courageous and independent heroine and a prince who treats her as an equal by acknowledging that her desire for adventure is equal to his own.

Prince Nautilus (Melmed, 1994) is a modern fairy tale about a kind and courageous young woman who frees a prince from an evil wizard's spell that imprisoned the prince in a seashell. She rejects his marriage proposal, explaining that for years she had longed to "see the wide world and its wonders" (n.p.). Unthreatened by her independence, the prince appreciates her inner qualities and offers to join her on her quest for adventure.

The Four Gallant Sisters (Kimmel, 1992) is another modern fairy tale in which four orphaned sisters disguise themselves as men to go out in the world to learn a trade. Later they use their skills to rescue a princess and her four brothers from a dragon.

The Enchanter's Daughter (Barber, 1987) is a modern fairy tale about a girl who rejects her life as a fairytale princess and escapes to the small house from which the Enchanter had stolen her as an infant. She takes control of her own destiny and chooses to live a simple life as a humble peasant girl caring for her family and the land—exchanging material wealth for freedom, knowledge, love, and meaningful work.

The King's Equal (Paterson, 1999). A dying king proclaims that his son cannot wear the crown of the kingdom until he marries a woman who is his equal in beauty, intelligence, and wealth. The arrogant prince believes this is impossible until Rosamund, a wise and kind shepherdess, uses her voice to prove that she is not only his equal, but is *more than equal* to him. Now he must prove that he is worthy to have Rosamund for his wife. At the end of his quest, he gains the self-knowledge, humility, kindness, and wisdom that enable him to win her heart and to serve as a good king.

The Glass Mountain (Wolkstein, 1999) is a retelling of a Grimm tale in which a king challenges his daughter's suitors to climb a glass mountain. Wolkstein's retelling challenges the patriarchal perspective found in the traditional tale. The princess insists on choosing her bridegroom, and she and her suitor are able to realize their own dreams and to help others as well. The story ends with a focus on love, generosity, and the creation of a new reign.

The Well at the End of the World (San Souci, 2004). This modern revision of a traditional British folktale features an independent and competent heroine who goes on a difficult quest to find the healing waters that will cure her father, the king. In response to her kindness, helper characters assist her on this quest. This practical princess chooses her bridegroom because of his "sense of fun," and his kindness, wisdom, and even temper. On the last page, the artist shows the happy couple enjoying each other's company in front of the fire. She is reading; he is knitting.

Novels

Bound (Napoli, 2004) is a novel based on a Chinese Cinderella story. Like most of the heroines in traditional Cinderella tales, Xing Xing is an independent young woman who takes control of her own destiny in spite of her life of neglect and servitude in her stepmother's home. "She [Xing Xing] felt strong. A strong woman in a world that tried to deny the very existence of such a thing. But she wouldn't be denied" (p. 176–77). When the prince asks Xing Xing to marry him, she responds only after she is able to accept his offer "with full understanding" (p. 184).

Ella Enchanted (Levine, 1997) is a novel about Ella, who struggles against the gift of obedience, the curse of an old fairy at her birth. Ella is an independent individual with a strong voice, and she is determined to take control of her own destiny. The prince and Ella's father present opposing models of male behavior: the prince is kind, considerate, caring, hardworking, and intelligent; Ella's father is unfeeling and self-centered, and he treats his daughter as an object. Ella and the prince become friends before they begin to love each other.

Littlejim (Houston, 1990, 1993). This novel, inspired by stories of the author's family, is about twelve-year-old Littlejim Houston, who lives with his family on a farm in the early years of the twentieth century. His mother, his sister, and his teacher recognize his special gift as a writer, but his father expresses only contempt for his son. To his father, reading and writing are not manly activities. Littlejim is deeply hurt by his father's contempt but is determined to earn his approval and respect. When his father forbids him to enter an essay contest, Littlejim works on his essay in secret. His decision to defy his father to prove his worth sets the stage for this story of a boy coming into manhood and pushing against the boundaries that constrain him.

Bridge to Terabithia (Paterson, 1977, 1987) is a novel about an isolated rural community in which Jess and a newcomer, Leslie, build a friendship and a secret kingdom where Leslie helps Jess discover worlds of imagination, learning, and language. When Leslie ignores the gender separation on the school playground and enters the boys' race and wins, only Jess supports her. He, too, pushes against the boundaries that define behavior according to gender: Jess's father is opposed to his son's deep interest in art and considers this an inappropriate and suspicious pursuit for a boy.

A Special Gift (M. L. Simon, 1978). In this novel, Peter's secret love of ballet is in conflict with his public image as an athlete. His father pressures him to pursue his athletic interests, suggesting that his interest in ballet is not natural for a boy. Peter struggles with his own inner doubts about his identity as a male.

Love That Dog (Creech, 2001). Jack tells his story in a poetry journal. His first entry reveals his acceptance of traditional gender roles: "I don't want to because boys don't write poetry. Girls do" (p. 1). However, in response to the poetry his teacher reads aloud, and inspired by other poets and by his dog, Sky, Jack gradually learns to love poetry and evolves into a poet himself.

Tuck Everlasting (Babbitt, 1975, 1999). At the beginning of this novel, the protagonist, Winnie Foster, is self-absorbed and sees herself as an object of parental authority. In the course of the narrative, moving from object to subject, Winnie develops a clear sense of her own autonomy and voice and takes an active part in shaping her destiny.

Holes (Sachar, 1998, 2002). In the beginning of this winner of the Newbery Medal, the protagonist, Stanley Yelnats, overweight, friendless, and a target for bullies, sees himself as object and victim, controlled by his past, a family curse, his family's poverty, the judge, and his peers. His name is a palindrome, and this is a story of reversals: Stanley moves from object to subject position as he gains inner strength and wisdom and begins to take control of his life.

Journey (MacLachlan, 1991). ". . . *Journey* is a feminist text that explores an adolescent male's subjectivity" (Trites, 1997, p. 35).

A Solitary Blue (Voigt, 1983, 2003). For years the protagonist, Jeff Greene, perceives himself as an object at home and school. He does what he is expected to do and seems to be voiceless and invisible in these settings. Like Journey, Jeff has been abandoned by his mother at a young age, and he struggles to confront his feelings as his mother betrays him again and again in his young life. He gradually finds his own voice and begins to develop a sense of self and to assert his personality until he is able to stand up to her and to take control of his life.

Sahara Special (Codell, 2003). Sahara Jones is repeating her fifth-grade year, and her mother requests that she be taken out of special ed and placed in a regular classroom. The narrative is structured around Sahara's two selves—her school self, represented by the thick file kept by the school counselor, and her private self, represented by the book she is writing about herself. These files are a barrier for her; she has already been labeled by the school. Fortunately, her new teacher does not read her students' files; she supports the individuality of each student, and, in particular, she supports Sahara's talents as a writer. When Sahara realizes she is not being prejudged, she begins to get involved in school and gains the self-confidence and faith in other people that enable her to reveal her private self and develop her inner qualities. In the school setting, she is finally able to move from object to subject position as she begins to take control of her own decisions and actions.

One Fat Summer (Lipsyte, 1977) is a first-person account of a "turning-point summer" by fourteen-year-old Bobby Marks, whose excessive weight functions as a barrier that separates him from his peers and keeps him from pursuing his love of swimming because of his body image in a bathing suit. However, Bobby gradually moves from object to subject position as a result of a job managing the lawn of a rich estate owner. He begins to take control of his eating habits and gradually loses weight. As he gains self-confidence and a stronger voice, he begins to stand up for himself and to take charge of his life.

The Ravenmaster's Secret: Escape from the Tower of London (Woodruff, 2003). Set in London, 1735, this story is told from the perspective of eleven-year-old Forrest Harper, who lives with his family at the Tower of London and helps his father tend the ravens and guard the prisoners. He longs to prove his courage to the bullies who treat him as an object of ridicule and, seeing him as too weak and cowardly for a boy, take advantage of his short height and sensitive nature. Forrest's inner struggle is intertwined with the drama of a tower escape. When he is confronted with the possibility of saving the lives of two friends, he draws from his inner strength and follows his moral sense and his commitment as a friend.

McKendree (Belton, 2000) is a novel that focuses on intraracial conflicts. The central character is a fourteen-year-old African American girl, Tilara Haynes, whose mother died before she was two and whose stern father teaches her to believe in the value of light skin over dark, "good hair" over kinky. The words and behavior of those around her reinforce this stereotype, and she passively accepts the notion that, with her own dark skin, "she could never be pretty" (p. 9). When Tilara spends the summer of 1948 with her aunt Cloelle in West Virginia, she learns to see herself in a different way and discovers the power of language as she begins to "assert her own personality" and to resist her father's attempt to control her behavior and self-image. By the end of the summer, she has gained self-confidence and a sense of her own worth.

Session 5

Prior to the fifth session, students wrote responses to the following questions in their journals:

1. What literary themes did you discover in the books you heard or read in this unit? Use symbols such as "walls," "barriers," and "bridges" to discuss these themes.

2. What connections did you find between the fiction and the nonfiction selections you heard or read?

3. What can you do to help break down barriers and build bridges in your own world?

After completing this assignment, students brought their response journals to this fifth session for a "synthesis discussion" in which they collaborated to pull together what they had learned about complex issues of race, class, and gender; injustices in the past and present; the nature of social barriers and bridges; the role of stereotypes and prejudice in sustaining these barriers; and individuals in fiction and real life who took action to break barriers and build bridges. Students consulted their journals as they participated in this synthesis discussion, which concluded with a focus on stereotypes and barriers in their own world. After this synthesis discussion, students worked in small groups to develop and implement plans of action for breaking down these barriers.

Action Plans: Several students identified "invisible walls" that seemed to exist in the cafeteria. They planned to eat lunch with kids they didn't know very well and who they thought were "sort of different." Students in another group who had engaged in a thoughtful discussion of *Say Something* (Moss, 2004) were inspired to get involved whenever they discovered barriers created by teasing or bullying. In this provocative picture book the young narrator is a passive witness to the abuse of "others." Although she doesn't participate in the teasing and bullying that degrades and marginalizes peers, the narrator is silent until one day she, too, becomes the victim of this cruelty. This experience convinces her to take action. Two pages of resources that follow the narrative include the words of Thom Harnett, a civil rights attorney:

"One person speaking up makes more noise than a thousand people who remain silent."

   After students had a chance to translate their plans into action, a follow-up session was scheduled to enable them to share their experiences. As students shared their "action plans," outcomes, and personal reflections in this follow-up session, they were able to find new meaning in the words of Jacqueline Woodson (2005), who explained in her Web site why she decided to write *The Other Side:* "I wanted to write about how powerful kids can be. Clover and Annie fight against segregation by becoming friends. They don't believe in the ideas the adults have about things so they do what they can to change the world. We all have this power."

   At the end of this fifth session, students were given a homework assignment to read *Maniac Magee* (Spinelli, 1990); to keep a running record of their personal responses to the unfolding text in their response journals; and to record connections between this novel and previous reading experiences in this unit. Students worked with partners to search the Internet for information about Spinelli and his work, and they were introduced to Spinelli's autobiography, *Knots in My Yo-Yo String: The Autobiography of a Kid* (Spinelli, 1998), in which the author reveals the way he has translated real life into fiction. The chapter entitled, "Dr. Winter's Finger" (pp. 102–9) provides fascinating insights about the origins of *Maniac Magee* and was read aloud to the whole class while they were reading this novel independently. In preparation for working in small dialogue groups to talk about this novel, the students were asked to formulate two or three questions that would be used to initiate literary analysis and to stimulate critical discussion of the complex issues addressed in this novel. In addition, they were asked to reflect on how the previous reading experiences in this unit might have prepared them for reading this novel. (See Strategy 2.)

   Maniac Magee is the story of a racially divided town, Two Mills, Pennsylvania, in which the East End and West End are two hostile camps separated by Hector Street. Maniac Magee, a legendary hero in a contemporary realistic novel, crosses Hector Street and moves between the East End and the West End in an attempt to break down barriers, build bridges between these two camps, and bring together those who have learned to see each other as the enemy. While others do not separate their observations from their preconceptions and see what they *expect,* Maniac sees what *is.* Maniac is a larger-than-life character who confronts the prejudice, ignorance, and fear that he finds on both sides of Hector

Street and searches for a way to bring about racial harmony. He is also a "regular kid" who is searching for a home and a family.

Small Dialogue Groups

Students consulted their journal entries and notes from Internet searches or Spinelli's autobiography to contribute ideas to the dialogue in these small groups. One participant in each group served as a scribe to record students' questions as well as key ideas, discoveries, and interpretations that emerged out of these conversations. Examples of student-initiated questions are included below. Students had posed some of these questions in response to their initial transactions with this novel and had found some, but not all, answers in the unfolding narrative. (See Strategy 8.)

1. What clues did the author give you to let you know this novel is both a tall tale and realism?
2. Why did the author put the jump-rope rhyme at the beginning of the story?
3. What was Maniac's quest as a tall-tale hero?
4. What was Maniac's quest as a regular kid?
5. How did Mars Bar and Amanda help Maniac with his quests?
6. Why did the author create a character without any prejudices?
7. Compare Maniac and Ruby Bridges that time at the end of first grade when the white boy told her *why* he couldn't play with her.
8. Compare Hector Street and the fence in *The Other Side*.
9. Compare Maniac and the two girls in *The Other Side*.
10. What barriers are in this novel? Why?
11. Which character showed how ignorance keeps a stereotype going?
12. Which characters showed how fear keeps prejudice going?
13. How come Maniac didn't go out on the trolley trestle to rescue Russell?
14. Did you predict what would happen when Maniac looked at the trestle? Explain what you were thinking when you read this part.
15. Why did Mars Bar say to Maniac: "Listen, man, I know you wasn't scared. I know it" (p. 175)?
16. How do you think Maniac felt when he finally told Mars Bar about his parents?

17. Compare Maniac and the civil rights workers.

18. How did Spinelli's autobiography help you figure out why he wrote this novel?

19. Hector was a Trojan prince and a noble warrior. Why did Spinelli decide to use "Hector Street" to separate the East End from the West End?

20. Compare Maniac's quest and our "action plans."

Assessment

Assessment is an ongoing process throughout each literature unit. Objectives that are used to develop the lesson plan are also used as criteria for assessment of students' involvement and their understanding as readers, writers, and thinkers in response to the literary experiences in the unit. During the "Barriers and Bridges" unit, the teacher kept a running record of students' participation in the cumulative group sessions and their contributions to group discussions. She evaluated entries in their response journals, including the written conversations when those took the form of "dialogue journals"; their responses to the three questions that served as a preparation for the synthesis discussion in Session 5; their own questions about *Maniac Magee,* as well as their developing habits of questioning and inquiry; and their "self-evaluation" reports, in which they shared what they had learned during the unit, what they needed to work on, and how they had grown as active readers and writers.

For example, the teacher noted that student-initiated questions and comments about the scene at the trolley trestle in *Maniac Magee* revealed their engagement in the story. That is, many of the students had entered into the story world and had used the "subtext strategy" to get inside the characters of Maniac and Mars Bar and to consider the thoughts and emotions behind their actions (Clyde, 2003). Student-initiated questions also revealed students' use of prior knowledge of genre, author's craft, and symbolism to engage in an analysis of this complex text. Students' written and oral work provided evidence of their strengths and weaknesses as learners and new understandings gained from this literary/literacy/social studies unit. For example, a student who read *Esperanza Rising* observed that "deep river" was used as a metaphor for the class differences that separate Esperanza, the daughter of the ranch owner, from Miguel, the son of her family's housekeeper. This student compared "deep river" to the "wall" (or laws) that separates black and white in the story of the Little Rock Nine; Hector Street, which separates black and white in *Maniac Magee;* and the "door" that separates rich and poor in *The Royal Bee.* Another student who read this novel described her cover-to-cover study of this book and explained that it wasn't until she finished the book that she understood the significance of the Mexican proverb that preceded the first chapter: "The rich person is richer when he becomes poor, than the poor person when he becomes rich." This student identified in this novel another "wall" created by cultural prejudice and stereotypes about Mexicans. At one point in the narrative, when Esperanza asks Miguel why they drive so far to shop at a Japanese market, he explains that the owner of this shop is kind to Mexicans and "treats us like people" (p. 186). He tells Esperanza that people here think all Mexicans are "uneducated, dirty, poor, and unskilled. It does not occur to them that many have been trained in professions in Mexico . . . . Americans see us as one big, brown group who are good for only manual labor" (p. 187). Another student shared his personal response to *Fly Away Home,* the story of a homeless child living in an airport: ". . . and when I went to the airport during our vacation I kept thinking about that boy and his dad and what it would be like to be them!" A student who read *La Mariposa* focused on the author's dedication: "To my teachers, whose faith in my ability and guidance helped me break the migrant circuit." This author's tribute to his teachers triggered a connection to the teacher in *The Royal Bee* who helped Song-ho "build a bridge out of poverty." This student identified another intertextual link with *Amelia's Road*: In each story the teacher displays the child's drawing in the classroom, and, for both Francisco, in *La Mariposa,* and Amelia, this act of recognition and appreciation plays a significant role in their struggle to define themselves and to find a place where they belong.

Oral and written responses to literature also revealed students' use of: (1) figurative language introduced in this literature unit; (2) comparative analysis and intertextual links among these diverse selections; and (3) reading-thinking strategies such as initiating cover-to-cover studies of new texts, activating prior knowledge, making predictions and inferences, engaging in metacognition, and reflecting on and identifying text-to-self and text-to-text connections that enrich transactions with literary texts. Students used the historical background found in nonfiction texts to help them understand the complex social issues in fiction. The literature selected for this unit promoted discussion about these complex social issues that revealed students' response to the injustices in the past and present as they discovered the realities of social barriers then and now and the way race, class, and gender can be used to define the powerful and the powerless. Many of these books elicited critical dialogues and inspired students to translate into practice their understanding that their own perceptions of "others" can change after they get to know them as individuals (Harste, 1999, p. 508). In these literary selections, students encountered individuals who took action against social injustices and who inspired them to reflect on what Woodson calls their own power to "change the world."

Standardized Tests

In a public school in Pittsford, New York, fourth-grade students who had studied literature in the context of several of the literature units featured in this book, including the "Barriers and Bridges" unit, took the New York State English Language Arts Test. Two teachers who had worked with these fourth graders were pleasantly surprised to see their scores on this test. These teachers reported that in the six years that they had administered this test to fourth graders, they had never seen such high scores achieved by their students, including the "Reading Resource" and "Special Education" students. The teachers concluded that *all* their students had clearly benefited from the rich literary/literacy experiences inherent in the literature units they had introduced into their curriculum that year. The New York State test assesses listening skills, reading comprehension, and the ability to write an essay requiring analysis and synthesis of multiple texts. These teachers attributed the high quality of their students' test performance to their involvement in literature units in which they entered into rich literary discussions, practiced reading-thinking strategies, engaged in literary analysis of single texts and synthesis of multiple texts, and studied the craft of authors and artists. They had observed their fourth graders becoming increasingly confident and competent as independent and thoughtful readers and writers as they became immersed in the study of literature in the context of the literature units featured in this book.[2]

Notes

1. Lesson plans designed for grades 3 to 5 and for grades 6 to 8, respectively, were first published in the NCTE/IRA "ReadWriteThink" Web site (http://www.ReadWriteThink.org) as "Literature as a Catalyst for Social Action: Breaking Barriers, Building Bridges" and "Breaking Barriers, Building Bridges: Critical Discussion of Social Issues." The material in this online resource was drawn from the literature unit described in this chapter. Embedded within this chap-

ter are selected student responses to the texts featured in this literature unit as it was introduced in diverse classrooms.

      2. The fourth graders mentioned in the last segment of this chapter were students of Jeanne Zettel and Nancy Campbell (Pittsford Central School District, Pittsford, New York), who shared with me the impact of the literature units on their students' growth as thoughtful and motivated readers and writers and on their performance on the standards test mandated by New York State since 1999. Zettel and Campbell explained that, for years, they had been using a prescribed basal reading series and concomitant materials in which skills were taught in isolation. However, as they prepared their students for this New York State test, they began looking for a better way to teach their students the reading-thinking strategies they would need to use on this test and that would enable them to find meaning in what they were reading. After attending a series of workshops in which I introduced the use of literature units as the core of a language arts curriculum, these two teachers decided to put away the basal readers and to develop a yearlong language arts program structured around a series of literature units. Campbell and Zettel shared with me what happened: "Teaching reading-thinking skills through the literature units caused each student's reading comprehension to improve significantly. This was the first time we had seen struggling students as well as highly able students become so completely engaged in literary and literacy experiences and exhibit so much progress as readers and writers. We were amazed to see the children's excitement about books and reading and their ability to understand and enjoy and discuss challenging books that our previous fourth graders had not been ready to comprehend. Our students' discussions about complex books were remarkable! We felt the whole year was such a powerful experience for us and for our students, and we became a real community of readers! For the first time in our years of teaching, we felt that our students really understood literature and that reading opened up new worlds for them. We felt we were making a difference in their lives by helping them learn to love reading!"

References

Chapter 1

Professional References

Adams, M. J., & Collins A. (1977). *A schema-theoretic view of reading* (Technical Rep. No. 32). Urbana: University of Illinois, Center for the Study of Reading. (ERIC, ED142971)

Allen, R. V. (1976). *Language experiences in communication*. Boston: Houghton Mifflin.

Almasi, J. F., McKeown, M. G., & Beck, I. L. (1996). The nature of engaged reading in classroom discussions of literature. *Journal of Literacy Research, 28*(1), 107–46.

Anderson, R. C. (1971). Encoding processes in the storage and retrieval of sentences. *Journal of Experimental Psychology, 91,* 338–41.

Anderson, R. C., & Pearson, P. D. (1984). A schema-theoretic view of basic processes in reading. In P. D. Pearson, R. Barr, M. L. Kamil, & P. Mosenthal (Eds.), *Handbook of Reading Research* (pp. 255–92). White Plains, NY: Longman.

Applebee, A. N., Langer, J. A., & Mullis, I.V. S. (1987). *Learning to be literate in America: Reading, writing, and reasoning*. Princeton, NJ: Educational Testing Service.

Ashton-Warner, S. (1958). *Spinster, a novel*. London: Secker & Warburg.

Ashton-Warner, S. (1963). *Teacher*. New York: Simon & Schuster.

Atwell, N. (1987). *In the middle: Writing, reading, and learning with adolescents*. Portsmouth, NH: Heinemann.

Barrentine, S. J. (1996). Engaging with reading through interactive read-alouds. *The Reading Teacher, 50*(1), 36–43.

Barton, J., & Sawyer, D. M. (2003/2004). Our students *are* ready for this: Comprehension instruction in the elementary school. *The Reading Teacher, 57,* 334–47.

Baumann, J. F., Jones, L. A., & Seifert-Kessell, N. (1993). Using think alouds to enhance children's comprehension monitoring abilities. *The Reading Teacher, 47*(3), 184–93.

Baumann, J. F., & Ivey, G. (1997). Delicate balances: Striving for curricular and instructional equilibrium in a second-grade, literature/strategy-based classroom. *Reading Research Quarterly, 32*(3), 244–75.

Beach, R. (1990). New directions in research on responses to literature. In E. J. Farrell, & J. R. Squire (Eds.), *Transactions with literature: A fifty-year perspective* (pp. 65–77). Urbana, IL: National Council of Teachers of English.

Block, C. C. (1993). Strategy instruction in a literature-based reading program. *Elementary School Journal, 94*(2), 139–51.

Block, C. C., Gambrell, L. B., & Pressley, M. (Eds.). (2002). *Improving comprehension instruction: Rethinking research, theory, and classroom practice* (1st ed.). San Francisco: Jossey-Bass.

Bromley, K. D. (1996). *Webbing with literature: Creating story maps with children's books* (2nd ed.). Boston: Allyn & Bacon.

Calkins, L. M. (1986). *The art of teaching writing*. Portsmouth, NH: Heinemann.

Calkins, L. M. (1994). *The art of teaching writing* (New ed.). Portsmouth, NH: Heinemann.

Cazden, C. (1981). *Peer dialogues across the curriculum*. Unpublished manuscript.

Chinn, C. A., Anderson, R. C., & Waggoner, M. A. (2001). Patterns of discourses in two kinds of literature discussion. *Reading Research Quarterly, 36*, 378–411.

Clark, M. M. (1976). *Young fluent readers: What can they teach us?* London: Heinemann.

Clyde, J. A. (2003). Stepping inside the story world: The subtext strategy—A tool for connecting and comprehending. *The Reading Teacher, 57*(2), 150–60.

Cole, A. D. (2003). *Knee to knee, eye to eye: Circling in on comprehension*. Portsmouth, NH: Heinemann.

Collins, A., & Smith, E. E. (1982). Teaching the process of reading comprehension. In D. K. Detterman & R. J. Sternberg (Eds.), *How and how much can intelligence be increased* (pp. 173–85). Norwood, NJ: Ablex.

Dole, J. A., Duffy, G. G., Roehler, L. R., & Pearson, P. D. (1991). Moving from the old to the new: Research on reading comprehension instruction. *Review of Educational Research, 61*(2), 239–64.

Durkin, D. (1961). Children who read before grade one. *The Reading Teacher, 14*, 163–66.

Durkin, D. (1978/1979). What classroom observations reveal about reading comprehension instruction. *Reading Research Quarterly, 14*(4), 481–533.

Fisher, B., & Medvic, E. F. (2003). *For reading out loud: Planning and practice*. Portsmouth, NH: Heinemann.

Fitzgerald, J., & Spiegel, D. L. (1983). Enhancing children's reading comprehension through instruction in narrative structure. *Journal of Reading Behavior, 15*(2), 1–17.

Fitzgerald, J., & Teasley, A. B. (1986). Effects of instruction in narrative structure on children's writing. *Journal of Educational Psychology, 78*(6), 424–32.

Freire, P. (2000). *Pedagogy of the oppressed* (30th anniversary ed.). New York: Continuum.

Golden, J. M., & Guthrie, J. T. (1986). Convergence and divergence in reader response to literature. *Reading Research Quarterly, 21*(4), 408–21.

Goldenberg, C. (1992/1993). Instructional conversations: Promoting comprehension through discussion. *The Reading Teacher, 46*(4), 316–26.

Goodman, K. (1985). Unity in reading. In H. Singer & R. B. Ruddell (Eds.), *Theoretical models and processes of reading* (3rd ed., pp. 813–40). Newark, DE: International Reading Association.

Goodman, K. S. (1967). Reading: A psycholinguistic guessing game. *Journal of the Reading Specialist, 6*(4), 126–35.

Graesser, A., Golding, J., & Long, D. (1991). Narrative representation and comprehension. In R. Barr, M. L. Kamil, P. Mosenthal, & P. D. Pearson (Eds.), *Handbook of reading research* (Vol. 2, pp. 171–205). White Plains, NY: Longman.

Graves, D. H. (1983). *Writing: Teachers and children at work*. Exeter, NH: Heinemann Educational Books.

Graves, D. H. (2003). *Writing: Teachers and children at work* (20th anniversary ed.). Portsmouth, NH: Heinemann.

Guthrie, J. T. (1973). Models of reading and reading disability. *Journal of Educational Psychology, 65*(3), 9–18.

Guthrie, J. T., Alverson, S., & Poundstone, C. (1999). Engaging students in reading. *Knowledge Quest, 27*(4), 8–16.

Hartman, D. K. (1995). Eight readers reading: The intertextual links of proficient readers reading multiple passages. *Reading Research Quarterly, 30*(3), 520–61.

Hefflin, B. R., & Hartman, D. K. (2002). Using writing to improve comprehension: A review of the writing-to-reading research. In C. C. Block, L. B. Gambrell, & M. Pressley (Eds.), *Improving comprehension instruction: Rethinking research, theory, and classroom practice* (pp. 199–228). San Francisco: Jossey-Bass.

Hepler, S. I., & Hickman, J. (1982). "The book was okay. I love you"—Social aspects of response to literature. *Theory into Practice, 21*(4), 278–83.

Higonnet, M. (1990). The playground of the peritext. *Children's Literature Association Quarterly, 15*(2), 47–49.

Huck, C. S., & Kiefer, B. Z. (2004). *Children's literature in the elementary school* (8th ed.). Boston: McGraw-Hill.

Hudelson, S. J., & Lindfors, J. W. (Eds.). (1993). *Delicate balances: Collaborative research in language education*. Urbana, IL: National Council of Teachers of English.

Keene, E. O. (2002). From good to memorable: Characteristics of highly effective comprehension teaching. In C. C. Block, L. B. Gambrell, & M. Pressley (Eds.). *Improving comprehension instruction: Rethinking research, theory, and classroom practice* (1st ed., pp. 80–105). San Francisco: Jossey-Bass.

Keene, E. O., & Zimmermann, S. (1997). *Mosaic of thought: Teaching comprehension in a reader's workshop*. Portsmouth, NH: Heinemann.

Kristeva, J. (1984). *Revolution in poetic language*. New York: Columbia University Press.

Kucan, L., & Beck, I. L. (1997). Thinking aloud and reading comprehension research: Inquiry, instruction, and social interaction. *Review of Educational Research, 67*(3), 271–99.

Langer, J. A. (1990). Understanding literature. *Language Arts, 67*(8), 812–16.

Langer, J. A. (1994). A response-based approach to reading literature. *Language Arts, 71*(3), 203–11.

Langer, J. A. (1995). *Envisioning literature: Literary understanding and literature instruction*. New York: Teachers College Press.

Langer, J. A. (1998). Thinking and doing literature: An eight-year study. *English Journal, 87*(2), 16–23.

Leland, C. H., & Harste, J. C. (2000). Critical literacy: Enlarging the space of the possible. *Primary Voices K–6, 9*(2), 3–7.

Leondar, B. (1977). Hatching plots: Genesis of storymaking. In D. N. Perkins & B. Leondar (Eds.), *The arts and cognition* (pp. 172–91). Baltimore: Johns Hopkins University Press.

Luke, A., & Freebody, P. (1997). Shaping the social practices of reading. In S. Muspratt, A. Luke, & P. Freebody (Eds.), *Constructing critical literacies* (pp. 185–225). Cresskill, NJ: Hampton Press.

Lukens, R. J. (2003). *A critical handbook of children's literature* (7th ed.). New York: Longman.

Mandler, J. M., & Johnson, N. S. (1977). Remembrance of things parsed: Story structure and recall. *Cognitive Psychology, 9*, 111–51.

McDaniel, C. (2004). Critical literacy: A questioning stance and the possibility for change. *The Reading Teacher, 57*(5), 472–81.

McGee, L. M. (1996). Response-centered talk: Windows on children's thinking. In L. Gambrell & J. F. Almasi (Eds.), *Lively discussions! Fostering engaged reading* (pp. 194–207). Newark, DE: International Reading Association.

Meyer, B. J. F., & Rice, G. E. (1984). The structure of text. In P. D. Pearson, R. Barr, M. L. Kamil, & P. Mosenthal (Eds.), *Handbook of reading research* (pp. 319–51). White Plains, NY: Longman.

Moss, J. F. (1982). Reading and discussing fairy tales—old and new. *The Reading Teacher, 35*(6), 656–60.

Moss, J. F. (1984). *Focus units in literature: A handbook for elementary school teachers*. Urbana, IL: National Council of Teachers of English.

Moss, J. F. (1990). *Focus on literature: A context for literacy learning*. Katonah, NY: R. C. Owen.

Moss, J. F. (1998). Literary discussion and the quest for meaning. *Teaching and Learning Literature with Children and Young Adults, 8*(1), 99–109.

Moss, J. F. (2000). *Teaching literature in the middle grades: A thematic approach* (2nd ed.). Norwood, MA: Christopher-Gordon.

Moss, J. F. (2002). *Literary discussion in the elementary school.* Urbana, IL: National Council of Teachers of English.

Moss, J. F., & Fenster, M. F. (2002). *From literature to literacy: Bridging learning in the library and the primary grade classroom.* Newark, DE: International Reading Association.

Nauman, A. D. (1990). Structure and perspective in reading and writing. In T. Shanahan (Ed.), *Reading and writing together: New perspectives for the classroom* (pp. 57–76). Norwood, MA: Christopher-Gordon.

Nystrand, M., & Gamoran, A. (1991). Instructional discourse, student engagement, and literature achievement. *Research in the Teaching of English, 25*(3), 261–90.

Ogle, D. M. (1986). K-W-L: A teaching model that develops active reading of expository text. *The Reading Teacher, 39*(6), 564–70.

Oster, L. (2001). Using the think-aloud for reading instruction. *The Reading Teacher, 55*(1), 64–69.

Paivio, A. (1971). *Imagery and verbal processes.* New York: Holt, Rinehart, and Winston.

Paivio, A. (1986). *Mental representations: A dual coding approach.* New York: Clarendon Press.

Palincsar, A. S., & Brown, A. L. (1984). Reciprocal teaching of comprehension-fostering and comprehension-monitoring activities. *Cognition and Instruction, 1*(2), 117–75.

Palincsar, A. S., & Brown, A. L. (1988). Teaching and practicing thinking skills to promote comprehension in the context of group problem solving. *Remedial and Special Education (RASE), 9*(1), 53–59.

Portalupi, J. (1999). Learning to write: Honoring both process and product. *Primary Voices K–6, 7,* 2–6.

Pressley, M., El-Dinary, P. B., Gaskins, I., Schuder, T., Bergman, J. L., Almasi, J., & Brown, R. (1992). Beyond direct explanation: Transactional instruction of reading comprehension strategies. *Elementary School Journal, 92*(5), 513–55.

Raphael, T. E., and McMahon, S. I. (1998). Book club: An alternative framework for reading instruction. *Reading Teacher, 48*(2), 102–16.

Ray, K. W. (1999). *Wondrous words: Writers and writing in the elementary classroom.* Urbana, IL: National Council of Teachers of English.

Ray, K. W. (2002). *What you know by heart: How to develop curriculum for your writing workshop.* Portsmouth, NH: Heinemann.

Ray, K. W., & Cleaveland, L. B. (2004). *About the authors: Writing workshop with our youngest writers*. Portsmouth, NH: Heinemann.

Ray, K. W., & Laminack, L. L. (2001). *The writing workshop: Working through the hard parts (and they're all hard parts)*. Urbana, IL: National Council of Teachers of English.

Reutzel, D. R., Camperell, K., & Smith, J. A. (2002). Hitting the wall: Helping struggling readers comprehend. In C. C. Block, L. B. Gambrell, & M. Pressley (Eds.), *Improving comprehension instruction: Rethinking research, theory, and classroom practice* (1st ed., pp. 321–53). San Francisco: Jossey-Bass.

Rosenblatt, L. M. (1978). *The reader, the text, the poem: The transactional theory of the literary work*. Carbondale: Southern Illinois University Press.

Rosenblatt, L. M. (1982). The literary transaction: Evocation and response. *Theory into Practice, 21*(4), 268–77.

Rosenblatt, L. M. (1991). Literature—S.O.S.! *Language Arts, 68*(6), 444–48.

Rosenshine, B. V. (1980). Skill hierarchies in reading comprehension. In R. J. Spiro, B. C. Bruce, & W. F. Brewer (Eds.), *Theoretical issues in reading comprehension: Perspectives from cognitive psychology, artificial intelligence, linguistics, and education* (pp. 535–54). Hillsdale, NJ: Erlbaum.

Routman, R. (1988). *Transitions: From literature to literacy* (1st ed.). Portsmouth, NH: Heinemann.

Routman, R. (1991). *Invitations: Changing as teachers and learners K–12*. Portsmouth, NH: Heinemann.

Rumelhart, D. E. (1976). *Toward an interactive model of reading*. La Jolla: Center for Human Information Processing, University of California, San Diego.

Rumelhart, D. E. (1980). Schemata: The building blocks of cognition. In R. J. Spiro, B. C. Bruce, & W. F. Brewer (Eds.), *Theoretical issues in reading comprehension: Perspectives from cognitive psychology, artificial intelligence, linguistics, and education* (pp. 33–58). Hillsdale, NJ: Erlbaum.

Serafini, F. (2004). *Lessons in comprehension: Explicit instruction in the reading workshop*. Portsmouth, NH: Heinemann.

Serafini, F., & Giorgis, C. (2003). *Reading aloud and beyond: Fostering the intellectual life with older readers*. Portsmouth, NH: Heinemann.

Shanahan, T. (1990). Reading and writing together: What does it really mean? In T. Shanahan (Ed.), *Reading and writing together: New perspectives for the classroom* (pp. 1–18). Norwood, MA: Christopher-Gordon.

Short, K. G. (1995). *Research and professional resources in children's literature: Piecing a patchwork quilt*. Newark, DE: International Reading Association.

Sipe, L. R. (2002). Talking back and taking over: Young children's expressive engagement during storybook read-alouds. *The Reading Teacher, 55*(5), 476–83.

Sipe, L. R. (2003). It's a matter of style: One teacher's storybook reading in an urban kindergarten. *The New Advocate, 16*(2), 161–70.

Smith, F. (1978). *Understanding reading: A psycholinguistic analysis of reading and learning to read* (2nd ed.). New York: Holt, Rinehart, and Winston.

Smith, F. (1982). *Writing and the writer.* New York: Holt, Rinehart, and Winston.

Smith, F. (1984). Reading like a writer. In J. M. Jensen (Ed.), *Composing and comprehending* (pp. 47–56). Urbana, IL: National Conference on Research in English, ERIC Clearinghouse on Reading and Communication Skills.

Smith, F. (1988). *Understanding reading: A psycholinguistic analysis of reading and learning to read* (4th ed.). Hillsdale, NJ: Erlbaum.

Smith, N. B. (1965). *American reading instruction: Its development and its significance in gaining a perspective on current practices in reading.* Newark, DE: International Reading Association.

Spiegel, D. L. (1998). Reader response approaches and the growth of readers. *Language Arts, 76*(1), 41–48.

Spiro, R. J. (1980). Constructive processes in prose comprehension. In R. J. Spiro, B. C. Bruce, & W. F. Brewer (Eds.), *Theoretical issues in reading comprehension: Perspectives from cognitive psychology, artificial intelligence, linguistics, and education* (pp. 245–78). Hillsdale, NJ: Erlbaum.

Staton, J. (1980). Writing and counseling: Using a dialogue journal. *Language Arts, 57*(5), 514–18.

Stauffer, R. G. (1970). *The language-experience approach to the teaching of reading.* New York: Harper & Row.

Stein, N. L. (1978). *How children understand stories: A developmental analysis* (Technical Rep. No. 69). Champaign: University of Illinois, Center for the Study of Reading. (ERIC, ED153205)

Stein, N. L., & Glenn, C. G. (1979). An analysis of story comprehension in elementary school children. In R. O. Freedle (Ed.), *New directions in discourse processing* (Vol. 2, pp. 53–120). Norwood, NJ: Ablex.

Stotsky, S. (1983). Research on reading/writing relationships: A synthesis and suggested directions. *Language Arts, 60*(5), 627–42.

Swift, K. (1993). Try reading workshop in your classroom. *The Reading Teacher, 46*(5), 366–71.

Vygotsky, L. S. (1978). *Mind in society: The development of higher psychological processes.* Cambridge, MA: Harvard University Press.

Walmsley, S. A. (1992). Reflections on the state of elementary literature instruction. *Language Arts, 69*(7), 508–14.

Wells, D. (1995). Leading grand conversations. In N. L. Roser & M. G. Martinez (Eds.), *Book talk and beyond: Children and teachers respond to literature* (pp. 132–39). Newark, DE: International Reading Association.

Whitehurst, G. J., Arnold, D. S., Epstein, J. N., Angell, A. L., Smith, M., & Fischel, J. E. (1994). A picture book reading intervention in day care and home for children from low-income families. *Developmental Psychology, 30*(5), 679–89.

Wolf, D. P. (1988). *Reading reconsidered: Literature and literacy in high school.* New York: College Entrance Examination Board.

Chapter 2

Professional References

Clyde, J. A. (2003). Stepping inside the story world: The subtext strategy—A tool for connecting and comprehending. *The Reading Teacher, 57*(2), 150–60.

Freire, P. (2000). *Pedagogy of the oppressed* (30th anniversary ed.). New York: Continuum.

Huck, C. S., & Kiefer, B. Z. (2004). *Children's literature in the elementary school* (8th ed). Boston: McGraw-Hill.

Langer, J. A. (1995). *Envisioning literature: Literary understanding and literature instruction.* New York: Teachers College Press.

Lukens, R. J. (2003). *A critical handbook of children's literature* (7th ed.). Boston: Allyn & Bacon.

Short, K. G., Harste, J. C., & Burke, C. (1996). *Creating classrooms for authors and inquirers* (2nd ed.). Portsmouth, NH: Heinemann.

Children's Books

Aardema, V. (1999). *Koi and the kola nuts: A tale from Liberia* (J. Cepeda, Illus.). New York: Atheneum Books for Young Readers.

Aesop & Lynch, T. (2000). *Fables from Aesop.* New York: Viking.

Aesop & Pinkney, J. (2000). *Aesop's fables.* New York: SeaStar Books.

Aylesworth, J. (1998). *The full belly bowl* (W. Halperin, Illus.). New York: Atheneum Books for Young Readers.

Aylesworth, J. (2003). *Goldilocks and the three bears* (B. McClintock, Illus.). New York: Scholastic Press.

Bahous, S. (1993). *Sitti and the cats: A tale of friendship* (N. Malick, Illus.). Niwot, CO: Roberts Rinehart.

Bloom, B. (2001). *Crackers* (P. Biet, Illus.). New York: Orchard Books.

Brett, J. (1987). *Goldilocks and the three bears.* New York: Dodd, Mead.

Cauley, L. B. (1981). *Goldilocks and the three bears.* New York: Putnam.

Daugherty, J. (1938). *Andy and the lion.* New York: Viking.

Daugherty, J. (1989). *Andy and the lion: A tale of kindness remembered or the power of gratitude.* New York: Puffin Books.

Donaldson, J. (2001). *Room on the broom* (A. Scheffler, Illus.). New York: Dial Books for Young Readers.

Eisen, A. (1987). *Goldilocks and the three bears* (L. B. Ferris, Illus.). New York: Ariel Books.

Ernst, L. C. (1998). *Stella Louella's runaway book.* New York: Simon & Schuster Books for Young Readers.

Ernst, L. C. (2000). *Goldilocks returns.* New York: Simon & Schuster Books for Young Readers.

Ezra, M. (1996). *The hungry otter* (G. Rowe, Illus.). New York: Crocodile Books.

Galdone, P. (1968). *Henny Penny.* New York: Seabury Press.

Galdone, P. (1970a). *Androcles and the lion.* New York: McGraw-Hill.

Galdone, P. (1970b). *The three little pigs.* New York: Clarion Books.

Galdone, P. (1972). *The three bears.* New York: Seabury Press.

Galdone, P. (1973a). *The little red hen.* New York: Seabury Press.

Galdone, P. (1973b). *The three billy goats Gruff.* New York: Seabury Press.

Galdone, P. (1974). *Little Red Riding Hood.* New York: McGraw-Hill.

Galdone, P. (1975). *The gingerbread boy.* New York: Seabury Press.

Galdone, P. (1976). *The magic porridge pot.* New York: Seabury Press.

Galdone, P. (1978). *Cinderella.* New York: McGraw-Hill.

Galdone, P. (1984). *The elves and the shoemaker.* New York: Clarion Books.

Galdone, P. (1985). *Rumpelstiltskin.* New York: Clarion Books.

Ginsburg, M. (1983). *The magic stove* (L. Heller, Illus.). New York: Coward, McCann & Geoghegan.

Godden, R. (1972). *The old woman who lived in a vinegar bottle* (M. Hedderwick, Illus.). New York: Viking.

Gorbachev, V. (2001). *Goldilocks and the three bears.* New York: North-South Books.

Grimm, J., Grimm, W., & Galdone, P. (1982). *Hansel and Gretel.* New York: McGraw-Hill.

Guthrie, D. (1993). *Nobiah's well: A modern African folktale* (R. Roth, Illus.). Nashville: Ideals Children's Books.

Herman, G., & Aesop. (1998). *The lion and the mouse* (L. McCue, Illus.). New York: Random House.

Herman, G., & Aesop. (2003). *The lion and the mouse* (L. McCue, Illus.). New York: Random House.

Hickox, R. (1998). *The golden sandal: A Middle Eastern Cinderella story* (W. Hillenbrand, Illus.). New York: Holiday House.

Jones, C. (1997). *The lion and the mouse.* Boston: Houghton Mifflin.

Kimmel, E. A. (1997). *Sirko and the wolf: A Ukrainian tale* (R. Sauber, Illus.). New York: Holiday House.

La Fontaine, J. de. (1963). *The lion and the rat: A fable* (B. Wildsmith, Illus.). New York: Watts.

La Fontaine, J. de. (1984). *The lion and the rat: A fable* (B. Wildsmith, Illus.). Oxford: Oxford University Press.

La Fontaine, J. de. (1999). *The lion and the rat: A fable* (B. Wildsmith, Illus.). Oxford: Oxford University Press.

Marshall, J. (1988). *Goldilocks and the three bears*. New York: Dial Books for Young Readers.

McPhail, D. (1995). *Goldilocks and the three bears*. New York: Scholastic.

Oppenheim, J. (1992). *One gift deserves another* (B. Zaunders, Illus.). New York: Dutton Children's Books.

Orgel, D., & Aesop. (2000). *The lion and the mouse: And other Aesop's fables* (B. Kitchen, Illus.). New York: Dorling Kindersley.

Paterson, K. (1998). *Celia and the sweet, sweet water* (V. Vagin, Illus.). New York: Clarion Books.

Peet, B. (1972). *The ant and the elephant*. Boston: Houghton Mifflin.

Petach, H. (1995). *Goldilocks and the three hares*. New York: Putnam & Grosset.

Reit, S. (1989). *The rebus bears* (K. Smith, Illus.). New York: Bantam Books.

Reit, S. (1997). *The rebus bears* (K. Smith, Illus.). Milwaukee: Gareth Stevens.

Renberg, D. H. (1994). *King Solomon and the bee* (R. Heller, Illus.). New York: HarperCollins.

Rosales, M. B. (1999). *Leola and the Honeybears: An African-American retelling of Goldilocks and the three bears*. New York: Scholastic.

Sanfield, S. (1996). *Just rewards, or, Who is that man in the moon and what's he doing up there anyway?* (E. Lisker, Illus.). New York: Orchard Books.

Sierra, J. (1997). *The mean hyena: A folktale from Malawi* (M. Bryant, Illus.). New York: Lodestar Books.

Sierra, J. (1999). *The dancing pig* (J. Sweetwater, Illus.). San Diego: Harcourt.

Smith, S. (2004). *Goldilocks and the three Martians* (M. Garland, Illus.). New York: Dutton Children's Books.

Stanley, D. (2003). *Goldie and the three bears*. New York: HarperCollins.

Steig, W. (1977). *Amos and Boris*. New York: Puffin Books.

Stevens, J. (1986). *Goldilocks and the three bears*. New York: Holiday House.

Turkle, B. (1976). *Deep in the forest*. New York: Dutton.

Watts, B. (1985). *Goldilocks and the three bears*. New York: North-South Books.

Watts, B., & Aesop. (2000). *The lion and the mouse: An Aesop fable*. New York: North-South Books.

Yolen, J. (1987). *The three bears rhyme book* (J. Dyer, Illus.). San Diego: Harcourt.

Chapter 3

Professional References

Dole, J. A., Duffy, G. G., Roehler, L. R., & Pearson, P. D. (1991). Moving from the old to the new: Research on reading comprehension instruction. *Review of Educational Research, 61*(2), 239–64.

Fitzgerald, J. (1983, April 11–15). *The relationship between reading ability and expectations for story structures.* Paper presented at the Annual Meeting of the American Educational Research Association, Montreal, Canada.

Hansen, J. (2001). *When writers read* (2nd ed.). Portsmouth, NH: Heinemann.

McConaughy, S. (1980). Using story structure in the classroom. *Language Arts, 57*(2), 157–65.

Nauman, A. D. (1990). Structure and perspective in reading and writing. In T. Shanahan (Ed.), *Reading and writing together: New perspectives for the classroom* (pp. 57–76). Norwood, MA: Christopher-Gordon.

Portalupi, J. (1999). Learning to write: Honoring both process and product. *Primary Voices K–6, 7,* 2–6.

Sadow, M. (1982). The use of story grammar in the design of questions. *The Reading Teacher, 35*(5), 518–22.

Smith, F. (1984). Reading like a writer. In J. M. Jensen (Ed.), *Composing and comprehending* (pp. 47–56). Urbana, IL: National Conference on Research in English, ERIC Clearinghouse on Reading and Communication Skills.

Stein, N. L., & Glenn, C. G. (1979). An analysis of story comprehension in elementary school children. In R. O. Freedle (Ed.), *New directions in discourse processing* (Vol. 2, pp. 53–120). Norwood, NJ: Ablex.

Wolf, S. A. (2004). *Interpreting literature with children.* Mahwah, NJ: Erlbaum.

Children's Books

Abercrombie, B. (1990). *Charlie Anderson* (M. Graham, Illus.). New York: McElderry Books.

Adamson, J. (1970). *Pippa, the cheetah, and her cubs.* New York: Harcourt.

Allen, J. (1992). *Tiger* (T. Humphries, Illus.). Cambridge, MA: Candlewick Press.

Arnold, C. (1993). *Cats: In from the wild* (R. Hewett, Illus.). Minneapolis: Carolrhoda Books.

Arnold, C. (1995). *Lion* (R. Hewett, Illus.). New York: Morrow Junior Books.

Arnold, C. (1999). *Cats* (R. Hewett, Illus.). Minneapolis: Lerner Publications.

Arnold, M. D., & Henterly, J. (1995). *Heart of a tiger*. New York: Dial Books for Young Readers.

Artell, M. (2001). *Petite Rouge: A Cajun Red Riding Hood* (J. Harris, Illus.). New York: Dial Books for Young Readers.

Bahous, S. (1993). *Sitti and the cats: A tale of friendship* (N. Malick, Illus.). Niwot, CO: Roberts Rinehart.

Baker, L. A. (1987). *The third-story cat*. Boston: Little, Brown.

Barber, A. (1990). *The mousehole cat* (N. Bayley, Illus.). New York: Macmillan.

Bateman, R., & Archbold, R. (1998). *Safari*. Boston: Little, Brown.

Beisner, M. (1990). *Catch that cat! A picture book of rhymes and puzzles*. New York: Farrar, Straus, and Giroux.

Bloom, B. (2001). *Crackers* (P. Biet, Illus.). New York: Orchard Books.

Brett, J. (1985). *Annie and the wild animals*. Boston: Houghton Mifflin.

Bryan, A. (1985). *The cat's purr*. New York: Atheneum.

Buck, P. S. (1971). *The Chinese story teller* (R. Shekerjian, Illus.). New York: John Day.

Calhoun, M. (1991). *High-wire Henry* (E. Ingraham, Illus.). New York: Morrow Junior Books.

Calhoun, M. (1994). *Henry the sailor cat* (E. Ingraham, Illus.). New York: Morrow Junior Books.

Calhoun, M. (1999). *Blue-ribbon Henry* (E. Ingraham, Illus.). New York: Morrow Junior Books.

Chancellor, D. (2000). *Tiger tales and big cat stories*. New York: Dorling Kindersley.

Choi, Y. (1998). *New cat*. New York: Frances Foster Books/Farrar, Straus, and Giroux.

Clements, A. (2002). *Dolores and the big fire: A true story* (E. Beier, Illus.). New York: Simon & Schuster.

Clutton-Brock, J. (1991). *Cat* (D. King, Illus.). New York: Knopf.

Coats, L. J. (1987). *Goodyear the city cat*. New York: Macmillan.

Cox, J. (2002). *Cool cat, school cat* (B. Sims, Illus.). New York: Holiday House.

Darling, K. (1998). *ABC cats* (T. Darling, Illus.). New York: Walker.

Dowson, N. (2004). *Tigress* (J. Chapman, Illus.). Cambridge, MA: Candlewick Press.

Egielski, R. (2001). *Slim and Jim*. New York: Laura Geringer Books/ HarperCollins.

Elzbieta. (1989). *Brave Babette and sly Tom*. New York: Dial Books for Young Readers.

Emberley, M. (1990). *Ruby*. Boston: Little, Brown.

Feder, J. (1982). *The life of a cat* (T. Michalski, Illus.). Chicago: Childrens Press International.

French, F. (1998). *Jamil's clever cat: A folk tale from Bengal* (D. Newby, Illus.). London: Frances Lincoln.

Galdone, P. (1976). *Puss in boots*. New York: Seabury Press.

George, J. C. (2000). *How to talk to your cat* (P. Meisel, Illus.). New York: HarperCollins.

Gibbons, G. (1996). *Cats*. New York: Holiday House.

Goode, D. (2001). *Tiger trouble!* New York: Blue Sky Press.

Grabianski, J. (1967). *Cats*. New York: Watts.

Hausman, G., & Hausman, L. (2000). *Cats of myth: Tales from around the world* (L. A. Baker, Illus.). New York: Simon & Schuster Books for Young Readers.

Hodges, M., & Hearn, L. (2002). *The boy who drew cats* (A. Sogabe, Illus.). New York: Holiday House.

Huling, J. (2002). *Puss in cowboy boots* (P. Huling, Illus.). New York: Simon & Schuster Books for Young Readers.

Hutchins, H. J. (2001). *One dark night* (S. K. Hartung, Illus.). New York: Viking.

Jeschke, S. (1987). *Lucky's choice*. New York: Scholastic.

Jones, C. (1997). *The lion and the mouse*. Boston: Houghton Mifflin.

Joosse, B. M. (1992). *Nobody's cat* (M. Sewell, Illus.). New York: HarperCollins.

Kellogg, S. (1981). *A Rose for Pinkerton*. New York: Dial Press.

Killilea, M. (1992). *Newf* (I. Schoenherr, Illus.). New York: Philomel Books.

Kimmel, E. A. (2003). *Three samurai cats: A story from Japan* (M. Gerstein, Illus.). New York: Holiday House.

King-Smith, D. (1989). *Martin's mice* (J. Alborough, Illus.). New York: Crown.

Lakin, P. (2002). *Clarence the copy cat* (J. Manders, Illus.). New York: Doubleday Books for Young Readers.

Lauber, P. (1998). *The true-or-false book of cats* (R. Schanzer, Illus.). Washington, DC: National Geographic Society.

Levine, A. A. (1994). *The boy who drew cats: A Japanese folktale* (F. Clément, Illus.). New York: Dial Books for Young Readers.

Light, S. (2002). *Puss in boots*. New York: Abrams.

Livingston, M. C. (1987). *Cat poems* (T. S. Hyman, Illus.). New York: Holiday House.

Lyon, G. E. (1998). *A traveling cat* (P. B. Johnson, Illus.). New York: Orchard Books.

MacDonald, M. R. (2001). *Mabela the clever* (T. Coffey, Illus.). Morton Grove, IL: Whitman.

Maitland, B. (1998). *The bookstore ghost* (N. B. Westcott, Illus.). New York: Dutton Children's Books.

Maitland, B. (2001). *The bookstore burglar* (N. B. Westcott, Illus.). New York: Dutton Children's Books.

Malkovych, I. (1995). *The cat and the rooster: A Ukrainian folktale* (K. Lavro, Illus., M. Onyschuk, Trans.). New York: Knopf.

Manning-Sanders, R. (1981). *A book of cats and creatures* (R. Jacques, Illus.). New York: Dutton Children's Books.

McCully, E. A. (2001). *Four hungry kittens*. New York: Dial Books for Young Readers.

McDonald, J. (1991). *Homebody* (K. W. Swanson, Illus.). New York: Putnam.

Micklethwait, L. (1995). *Spot a cat*. Boston: Houghton Mifflin.

Miles, M. (1969). *Nobody's cat* (J. Schoenherr, Illus.). Boston: Little, Brown.

Monson, A. M. (1997). *Wanted: Best friend* (L. Munsinger, Illus.). New York: Dial Books for Young Readers.

Oakley, G. (1972). *The church mouse*. New York: Atheneum.

Oakley, G. (1987). *The church mouse*. New York: Atheneum.

O'Neill, A. (1998). *Cats*. New York: Kingfisher.

Parsons, A. (1990). *Amazing cats* (J. Young, Illus.). New York: Knopf.

Patterson, F. (1985). *Koko's kitten*. New York: Scholastic.

Perrault, C. (1990). *Puss in boots* (F. Marcellino, Illus., M. Arthur, Trans.). New York: Farrar, Straus, and Giroux.

Purdy, C. (1994). *Mrs. Merriwether's musical cat* (P. Mathers, Illus.). New York: Putnam.

Richard, F., & Levine, A. A. (1994). *On cat mountain* (A. Buguet, Illus.). New York: Putnam's.

Robertus, P. M. (1991). *The dog who had kittens* (J. Stevens, Illus.). New York: Holiday House.

Rowland, D. (1989). *A world of cats* (J. Gurney & R. Himler, Illus.). Chicago: Contemporary Books.

San Souci, R. D., & Aulnoy, [M.-C.] d'. (1990). *The white cat: An old French fairy tale* (G. Spirin, Illus.). New York: Orchard Books.

Sara. (1991). *Across town*. New York: Orchard Books.

Schwartz, A. (1992). *Stories to tell a cat* (C. Huerta, Illus.). New York: HarperCollins.

Sepúlveda, L. (2003). *The story of the seagull and the cat who taught her to fly* (C. Sheban, Illus., M. S. Peden, Trans.). New York: Levine Books.

Simon, S. (1991). *Big cats*. New York: HarperCollins.

Stainton, S. (2004). *The lighthouse cat* (A. Mortimer, Illus.). New York: Katherine Tegen Books.

Steig, W. (1985). *Solomon: The rusty nail.* New York: Farrar, Straus, and Giroux.

Stevens, J. (1990). *How the Manx cat lost its tail.* San Diego: Harcourt.

Stone, L. M. (1989a). *The cheetah.* Vero Beach, FL: Rourke.

Stone, L. M. (1989b). *The cougar.* Vero Beach, FL: Rourke.

Stone, L. M. (1989c). *The leopard.* Vero Beach, FL: Rourke.

Stone, L. M. (1999a). *Bengal cats.* Vero Beach, FL: Rourke.

Stone, L. M. (1999b). *Siamese cats.* Vero Beach, FL: Rourke.

Titus, E. (1957). *Anatole and the cat* (P. Galdone, Illus.). New York: McGraw-Hill.

Titus, E. (1990). *Anatole and the cat* (P. Galdone, Illus.). New York: Bantam Books.

Turkle, B. (1981). *Do not open.* New York: Dutton.

Voake, C. (2003). *Ginger finds a home.* Cambridge, MA: Candlewick Press.

Weaver, T. (2002). *Opera cat* (A. Wesson, Illus.). New York: Clarion Books.

West, J., & Izen, M. (2004). *The dog who sang at the opera* (E. Oller, Illus.). New York: Abrams.

Wilcox, C. (1999). *The Newfoundland.* Mankata, MN: Capstone High/Low Books.

Winston, P. D. (1981). *Wild cats.* Washington, DC: National Geographic Society.

Woelfle, G. (2001). *Katje, the windmill cat* (N. Bayley, Illus.). Cambridge, MA: Candlewick Press.

Yeoman, J. (1976). *Mouse trouble: Story* (Q. Blake, Illus.). New York: Collier Books.

Yep, L. (1997). *The dragon prince: A Chinese Beauty and the beast* (K. Mak, Illus.). New York: HarperCollins.

Yoshida, T. (1989). *Young lions.* New York: Philomel Books.

Chapter 4

Professional References

Bromley, K. D. (1996). *Webbing with literature: Creating story maps with children's books* (2nd ed.). Boston: Allyn & Bacon.

Calkins, L. M. (1994). *The art of teaching writing* (New ed.). Portsmouth, NH: Heinemann.

Moss, J. F. (1996). *Teaching literature in the elementary school: A thematic approach.* Norwood, MA: Christopher-Gordon.

Children's Books

Ackerman, K. (1990). *The tin heart* (M. Hays, Illus.). New York: Atheneum.

Anholt, L. (1994). *Camille and the sunflowers: A story about Vincent van Gogh.* Hauppauge, NY: Barron's.

Armstrong, W. H. (1979). *The tale of Tawny and Dingo* (C. Mikolaycak, Illus.). New York: Harper & Row.

Barrett, M. B. (1994). *Sing to the stars* (S. Speidel, Illus.). Boston: Little, Brown.

Bauer, M. D. (2004). *The double-digit club.* New York: Holiday House.

Bluthenthal, D. C. (2003). *I'm not invited?* New York: Atheneum Books for Young Readers.

Bogacki, T. (2001). *Circus girl.* New York: Farrar, Straus, and Giroux.

Borton, L. (1997). *Junk pile!* (K. B. Root, Illus.). New York: Philomel Books.

Boyd, L. (1989). *Bailey, the big bully.* New York: Viking Kestrel.

Brimner, L. (1990). *Cory Coleman, grade 2* (K. Ritz, Illus.). New York: Holt.

Brinson, C. L. (2003). *Seeing sugar.* New York: Viking.

Bulla, C. R. (1975). *Shoeshine girl* (L. Grant, Illus.). New York: Crowell.

Bulla, C. R. (1987). *The chalk box kid* (T. B. Allen, Illus.). New York: Random House.

Bulla, C. R. (2000). *Shoeshine girl* (J. Burke, Illus.). New York: HarperTrophy.

Bunting, E. (1992). *Summer wheels* (T. B. Allen, Illus.). San Diego: Harcourt.

Calmenson, S., & Cole, J. (1997). *Rockin' reptiles* (L. Munsinger, Illus.). New York: Morrow Junior Books.

Champion, J. (1993). *Emily and Alice* (S. Stevenson, Illus.). San Diego: Harcourt.

Champion, J. (1995). *Emily and Alice again* (S. Stevenson, Illus.). San Diego: Gulliver Books.

Champion, J. (2001a). *Emily and Alice baby-sit Burton* (J. Parazette, Illus.). San Diego: Gulliver Books.

Champion, J. (2001b). *Emily and Alice, best friends* (S. Stevenson, Illus.). San Diego: Gulliver Books.

Chang, H. (1988). *Elaine, Mary Lewis, and the frogs.* New York: Crown Publishers.

Chang, H. (1991). *Elaine and the flying frog.* New York: Random House.

Christiansen, C. B. (1993). *Sycamore street* (M. Sweet, Illus.). New York: Atheneum.

Clements, A. (2001). *Jake Drake know-it-all* (D. Avendaño, Illus.). New York: Simon & Schuster Books for Young Readers.

Clifton, L. (1992). *Three wishes* (M. Hays, Illus.). New York: Doubleday Books for Young Readers.

Cole, J. (1989). *Bully trouble* (M. Hafner, Illus.). New York: Random House.

Cole, J. (2003). *Bully trouble* (M. Hafner, Illus.). New York: Random House.

Conford, E. (1991). *Can do, Jenny Archer* (D. Palmisciano, Illus.). Boston: Springboard Books.

Cooper, I. (2000). *Absolutely Lucy* (A. Harvey, Illus.). New York: Golden Books.

Coutant, H. (1983). *The gift* (D. M. Vo, Illus.). New York: Knopf.

Coxe, M. (1994). *The great snake escape*. New York: HarperCollins.

Cristaldi, K. (1994). *Samantha the snob* (D. Brunkus, Illus.). New York: Random House.

Cristaldi, K. (2003). *Samantha the snob* (D. Brunkus, Illus.). New York: Random House.

Crowley, M. (1993). *Shack and back* (A. Carter, Illus.). Boston: Little, Brown.

Danziger, P. (1994). *Amber Brown is not a crayon* (T. Ross, Illus.). New York: Putnam's.

Danziger, P. (1995). *Amber Brown goes fourth*. New York: Putnam's.

DePaolo, P. (1992). *Rosie and the yellow ribbon* (J. Wolf, Illus.). Boston: Joy Street Books.

Doyle, M. (2002). *Storm cats* (S. Trotter, Illus.). New York: McElderry Books.

Dugan, B. (1992). *Loop the loop* (J. Stevenson, Illus.). New York: Greenwillow Books.

Falwell, C. (2001). *David's drawings*. New York: Lee & Low Books.

Fleischman, S. (1988). *The scarebird* (P. Sís, Illus.). New York: Greenwillow Books.

Fleischman, S. (1994). *The scarebird* (P. Sís, Illus.). New York: Mulberry Books.

Foley, P. (1990). *John and the fiddler* (M. Sewall, Illus.). New York: Harper & Row.

Fowler, S. G. (2000). *Albertina, the animals, and me* (J. Fowler, Illus.). New York: Greenwillow Books.

Grimes, N. (1994). *Meet Danitra Brown* (F. Cooper, Illus.). New York: Lothrop, Lee & Shepard.

Havill, J. (1993). *Jamaica and Brianna* (A. S. O'Brien, Illus.). Boston: Houghton Mifflin.

Henkes, K. (1988). *Chester's way*. New York: Greenwillow Books.

Henkes, K. (1989). *Chester's way*. New York: Puffin Books.

Hesse, K. (1993). *Lester's dog* (N. Carpenter, Illus.). New York: Crown.

Hest, A. (1989). *The best-ever good-bye party* (D. DiSalvo-Ryan, Illus.). New York: Morrow Junior Books.

Hooks, W. H. (1995). *The girl who could fly* (K. de Kiefte, Illus.). New York: Macmillan Books for Young Readers.

Hurwitz, J. (1988). *Teacher's pet* (S. Hamanaka, Illus.). New York: Morrow Junior Books.

Jacobson, J. (2001). *Winnie (dancing) on her own* (A. I. Geis, Illus.). Boston: Houghton Mifflin.

Jacobson, J. (2003). *Truly Winnie* (A. I. Geis, Illus.). Boston: Houghton Mifflin.

Jahn-Clough, L. (2001). *Simon and Molly plus Hester*. Boston: Houghton Mifflin.

James, S. (1997). *Leon and Bob*. Cambridge, MA: Candlewick Press.

Johnston, T. (1993). *The last snow of winter* (F. Henstra, Illus.). New York: Tambourine Books.

Johnston, T. (1994). *Amber on the mountain* (R. Duncan, Illus.). New York: Dial Books for Young Readers.

Jones, R. C. (1991). *Matthew and Tilly* (B. Peck, Illus.). New York: Dutton Children's Books.

Kamen, G. (1988). *The ringdoves: From the fables of Bidpai*. New York: Atheneum.

Keller, H. (1987). *Lizzie's invitation*. New York: Greenwillow Books.

Keller, H. (1992). *Island baby*. New York: Greenwillow Books.

Keller, H. (1998). *Angela's top-secret computer club*. New York: Greenwillow Books.

Keller, H. (2002). *Farfallina and Marcel*. New York: Greenwillow Books.

Kellogg, S. (1986). *Best friends: Story and pictures*. New York: Dial Books for Young Readers.

Kherdian, D. (1991). *The great fishing contest* (N. Hogrogian, Illus.). New York: Philomel Books.

Kliphuis, C. (2002). *Robbie and Ronnie* (C. Dematons, Illus.). New York: North-South Books.

Kroll, V. L. (1994). *Pink paper swans* (N. L. Clouse, Illus.). Grand Rapids, MI: Eerdmans.

Lasky, K. (1991). *Fourth of July bear* (H. Cogancherry, Illus.). New York: Morrow Junior Books.

Lindgren, B. (1988). *A worm's tale* (C. Torudd, Illus., D. Jonasson, Trans.). New York: R & S Books.

Little, J. (1998). *Emma's magic winter* (J. Plecas, Illus.). New York: HarperCollins.

Luthardt, K. (2004). *Hats!* Morton Grove, IL: Whitman.

Lyon, G. E. (1989). *Together* (V. Rosenberry, Illus.). New York: Orchard Books.

Marsden, C. (2002). *The gold-threaded dress*. Cambridge, MA: Candlewick Press.

Marshall, J. (1988). *George and Martha 'round and 'round*. Boston: Houghton Mifflin.

Marzollo, J. (1988). *Red Ribbon Rosie* (B. Sims, Illus.). New York: Random House.

Mason, J. B. (2004). *If the shoe fits* (S. S. Hines, Illus.). New York: Scholastic.

McDonald, M. (1995). *Insects are my life* (P. B. Johnson, Illus.). New York: Orchard Books.

McLerran, A. (1991). *Roxaboxen* (B. Cooney, Illus.). New York: Lothrop, Lee & Shepard.

McMullan, K. (2003). *Pearl and Wagner: Two good friends* (R. W. Alley, Illus.). New York: Dial Books for Young Readers.

McPhail, D. (1990). *Lost*. Boston: Little, Brown.

McPhail, D. (2002). *Jack and Rick*. San Diego: Harcourt.

Moore, I. (1991). *Little dog lost*. New York: Macmillan.

Myers, L. (1994). *Guinea pigs don't talk* (C. Taylor, Illus.). New York: Clarion Books.

Nagda, A. W. (2000). *Dear Whiskers* (S. Roth, Illus.). New York: Holiday House.

Naylor, P. R. (1991). *King of the playground* (N. L. Malone, Illus.). New York: Atheneum.

Naylor, P. R. (1994). *King of the playground* (N. L. Malone, Illus.). New York: Aladdin Paperbacks.

O'Neill, A. (2002). *The recess queen* (L. Huliska-Beith, Illus.). New York: Scholastic.

Polacco, P. (1992). *Mrs. Katz and Tush*. New York: Bantam Books.

Priceman, M. (1989). *Friend or frog*. Boston: Houghton Mifflin.

Ransom, C. F. (1992). *Shooting star summer* (K. Milone, Illus.). Honesdale, PA: Caroline House, Boyds Mills Press.

Rascal. (1995). *Orson* (M. Ramos, Illus.). New York: Lothrop, Lee & Shepard.

Rathmann, P. (1991). *Ruby the copycat*. New York: Scholastic.

Robins, J. (1993). *Addie's bad day* (S. Truesdell, Illus.). New York: HarperCollins.

Rosen, M. J. (1992). *Elijah's angel: A story for Chanukah and Christmas* (A. B. L. Robinson, Illus.). San Diego: Harcourt.

Roth, R. (1998). *Fishing for Methuselah*. New York: HarperCollins.

Russo, M. (1992). *Alex is my friend*. New York: Greenwillow Books.

Ryden, H. (1994). *Backyard rescue* (T. Rand, Illus.). New York: Tambourine Books.

Sharmat, M. W., & Sharmat, M. (1989). *The pizza monster* (D. Brunkus, Illus.). New York: Delacorte.

Silverman, E. (1994). *Don't fidget a feather!* (S. D. Schindler, Illus.). New York: Macmillan.

Soto, G. (1992). *The skirt* (E. Velasquez, Illus.). New York: Delacorte Press.

Staunton, T. (1990). *Maggie and me*. New York: Viking.

Tsutsui, Y. (1987). *Anna's secret friend* (A. Hayashi, Illus.). Harmondsworth: Viking Kestrel.

Uchida, Y. (1993). *The bracelet* (J. Yardley, Illus.). New York: Philomel.

Van Draanen, W. (2004) *Shredderman: Secret identity* (B. Biggs, Illus.). New York: Knopf.

Van Leeuwen, J. (2000). *Oliver and Albert, friends forever* (A. Schweninger, Illus.). New York: Fogelman Books.

Vaughan, R. L. (2000). *Eagle boy: A Pacific Northwest native tale* (L. Christiansen, Illus.). Seattle: Sasquatch Books.

Waber, B. (1988). *Ira says goodbye*. Boston: Houghton Mifflin.

Weisman, J. (1993). *The storyteller* (D. Bradley, Illus.). New York: Rizzoli.

Weninger, B. (1999). *Why are you fighting, Davy?* (E. Tharlet, Illus., R. Lanning, Trans.). New York: North-South Books.

Wheeler, L. (2003). *New pig in town* (F. Ansley, Illus.). New York: Atheneum Books for Young Readers.

Wiles, D. (2001). *Freedom summer* (J. Lagarrigue, Illus.). New York: Atheneum Books for Young Readers.

Willner-Pardo, G. (1992). *Natalie Spitzer's turtles* (M. Delaney, Illus.). Morton Grove, IL: Whitman.

Winthrop, E. (1989). *The best friends club: A Lizzie and Harold story* (M. Weston, Illus.). New York: Lothrop, Lee & Shepard Books.

Yeoman, J. (1970). *The bear's water picnic* (Q. Blake, Illus.). New York: Macmillan.

Chapter 5

Professional Reference

Huck, C. S., & Kiefer, B. Z. (2004). *Children's literature in the elementary school* (8th ed.). Boston: McGraw-Hill.

Children's Books

Adler, D. A. (2002). *A hero and the Holocaust: The story of Janusz Korczak and his children* (B. Farnsworth, Illus.). New York: Holiday House.

Aller, S. B. (1997). *Emma and the night dogs* (M. Backer, Illus.). Morton Grove, IL: Whitman.

Asare, M. (2002). *Sosu's call*. La Jolla, CA: Kane/Miller.

Blake, R. J. (2002). *Togo*. New York: Philomel Books.

Brenner, B. (1977). *Little one inch* (F. Brenner, Illus.). New York: Coward, McCann & Geoghegan.

Bridges, R. (1999). *Through my eyes*. New York: Scholastic.

Byrd, R. (1999). *Finn MacCoul and his fearless wife: A giant of a tale from Ireland*. New York: Dutton Children's Books.

Clements, A. (2002). *Dolores and the big fire: A true story* (E. Beier, Illus.). New York: Simon & Schuster.

Cole, J. (1982). *Best-loved folktales of the world* (J. K. Schwarz, Illus.). Garden City, NY: Doubleday.

Coles, R. (1995). *The story of Ruby Bridges* (G. Ford, Illus.). New York: Scholastic.

Cooper, S. (1991). *Tam Lin* (W. Hutton, Illus.). New York: McElderry Books.

Crisman, R. (1993). *Racing the Iditarod Trail*. New York: Dillon Press.

Diakité, B. W. (2003). *The magic gourd*. New York: Scholastic.

Flowers, P., & Dixon, A. (2003). *Big-enough Anna: The little sled dog who braved the Arctic* (B. Farnsworth, Illus.). Anchorage: Alaska Northwest Books.

Gallico, P. (1992). *The snow goose* (B. Peck, Illus.). New York: Knopf.

Gardiner, J. R. (1980). *Stone fox* (M. Sewall, Illus.). New York: Crowell.

Gardiner, J. R. (2003). *Stone fox* (G. Hargreaves, Illus.). New York: HarperTrophy.

Gibbons, G. (1990). *Beacons of light: Lighthouses*. New York: Morrow Junior Books.

Gold, A. L. (2000). *A special fate: Chiune Sugihara, hero of the Holocaust*. New York: Scholastic.

Greenfield, E. (1973). *Rosa Parks* (E. Marlow, Illus.). New York: Crowell.

Greenfield, E. (1996). *Rosa Parks* (G. Ashby, Illus.). New York: HarperCollins.

Guthrie, D. (1993). *Nobiah's well: A modern African folktale* (R. Roth, Illus.). Nashville: Ideals Children's Books.

Hall, L. (1973). *Barry, the bravest Saint Bernard* (G. Cohen, Illus.). Champaign, IL: Garrard.

Hall, L. (1992). *Barry, the bravest Saint Bernard* (A. Castro, Illus.). New York: Random House.

Hayes, S. (1989). *Robin Hood* (P. Benson, Illus.). New York: Holt.

Helldorfer, M.-C. (1991). *The mapmaker's daughter* (J. Hunt, Illus.). New York: Bradbury Press.

Hesse, K. (2004). *The cats in Krasinski Square* (W. Watson, Illus.). New York: Scholastic.

Hodges, M. (1990). *The kitchen knight: A tale of King Arthur* (T. S. Hyman, Illus.). New York: Holiday House.

Hodges, M. (1993). *The hero of Bremen* (C. Mikolaycak, Illus.). New York: Holiday House.

Hopkinson, D. (1997). *Birdie's lighthouse* (K. B. Root, Illus.). New York: Atheneum Books for Young Readers.

Hughes, M. (1992). *Little Fingerling: A Japanese folktale* (B. Clark, Illus.). Nashville: Ideals Children's Books.

Innocenti, R., & Gallaz, C. (1985). *Rose Blanche* (American ed.). Mankato, MN: Creative Education.

Innocenti, R., & Gallaz, C. (1996). *Rose Blanche.* San Diego: Creative Editions/ Harcourt.

Isaacs, A. (1994). *Swamp Angel* (P. O. Zelinsky, Illus.). New York: Dutton Children's Books.

Ishii, M. (1967). *Issun Boshi, the inchling: An old tale of Japan* (F. Akino, Illus., K. Paterson, Trans.). New York: Walker.

Jackson, D. M. (2003). *Hero dogs: Courageous canines in action.* New York: Little, Brown.

Kellogg, S. (1984). *Paul Bunyan, a tall tale.* New York: Morrow.

Kimmel, E. A. (1992a). *Boots and his brothers: A Norwegian tale* (K. B. Root, Illus.). New York: Holiday House.

Kimmel, E. A. (1992b). *The four gallant sisters* (T. Yuditskaya, Illus.). New York: Holt.

Kimmel, E. A. (1995). *Rimonah of the flashing sword: A North African tale* (O. Rayyan, Illus.). New York: Holiday House.

Kimmel, E. C. (1999). *Balto and the great race* (N. Koerber, Illus.). New York: Random House.

Korschunow, I. (1984). *The foundling fox: How the little fox got a mother* (R. Michl, Illus.). New York: Harper & Row.

Kramer, S. (1993). *Adventure in Alaska: An amazing true story of the world's longest, toughest dog sled race* (K. Meyer, Illus.). New York: Bullseye Books.

Kroll, V. L. (2003). *Especially heroes* (T. Ladwig, Illus.). Grand Rapids, MI: Eerdmans Books for Young Readers.

Le Guin, U. K. (1992). *A ride on the red mare's back* (J. Downing, Illus.). New York: Orchard Books.

Lester, J. (1994). *John Henry* (J. Pinkney, Illus.). New York: Dial Books.

Littlesugar, A. (2001). *Freedom school, yes!* (F. Cooper, Illus.). New York: Philomel Books.

Lucas, E. (1997). *Cracking the wall: The struggles of the Little Rock Nine* (M. Anthony, Illus.). Minneapolis: Carolrhoda Books.

Lunn, J. L. S. (2001). *Laura Secord: A story of courage* (M. Newhouse, Illus.). Plattsburgh, NY: Tundra Books.

MacGill-Callahan, S. (1997). *To capture the wind* (G. Manchess, Illus.). New York: Dial Books for Young Readers.

Manning-Sanders, R. (1982). *A book of heroes and heroines* (R. Jacques, Illus.). London: Methuen Children's Books.

Martin, R. (1998). *The brave little parrot* (S. Gaber, Illus.). New York: Putnam's.

McCarthy, R. F. (1993). *The inch-high samurai* (S. Kasamatsu, Illus.). Tokyo: Kodansha International.

McCully, E. A. (1996). *The ballot box battle*. New York: Knopf.

McCully, E. A. (1998). *Beautiful warrior: The legend of the nun's kung fu* (2nd ed.). New York: Levine Books.

McCully, E. A. (2002). *The battle for St. Michaels*. New York: HarperCollins.

Miller, D. S. (2002). *The great serum race: Blazing the Iditarod Trail* (J. Van Zyle, Illus.). New York: Walker.

Minahan, J. A. (1995). *Abigail's drum* (R. M. Quackenbush, Illus.). New York: Pippin Press.

Mochizuki, K. (1997). *Passage to freedom: The Sugihara story* (D. Lee, Illus.). New York: Lee & Low Books.

Morimoto, J. (1986). *The inch boy*. New York: Viking Kestrel.

Nolen, J. (2000). *Big Jabe* (K. Nelson, Illus.). New York: Lothrop, Lee & Shepard Books.

Olson, A. N. (1987). *The lighthouse keeper's daughter* (E. Wentworth, Illus.). Boston: Little, Brown.

Oppenheim, S. L. (1992). *The lily cupboard* (R. Himler, Illus.). New York: HarperCollins.

Osborne, M. P. (1991). *American tall tales* (M. McCurdy, Illus.). New York: Knopf.

Osborne, M. P. (2002). *New York's bravest* (S. Johnson & L. Fancher, Illus.). New York: Knopf.

O'Shea, P. (1987). *Finn Mac Cool and the small men of deeds* (S. Lavis, Illus.). New York: Holiday House.

Park, L. S. (2003). *The firekeeper's son* (J. Downing, Illus.). New York: Clarion Books.

Paul, A. W. (1999). *All by herself: 14 girls who made a difference: Poems* (M. Steirnagle, Illus.). San Diego: Browndeer Press/Harcourt.

Perrow, A. (2000). *Lighthouse dog to the rescue* (E. Harris, Illus.). Camden, ME: Down East Books.

Perrow, A. (2003). *Lighthouse dog to the rescue* (E. Harris, Illus.). Camden, ME: Down East Books.

Polacco, P. (2000). *The butterfly*. New York: Philomel Books.

Porazinska, J. (1987). *The enchanted book: A tale from Krakow* (J. Brett, Illus., B. Smith, Trans.). San Diego: Harcourt.

Quayle, E. (1989). *The shining princess and other Japanese legends* (M. Foreman, Illus.). New York: Arcade.

Ringgold, F. (1999). *If a bus could talk: The story of Rosa Parks*. New York: Simon & Schuster Books for Young People.

Riordan, J. (1980). *The three magic gifts* (E. Le Cain, Illus.). New York: Oxford University Press.

Rogasky, B. (1986). *The water of life: A tale from the Brothers Grimm* (T. S. Hyman, Illus.). New York: Holiday House.

Roop, P., & Roop, C. (1985). *Keep the lights burning, Abbie* (P. E. Hanson, Illus.). Minneapolis: Carolrhoda Books.

San Souci, R. D. (1992). *The samurai's daughter: A Japanese legend* (S. Johnson, Illus.). New York: Dial Books for Young Readers.

San Souci, R. D. (1993). *Cut from the same cloth: American women of myth, legend, and tall tale* (J. B. Pinkney, Illus., J. Yolen, Intro.). New York: Philomel Books.

San Souci, R. D. (1995). *Kate Shelley: Bound for legend*. New York: Dial.

San Souci, R. D. (1998). *Fa Mulan: The story of a woman warrior* (J. Tseng & M.-S. Tseng, Illus.). New York: Hyperion Books for Children.

San Souci, R. D. (1998a). *A weave of words: An Armenian tale* (R. Colón, Illus.). New York: Orchard Books.

San Souci, R. D. (1999). *Brave Margaret: An Irish adventure* (S. W. Comport, Illus.). New York: Simon & Schuster Books for Young Readers.

San Souci, R. D. (2002). *The twins and the Bird of Darkness: A hero tale from the Caribbean* (T. Widener, Illus.). New York: Simon & Schuster Books for Young Readers.

Sanderson, R. (2001). *The Golden Mare, the Firebird, and the magic ring*. Boston: Little, Brown.

Sanfield, S. (1989). *The adventures of High John the Conqueror* (J. Ward, Illus.). New York: Orchard Books.

Sanfield, S. (1995). *The adventures of High John the Conqueror* (J. Ward, Illus.). Little Rock: August House.

Saxby, M. (1992). *The great deeds of heroic women* (R. Ingpen, Illus.). New York: Bedrick Books.

Sherman, J. (1988). *Vassilisa the wise: A tale of medieval Russia* (D. San Souci, Illus). Boston: Houghton Mifflin.

Shute, L. (1986). *Momotaro, the peach boy: A traditional Japanese tale*. New York: Lothrop, Lee & Shepard Books.

Souhami, J. (2002). *Mrs. McCool and the giant Cuhullin: An Irish tale*. New York: Holt.

Standiford, N. (1989). *The bravest dog ever: The true story of Balto* (D. Cook, Illus.). New York: Random House.

Standiford, N. (2003). *The bravest dog ever: The true story of Balto* (D. Cook, Illus.). New York: Random House.

Steptoe, J. (1984). *The story of Jumping Mouse: A Native American legend*. New York: Lothrop, Lee & Shepard Books.

Talbott, H. (1991). *The sword in the stone*. New York: Morrow Junior Books.

Talbott, H. (1995). *King Arthur and the Round Table*. New York: Morrow Junior Books.

Tchana, K. (2002). *Sense Pass King: A story from Cameroon* (T. S. Hyman, Illus.). New York: Holiday House.

Torre, B. L (1990). *The luminous pearl: A Chinese folktale* (C. Inouye, Illus.). New York: Orchard Books.

Towle, F. M. (1975). *The magic cooking pot: A folktale of India*. Boston: Houghton Mifflin.

Valgardson, W. D. (1995). *Winter rescue* (A. Zhang, Illus.). New York: McElderry Books.

Wang, R. C. (1991). *The fourth question: A Chinese tale* (J.-H. Chen, Illus.). New York: Holiday House.

Wetterer, M. K. (1990). *Kate Shelley and the midnight express* (K. Ritz, Illus.). Minneapolis: Carolrhoda Books.

Wetterer, M. K. (1991). *The boy who knew the language of the birds* (B. Wright, Illus.). Minneapolis: Carolrhoda Books.

Wood, T. (1996). *Iditarod dream: Dusty and his sled dogs compete in Alaska's Jr. Iditarod*. New York: Walker.

Yolen, J. (1989). *Dove Isabeau* (D. Nolan, Illus.). San Diego: Harcourt.

Yolen, J. (1990). *Tam Lin: An old ballad* (C. Mikolaycak, Illus.). San Diego: Harcourt.

Yolen, J. (1995). *Merlin and the dragons* (M. Li, Illus.). New York: Cobblehill Books, Dutton.

Young, E. (1989). *Lon Po Po: A Red-Riding Hood story from China*. New York: Philomel Books.

Zeman, L. (2003). *Sindbad's secret*. Toronto: Tundra Books.

Chapter 6

Professional References

Campbell, J. (1968). *The hero with a thousand faces* (2nd ed.). Princeton, NJ: Princeton University Press.

Frye, N. (1964). *The educated imagination*. Bloomington: Indiana University Press.

Huck, C. S., & Kiefer, B. Z. (2004). *Children's literature in the elementary school* (8th ed.). Boston: McGraw-Hill.

Lukens, R. J. (2003). *A critical handbook of children's literature* (7th ed.). Boston: Allyn & Bacon.

Roberts, W. E. (1994). *The tale of the kind and the unkind girls: AA-TH 480 and related titles*. Detroit: Wayne State University Press.

Smith, F. (1984). Reading like a writer. In J. M. Jensen (Ed.), *Composing and comprehending* (pp. 47–56). Urbana, IL: National Conference on Research in English, ERIC Clearinghouse on Reading and Communication Skills.

Yolen, J. (2000). *Touch magic: Fantasy, faerie and folklore in the literature of childhood* (Expanded ed.). Little Rock: August House.

Children's Books

Ada, A. F. (1991). *The gold coin* (N. Waldman, Illus.). New York: Atheneum.

Ada, A. F. (1994). *The gold coin* (N. Waldman, Illus.). New York: Aladdin Books.

Aiken, J. (1968). *A necklace of raindrops and other stories* (J. Pienkowski, Illus.). Garden City, NY: Doubleday.

Aiken, J. (1978). *Tale of a one-way street and other stories* (J. Pienkowski, Illus.). London: J. Cape.

Aiken, J. (2001). *A necklace of raindrops and other stories* (K. Hawkes, Illus.). New York: Knopf.

Aksakov, S. T. (1989). *The scarlet flower: A Russian folk tale* (B. Diodorov, Illus., I. Levine, Trans.). San Diego: Harcourt.

Araujo, F. P. (1994). *The perfect orange: A tale from Ethiopia* (X. J. Li, Illus.). Windsor, CA: Rayve.

Babbitt, N. (1998). *Ouch! A tale from Grimm* (F. Marcellino, Illus.). New York: HarperCollins.

Bahous, S. (1993). *Sitti and the cats: A tale of friendship* (N. Malick, Illus.). Niwot, CO: Roberts Rinehart.

Bang, M. (1981). *Tye May and the magic brush*. New York: Greenwillow Books.

Bass, L. G., Grimm, J., & Grimm, W. (1994). *The seven ravens* (E. S. Gazsi, Illus.). New York: HarperCollins.

Bender, R., & Perrault, C. (1995). *Toads and diamonds*. New York: Lodestar Books.

Berenzy, A. (1989). *A frog prince*. New York: Holt.

Biddle, S., & Biddle, M. (1994). *The crane's gift: A Japanese folktale*. Boston: Barefoot Books.

Bodkin, O. (1998). *The crane wife* (G. Spirin, Illus.). San Diego: Harcourt.

Brett, J. (1989). *Beauty and the beast*. New York: Clarion Books.

Brooke, W. J. (1993). *A brush with magic: Based on a traditional Chinese story* (M. Koelsch, Illus.). New York: HarperCollins Children's Books.

Climo, S. (1994). *Stolen thunder: A Norse myth* (A. Koshkin, Illus.). New York: Clarion Books.

Climo, S. (1995). *Atalanta's race: A Greek myth* (A. Koshkin, Illus.). New York: Clarion Books.

Coburn, J. R. (1998). *Angkat: The Cambodian Cinderella* (E. Flotte, Illus.). Fremont, CA: Shen's Books.

Coburn, J. R., & Lee, T. C. (1996). *Jouanah, a Hmong Cinderella* (A. S. O'Brien, Illus.). Arcadia, CA: Shen's Books.

Coville, B. (1992). *Jennifer Murdley's toad* (G. A. Lippincott, Illus.). San Diego: Harcourt.

Coville, B. (2002). *Jennifer Murdley's toad* (G. A. Lippincott, Illus.). San Diego: Harcourt.

Craft, C. (1999). *King Midas and the golden touch* (K. Craft, Illus.). New York: Morrow Junior Books.

Craig, M. J. (1977). *The donkey prince* (B. Cooney, Illus.). Garden City, NY: Doubleday.

Dasent, G. W. (1992). *East o' the sun and west o' the moon* (P. J. Lynch, Illus.). Cambridge, MA: Candlewick Press.

Demi. (1980). *Liang and the magic paintbrush*. New York: Holt, Rinehart, and Winston.

Demi. (1987). *Chen Ping and his magic axe*. New York: Dodd, Mead.

Demi. (1990). *The magic boat*. New York: Holt.

Diakité, B. W. (2003). *The magic gourd*. New York: Scholastic.

Domanska, J. (1967). *Palmiero and the ogre*. New York: Macmillan.

Dugin, A. (1993). *Dragon feathers* (O. Dugina, Illus.). Charlottesville, VA: Thomasson-Grant.

Erickson, R. E. (1998). *A toad for Tuesday* (L. Di Fiori, Illus.). New York: Beech Tree.

Gerstein, M. (1984). *Prince Sparrow*. New York: Four Winds Press.

Ginsburg, M. (1983). *The magic stove* (L. Heller, Illus.). New York: Coward, McCann & Geoghegan.

Grimm, J., & Grimm, W. (1989). *The Frog Prince, or, Iron Henry* (B. Schroeder, Illus., N. Lewis, Trans.). New York: North-South Books.

Grimm, J., & Grimm, W. (1996). *Little brother and little sister: A fairy tale* (B. Watts, Illus., A. Bell, Trans.). New York: North-South Books.

Hastings, S. (1988). *The singing ringing tree* (L. Brierley, Illus.). New York: Holt.

Helldorfer, M.-C. (1991). *The mapmaker's daughter* (J. Hunt, Illus.). New York: Bradbury Press.

Helldorfer, M.-C. (1993). *Cabbage Rose* (J. Downing, Illus.). New York: Bradbury Press.

Hewitt, K., & Hawthorne, N. (1987). *King Midas and the golden touch*. San Diego: Harcourt.

Heyer, M. (1986). *The weaving of a dream: A Chinese folktale*. New York: Viking Kestrel.

Heyer, M. (1995). *The girl, the fish and the crown: A Spanish folktale*. New York: Viking.

Heymsfeld, C. (2001). *The narwhal's tusk* (X. Li, Illus.). Los Altos, CA: Owl's House Press.

Hieatt, C. B. (1967). *Sir Gawain and the Green Knight* (W. H. Lorraine, Illus.). New York: Crowell.

Hodges, M. (1972). *The Gorgon's head: A myth from the isles of Greece* (C. Mikolaycak, Illus.). Boston: Little, Brown.

Hogrogian, N. (1983). *The devil with the three golden hairs: A tale from the Brothers Grimm*. New York: Knopf.

Hogrogian, N. (1985). *The glass mountain*. New York: Knopf.

Hooks, W. H. (1987). *Moss gown* (D. Carrick, Illus.). New York: Clarion Books.

Hooks, W. H. (1994). *Snowbear Whittington, an Appalachian Beauty and the beast* (V. Lisi, Illus.). New York: Macmillan.

Hopkins, J. (2000). *The horned toad prince* (M. Austin, Illus.). Atlanta: Peachtree.

Huck, C. S. (1995). *Toads and diamonds* (A. Lobel, Illus.). New York: Greenwillow Books.

Huck, C. S. (2001). *The black bull of Norroway: A Scottish tale* (A. Lobel, Illus.). New York: Greenwillow Books.

Hughes, S. (2004). *Ella's big chance: A Jazz-age Cinderella*. New York: Simon & Schuster Books for Young Readers.

Hunter, M. (1994). *Gilly Martin the fox* (D. McDermott, Illus.). New York: Hyperion Books for Children.

Hutton, W. (1981). *The nose tree*. New York: Atheneum.

Hutton, W. (1993). *Perseus*. New York: McElderry Books.

Isele, E. (1984). *The frog princess* (M. Hague, Illus.). New York: Crowell.

Ishii, M. (1987). *The tongue-cut sparrow* (S. Akaba, Illus.). New York: Lodestar Books.

Jackson, E. B. (1994). *Cinder Edna* (K. O'Malley, Illus.). New York: Lothrop, Lee & Shepard.

Johnston, T. (1995). *Alice Nizzy Nazzy: The witch of Santa Fe* (T. De Paola, Illus.). New York: Scholastic.

Kherdian, D. (1997a). *The golden bracelet* (N. Hogrogian, Illus.). New York: Holiday House.

Kherdian, D. (1997b). *The rose's smile: Farizad of the Arabian nights* (S. Vitale, Illus.). New York: Holt.

Kimmel, E. A. (1991). *Baba Yaga: A Russian folktale* (M. Lloyd, Illus.). New York: Holiday House.

Kimmel, E. A. (1992a). *Boots and his brothers: A Norwegian tale* (K. B. Root, Illus.). New York: Holiday House.

Kimmel, E. A. (1992b). *The four gallant sisters* (T. Yuditskaya, Illus.). New York: Holt.

Kimmel, E. A. (1994). *I-know-not-what, I-know-not-where: A Russian tale* (R. Sauber, Illus.). New York: Holiday House.

Kimmel, E. A., Grimm, J., & Grimm, W. (1994). *The goose girl: A story from the Brothers Grimm* (R. Sauber, Illus.). New York: Holiday House.

King-Smith, D. (2001). *Lady Lollipop* (J. Barton, Illus.). Cambridge, MA: Candlewick Press.

Kismaric, C. (1988). *The rumor of Pavel and Paali: A Ukrainian folktale* (C. Mikolaycak, Illus.). New York: Harper & Row.

Lang, A. (1981). *Aladdin and the wonderful lamp* (E. Le Cain, Illus.). New York: Viking.

Langton, J. (1985). *The hedgehog boy: A Latvian folktale* (I. Plume, Illus.). New York: Harper & Row.

Laroche, S., & Laroche, M. (1986). *The snow rose*. New York: Holiday House.

Levitin, S. (1982). *The fisherman and the bird* (F. Livingston, Illus.). Oakland, CA: Parnassus Press.

Littledale, F. (1988). *Peter and the North Wind* (T. Howell, Illus.). New York: Scholastic.

MacGill-Callahan, S. (1993). *The children of Lir* (G. Spirin, Illus.). New York: Dial Books.

MacGill-Callahan, S. (1997). *To capture the wind* (G. Manchess, Illus.). New York: Dial Books for Young Readers.

Marmur, M. (1960). *Japanese fairy tales*. New York: Golden Press.

Marshak, S. (1983). *The Month-Brothers: A Slavic tale* (D. Stanley, Illus., T. P. Whitney, Trans.). New York: Morrow.

Martin, R. (1998). *The brave little parrot* (S. Gaber, Illus.). New York: Putnam's.

Martin, R. (2000). *The language of birds* (S. Gaber, Illus.). New York: Putnam's.

Martin, R. (2005). *Birdwing* (D. Bellm, Trans.). New York: Arthur A. Levine Books.

Mayer, M. (1988). *Iduna and the magic apples* (L. Gál, Illus.). New York: Macmillan.

Mayer, M. (1990). *The spirit of the blue light* (L. Gál, Illus.). New York: Macmillan.

Mayer, M. (1997). *Pegasus* (K. Craft, Illus.). New York: Morrow Junior Books.

Mayer, M. (2002). *Perseus* (J. Spector, Illus.). New York: Fogelman Books.

Meddaugh, S. (1997). *Cinderella's rat*. Boston: Houghton Mifflin.

Melmed, L. K. (1994). *Prince Nautilus* (H. Sorensen, Illus.). New York: Lothrop, Lee & Shepard.

Mills, L. A. (2001). *The dog prince: An original fairy tale* (D. Nolan, Illus.). Boston: Little, Brown.

Muller, R. (1990). *The magic paintbrush.* New York: Viking Kestrel.

Muth, J. J. (2003). *Stone soup.* New York: Scholastic.

Newton, P. M. (1982). *The five sparrows: A Japanese folktale.* New York: Atheneum.

Nones, E. J. (1991). *The canary prince.* New York: Farrar, Straus, and Giroux.

Ogburn, J. K. (2000). *The magic nesting doll* (L. Long, Illus.). New York: Dial Books.

Paterson, K. (1992). *The king's equal* (V. V. Vagin, Illus.). New York: HarperCollins.

Paterson, K. (1999). *The king's equal* (C. Woodbridge, Illus.). New York: HarperTrophy.

Pyle, H. (1997). *Bearskin* (T. S. Hyman, Illus.). New York: Morrow Junior Books.

Rayevsky, I. (1990). *The talking tree: An old Italian tale* (R. Rayevsky, Illus.). New York: Putnam.

Richard, F., & Levine, A. A. (1994). *On cat mountain* (A. Buguet, Illus.). New York: Putnam's.

Riordan, J. (1980). *The three magic gifts* (E. Le Cain, Illus.). New York: Oxford University Press.

Rogasky, B., & Grimm, J. (1986). *The water of life: A tale from the Brothers Grimm* (T. S. Hyman, Illus.). New York: Holiday House.

Sadler, C. E. (1982). *Treasure mountain: Folktales from southern China* (J. Cheng, Illus.). New York: Atheneum.

San Souci, R. D. (1987). *The enchanted tapestry—A Chinese tale* (L. Gál, Illus.). New York: Dutton Children's Books.

San Souci, R. D. (1988). *Robert D. San Souci's the six swans* (D. San Souci, Illus.). New York: Simon & Schuster Books for Young Readers.

San Souci, R. D. (1989). *The talking eggs: A folktale from the American South* (J. Pinkney, Illus.). New York: Dial Books for Young Readers.

San Souci, R. D. (1992). *The samurai's daughter: A Japanese legend* (S. Johnson, Illus.). New York: Dial Books for Young Readers.

San Souci, R. D. (1998). *A weave of words: An Armenian tale* (R. Colón, Illus.). New York: Orchard Books.

San Souci, R. D. (2002a). *The silver charm: A folktale from Japan* (Y. Ito, Illus.). New York: Doubleday Books for Young Readers.

San Souci, R. D. (2002b). *The twins and the Bird of Darkness: A hero tale from the Caribbean* (T. Widener, Illus.). New York: Simon & Schuster Books for Young Readers.

San Souci, R. D. (2004). *The well at the end of the world* (R. Walsh, Illus.). San Francisco: Chronicle Books.

San Souci, R. D., & Aulnoy, [M.-C.] d'. (1990). *The white cat: An old French fairy tale* (G. Spirin, Illus.). New York: Orchard Books.

Sanderson, R. (1991). *The enchanted wood: An original fairy tale*. Boston: Little, Brown.

Sanderson, R. (1995). *Papa Gatto: An Italian fairy tale*. Boston: Little, Brown.

Sanderson, R. (1999). *The crystal mountain*. Boston: Little, Brown.

Sanfield, S. (1996). *Just rewards, or, Who is that man in the moon and what's he doing up there anyway?* (E. Lisker, Illus.). New York: Orchard Books.

Schroeder, A. (1994). *The stone lion* (T. L. W. Doney, Illus.). New York: Scribner's.

Scott, S. (1985). *The magic horse*. New York: Greenwillow Books.

Scott, S. (1987). *The three wonderful beggars*. New York: Greenwillow Books.

Sendak, M. (1963). *Where the wild things are*. New York: Harper & Row.

Sendak, M. (1988). *Where the wild things are* (25th anniversary ed.). New York: HarperCollins.

Singer, M. (1991). *The Golden Heart of winter* (R. Rayevsky, Illus.). New York: Morrow Junior Books.

Snyder, Z. K. (1992). *The changing maze* (C. Mikolaycak, Illus.). New York: Aladdin Books.

Spirin, G. (2002). *The tale of the Firebird*. New York: Philomel Books.

Stanley, D. (1990). *Fortune*. New York: Morrow Junior Books.

Stanley, D. (1997). *Rumpelstiltskin's daughter*. New York: Morrow Junior Books.

Steptoe, J. (1984). *The story of Jumping Mouse: A Native American legend*. New York: Lothrop, Lee & Shepard Books.

Steptoe, J. (1987). *Mufaro's beautiful daughters: An African tale*. New York: Lothrop, Lee & Shepard Books.

Stern, S. (1982). *Vasily and the dragon: An epic Russian fairy tale*. London: Pelham Books.

Stewig, J. W. (1995). *Princess Florecita and the iron shoes: A Spanish fairy tale* (W. Popp, Illus.). New York: Knopf.

Stewig, J. W. (1999). *King Midas: A golden tale* (O. Rayyan, Illus.). New York: Holiday House.

Stewig, J. W., Grimm, J., & Grimm, W. (2001). *Mother Holly: A retelling from the Brothers Grimm* (J. Westerman, Illus.). New York: North-South Books.

Talbott, H. *O'Sullivan stew: A tale cooked up in Ireland*. New York: Putnam's.

Torre, B. L. (1990). *The luminous pearl: A Chinese folktale* (C. Inouye, Illus.). New York: Orchard Books.

Towle, F. M. (1975). *The magic cooking pot: A folktale of India*. Boston: Houghton Mifflin.

Uchida, Y. (1955). *The magic listening cap: More folk tales from Japan*. New York: Harcourt.

Walker, B. K. (1988). *A treasury of Turkish folktales for children*. Hamden, CT: Linnet Books.

Wallace, I. (1986). *Sparrow's song*. New York: Viking Kestrel.

Wang, R. C. (1991). *The fourth question: A Chinese tale* (J.-H. Chen, Illus.). New York: Holiday House.

Wang, R. C. (1995). *The treasure chest: A Chinese tale* (W. Hillenbrand, Illus.). New York: Holiday House.

Watts, B., & La Fontaine, J. de. (2002). *The rich man and the shoemaker: A fable*. New York: North-South Books.

Wetterer, M. K. (1991). *The boy who knew the language of the birds* (B. Wright, Illus.). Minneapolis: Carolrhoda Books.

Whitney, T. P. (1970). *Vasilisa the beautiful* (N. Hogrogian, Illus.). New York: Macmillan.

Wiesner, D., & Kahng, K. (1987). *The loathsome dragon*. New York: Putnam.

Wiesner, D., & Kahng, K. (2005). *The loathsome dragon*. New York: Clarion.

Willard, N. (1992). *Beauty and the beast* (B. Moser, Illus.). San Diego: Harcourt.

Winthrop, E. (1991). *Vasilissa the beautiful: A Russian folktale* (A. Koshkin, Illus.). New York: HarperCollins.

Wolkstein, D. (1991). *Oom Razoom, or, Go I know not where, bring back I know not what: A Russian tale* (D. McDermott, Illus.). New York: Morrow Junior Books.

Yagawa, S. (1981). *The crane wife* (S. Akaba, Illus., K. Paterson, Trans.). New York: Morrow.

Yep, L. (1997a). *The dragon prince: A Chinese Beauty and the beast* (K. Mak, Illus.). New York: HarperCollins.

Yep, L. (1997b). *The Khan's daughter: A Mongolian folktale* (J. Tseng & M.-S. Tseng, Illus.). New York: Scholastic.

Yolen, J. (1968). *Greyling: A picture story from the islands of Shetland* (W. Stobbs, Illus.). Cleveland: World.

Yolen, J. (1991). *Greyling* (D. Ray, Illus.). New York: Philomel Books.

Chapter 7

Professional References

Atwell, N. (1987). *In the middle: Writing, reading, and learning with adolescents*. Upper Montclair, NJ: Boynton/Cook.

Benedict, S., & Carlisle, L. (1992). *Beyond words: Picture books for older readers and writers*. Portsmouth, NH: Heinemann.

Bode, B. (1989). Dialogue journal writing. *The Reading Teacher*, 42(8), 568–71.

Brooks, W., & Hampton, G. (2005). Safe discussions rather than first hand encounters: Adolescents examine racism through one historical fiction text. *Children's Literature in Education*, 36(1), 83–98.

Clyde, J. A. (2003). Stepping inside the story world: The subtext strategy—a tool for connecting and comprehending. *The Reading Teacher, 57*(2), 150–60.

Harste, J. C. (1999). Supporting critical conversation in classrooms. In K. M. Pierce (Ed.), *Adventuring with books: A booklist for pre-K–grade 6* (12th ed., pp. 507–54). Urbana, IL: National Council of Teachers of English.

Kiefer, B. Z. (1995). *The potential of picturebooks: From visual literacy to aesthetic understanding*. Englewood Cliffs, NJ: Merrill.

Krashen, Stephen (2004). *The power of reading: Insights from the research*. Westport, CT: Libraries Unlimited.

Leland, C. H., & Harste, J. C. (2000). Critical literacy: Enlarging the space of the possible. *Primary Voices K–6, 9*(2), 3–7.

Lukens, R. J. (2003). *A critical handbook of children's literature* (7th ed.). Boston: Allyn & Bacon.

McDaniel, C. (2004). Critical literacy: A questioning stance and the possibility for change. *The Reading Teacher, 57*(5), 472–81.

Moss, J. (2004). Breaking barriers, building bridges: Critical discussion of social issues. Retrieved June 30, 2005, from the NCTE/IRA ReadWriteThink Web site: http://www.readwritethink.org/lessons/lesson_view.asp?id=86.

Moss, J. (2005). Literature as a catalyst for social action: Breaking barriers, building bridges. Retrieved June 30, 2005, from the NCTE/IRA ReadWriteThink Web site: http://www.readwritethink.org/lessons/lesson_view.asp?id=105.

Parsons, L. (2004). Ella evolving: Cinderella stories and the construction of gender-appropriate behavior. *Children's Literature in Education, 35*(2), 135–54.

Saunders, S. L. (1999). *Look—and learn! Using picture books in grades five through eight*. Portsmouth, NH: Heinemann.

Serafini, F., & Giorgis, C. (2003). *Reading aloud and beyond: Fostering the intellectual life with older readers*. Portsmouth, NH: Heinemann.

Staton, J. (1988). *Dialogue journal communication: Classroom, linguistic, social, and cognitive views*. Norwood, NJ: Ablex.

Tiedt, I. M. (2000). *Teaching with picture books in the middle school*. Newark, DE: International Reading Association.

Trites, R. S. (1997). *Waking Sleeping Beauty: Feminist voices in children's novels*. Iowa City: University of Iowa Press.

Wolk, S. (2004). Literacy and democracy: Using picture books to teach for democracy. *Language Arts, 82*(1), 26–35.

Woodson, J. (2005). Picture books. Retrieved June 30, 2005, from the Jacqueline Woodson Web site: http://www.jacquelinewoodson.com/pb.html.

Children's Books

Ackerman, K. (1990). *The tin heart* (M. Hays, Illus.). New York: Atheneum.

Ada, A. F. (1997). *Gathering the sun: An ABC in Spanish and English* (S. Silva, Illus.). New York: Lothrop, Lee & Shepard Books.

Ada, A. F. (1998). *The malachite palace* (L. Gore, Illus., R. Zubizarreta-Ada, Trans.). New York: Atheneum Books for Young Readers.

Adler, D. A. (1993). *A picture book of Rosa Parks* (R. Casilla, Illus.). New York: Holiday House.

Altman, L. J. (1993a). *Amelia's road* (E. O. Sanchez, Illus.). New York: Lee & Low Books.

Altman, L. J. (1993b). *El camino de Amelia* (E. O. Sanchez, Illus., D. Santacruz, Trans.). New York: Lee & Low Books.

Babbitt, N. (1975). *Tuck everlasting*. New York: Farrar, Straus, and Giroux.

Babbitt, N. (1999). *Tuck everlasting*. Austin: Holt, Rinehart, and Winston.

Barber, A. (1987). *The enchanter's daughter* (E. Le Cain, Illus.). London: Cape.

Battle-Lavert, G. (2003). *Papa's mark* (C. Bootman, Illus.). New York: Holiday House.

Behrens, J. (1984). *Sally Ride, astronaut: An American first*. Chicago: Children's Press.

Belton, S. (2000). *McKendree*. New York: Greenwillow Books.

Bolden, T. (2003). *Portraits of African-American heroes* (A. Pitcairn, Illus.). New York: Dutton Children's Books.

Bridges, R. (1999). *Through my eyes*. New York: Scholastic.

Bridges, S. Y. (2002). *Ruby's wish* (S. Blackall, Illus.). San Francisco: Chronicle Books.

Bunting, E. (1991). *Fly away home* (R. Himler, Illus.). New York: Clarion Books.

Carlson, J. (1989). *Harriet Tubman: Call to freedom*. New York: Fawcett Columbine.

Cline-Ransome, L. (2004). *Major Taylor, champion cyclist* (J. E. Ransome, Illus.). New York: Atheneum Books for Young Readers.

Codell, E. R. (2003). *Sahara special*. New York: Hyperion Books for Children.

Coles, R. (1995). *The story of Ruby Bridges* (G. Ford, Illus.). New York: Scholastic.

Creech, S. (2001). *Love that dog*. New York: HarperCollins.

Curtis, C. P. (1995). *The Watsons go to Birmingham—1963*. New York: Delacorte Press.

Curtis, G. (1998). *The bat boy and his violin* (E. B. Lewis, Illus.). New York: Simon & Schuster Books for Young Readers.

Daly, N. (2003). *Once upon a time*. New York: Farrar, Straus, and Giroux.

Davidson, M. (1988). *The story of Jackie Robinson, bravest man in baseball* (F. Cooper, Illus.). New York: Dell.

Fenner, C. (1991). *Randall's wall*. New York: McElderry Books.

Ferris, J. (1988). *Go free or die: A story about Harriet Tubman* (K. Ritz, Illus.). Minneapolis: Carolrhoda Books.

Fleischman, P. (1997). *Seedfolks* (J. Pederson, Illus.). New York: HarperCollins.

Fox, P. (1991). *Monkey Island*. New York: Orchard Books.

Freedman, R. (2004). *The voice that challenged a nation: Marian Anderson and the struggle for equal rights*. New York: Clarion Books.

Fritz, J. (1995). *You want women to vote, Lizzie Stanton?* (D. DiSalvo-Ryan, Illus.). New York: Putnam's.

Gehret, J. (1994). *Susan B. Anthony: And justice for all* (J. Lennox, Illus.). Fairport, NY: Verbal Images Press.

Golenbock, P. (1990). *Teammates* (P. Bacon, Illus.). San Diego: Harcourt.

Greene, C. (1982). *Sandra Day O'Connor: First woman on the Supreme Court*. Chicago: Children's Press.

Greenfield, E. (1996). *Rosa Parks* (G. Ashby, Illus.). New York: HarperCollins.

Grimes, N. (2002). *Talkin' about Bessie: The story of aviator Elizabeth Coleman* (E. B. Lewis, Illus.). New York: Orchard Books.

Grimm, J., & Grimm, W. (1993). *Rumpelstiltskin: A fairy tale* (B. Watts, Illus., A. Bell, Trans.). New York: North-South Books.

Hamilton, V. (1993). *Many thousand gone: African Americans from slavery to freedom* (L. Dillon & D. Dillon, Illus.). New York: Knopf.

Hansen, J., & McGowan, G. (2003). *Freedom roads: Searching for the Underground Railroad* (J. E. Ransome, Illus.). Chicago: Cricket Books.

Harrington, J. N. (2004). *Going north* (J. Lagarrigue, Illus.). New York: Kroupa Books.

Haskins, J., & King, M. L. (1992). *I have a dream: The life and words of Martin Luther King, Jr.* Brookfield, CT: Millbrook Press.

Helldorfer, M.-C. (1991). *The mapmaker's daughter* (J. Hunt, Illus.). New York: Bradbury Press.

Hesse, K., & Parker, R. A. (1998). *Just Juice*. New York: Scholastic.

Hopkinson, D. (2002). *Under the quilt of night* (J. E. Ransome, Illus.). New York: Atheneum Books for Young Readers.

Hopkinson, D. (2003). *Girl wonder: A baseball story in nine innings* (T. Widener, Illus.). New York: Atheneum Books for Young Readers.

Houston, G. (1990). *Littlejim* (T. B. Allen, Illus.). New York: Philomel Books.

Houston, G. (1993). *Littlejim* (T. B. Allen, Illus.). New York: Beech Tree Books.

Howard, E. F. (1999). *Virgie goes to school with us boys* (E. B. Lewis, Illus.). New York: Simon & Schuster Books for Young Readers.

Howard, M. (1998). *Madeleine Albright*. Minneapolis: Lerner.

Hudson, W. (2004). *Powerful words: More than 200 years of extraordinary writing by African Americans*. New York: Scholastic Nonfiction.

Hurwitz, J., & Hurwitz, S. (1989). *Sally Ride: Shooting for the stars*. New York: Fawcett Columbine.

Jiménez, F. (1998). *La mariposa* (S. Silva, Illus.). Boston: Houghton Mifflin.

Kadohata, C. (2004). *Kira-kira*. New York: Atheneum.

Kimmel, E. A. (1992). *The four gallant sisters* (T. Yuditskaya, Illus.). New York: Holt.

Kroll, V. L. (2003). *Especially heroes* (T. Ladwig, Illus.). Grand Rapids, MI: Eerdmans Books for Young Readers.

Krull, K. (2003). *Harvesting hope: The story of Cesar Chavez* (Y. Morales, Illus.). San Diego: Harcourt.

Lasky, K. (2003). *A voice of her own: The story of Phillis Wheatley, slave poet* (P. Lee, Illus.). Cambridge, MA: Candlewick Press.

Leeper, A. (2003). *Juneteenth: A day to celebrate freedom from slavery*. Berkeley Heights, NJ: Enslow.

Levine, G. C. (1997). *Ella enchanted*. New York: HarperCollins.

Lewis, J. P. (2000). *Freedom like sunlight: Praisesongs for black Americans*. Mankato, MN: Creative Editions.

Lipsyte, R. (1977). *One fat summer*. New York: Harper & Row.

Littlesugar, A. (2001). *Freedom school, yes!* (F. Cooper, Illus.). New York: Philomel Books.

Lucas, E. (1997). *Cracking the wall: The struggles of the Little Rock Nine* (M. Anthony, Illus.). Minneapolis: Carolrhoda Books.

MacLachlan, P. (1991). *Journey*. New York: Delacorte Press.

McCully, E. A. (1996). *The ballot box battle*. New York: Knopf.

McKissack, P. (1997). *Run away home*. New York: Scholastic.

McKissack, P., & McKissack, F. (1992). *Zora Neale Hurston, writer and storyteller*. Hillside, NJ: Enslow.

McKissack, P., & McKissack, F. (2002). *Zora Neale Hurston, writer and storyteller* (Rev. ed.). Berkeley Heights, NJ: Enslow.

McWhorter, D. (2004). *A dream of freedom: The civil rights movement from 1954 to 1968*. New York: Scholastic.

Medearis, A. S. (1997). *Princess of the press: The story of Ida B. Wells-Barnett*. New York: Lodestar Books.

Melmed, L. K. (1994). *Prince Nautilus* (H. Sorensen, Illus.). New York: Lothrop, Lee & Shepard.

Miller, W. (1994). *Zora Hurston and the chinaberry tree* (C. Van Wright & Y.-H. Hu, Illus.). New York: Lee & Low Books.

Miller, W. (1997). *Richard Wright and the library card* (G. Christie, Illus.). New York: Lee & Low Books.

Millman, I. (2004). *Moses sees a play*. New York: Farrar, Straus, and Giroux.

Moore, C. (2002). *The daring escape of Ellen Craft* (M. O. Young, Illus.). Minneapolis: Carolrhoda Books.

Mora, P. (1997). *Tomás and the library lady* (R. Colón, Illus.). New York: Knopf.

Morrison, T. (2004). *Remember: The journey to school integration*. Boston: Houghton Mifflin.

Morrow, B. O. (2004). *A good night for freedom* (L. Jenkins, Illus.). New York: Holiday House.

Moss, M. (2004). *Mighty Jackie: The strike-out queen* (C. F. Payne, Illus.). New York: Simon & Schuster Books for Young Readers.

Moss, P. (2004). *Say something* (L. Lyon, Illus.). Gardiner, ME: Tilbury House.

Napoli, D. J. (2004). *Bound*. New York: Atheneum Books for Young Readers.

Nelson, M. (2005). *A wreath for Emmett Till* (P. Lardy, Illus.). Boston: Houghton Mifflin.

Nelson, V. M. (2003). *Almost to freedom* (C. Bootman, Illus.). Minneapolis: Carolrhoda Books.

Park, F., & Park, G. (2000). *The royal bee* (C. Z.-Y. Zhang, Illus.). Honesdale, PA: Boyds Mills Press.

Parks, R., & Haskins, J. (1997). *I am Rosa Parks* (W. Clay, Illus.). New York: Dial Books for Young Readers.

Paterson, K. (1977). *Bridge to Terabithia* (D. Diamond, Illus.). New York: Crowell.

Paterson, K. (1987). *Bridge to Terabithia* (D. Diamond, Illus.). New York: HarperTrophy.

Paterson, K. (1999). *The king's equal* (C. Woodbridge, Illus.). New York: HarperTrophy.

Patrick, J. L. S. (2000). *The girl who struck out Babe Ruth* (J. Reeves, Illus.). Minneapolis: Carolrhoda Books.

Patterson, L. (1989). *Martin Luther King, Jr., and the freedom movement*. New York: Facts on File.

Pinkney, A. D. (2000). *Let it shine: Stories of black women freedom fighters* (S. Alcorn, Illus.). San Diego: Harcourt.

Pinkney, A. D. (2003). *Fishing day* (S. W. Evans, Illus.). New York: Jump at the Sun, Hyperion Books for Children.

Polacco, P. (1998). *Thank you, Mr. Falker*. New York: Philomel Books.

Porter, P. P. (2004). *Sky* (M. J. Gerber, Illus.). Toronto: Groundwood Books.

Ransom, C. F. (2003). *Liberty street* (E. Velasquez, Illus.). New York: Walker.

Rappaport, D. (2001). *Martin's big words: The life of Dr. Martin Luther King, Jr.* (B. Collier, Illus.). New York: Hyperion Books for Children.

Rappaport, D. (2004). *Free at last! Stories and songs of Emancipation* (S. W. Evans, Illus.). Cambridge, MA: Candlewick Press.

Rappaport, D., & Callan, L. (2000). *Dirt on their skirts: The story of the young women who won the world championship* (E. B. Lewis, Illus.). New York: Dial Books for Young Readers.

Ringgold, F. (1999). *If a bus could talk: The story of Rosa Parks*. New York: Simon & Schuster Books for Young People.

Ritchie, N. (2003). *The civil rights movement*. Hauppauge, NY: Barron's.

Robinet, H. (2000). *Walking to the bus-rider blues*. New York: Atheneum Books for Young Readers.

Robinson, S. (2004). *Promises to keep: How Jackie Robinson changed America*. New York: Scholastic.

Rochelle, B. (1993). *Witnesses to freedom: Young people who fought for civil rights*. New York: Lodestar Books.

Rockwell, A. F. (2000). *Only passing through: The story of Sojourner Truth* (G. Christie, Illus.). New York: Knopf.

Rodman, M. A. (2004). *Yankee girl*. New York: Farrar, Straus, and Giroux.

Rosenthal, B. (1986). *Lynette Woodard: The first female Globetrotter*. Chicago: Children's Press.

Ryan, P. M. (2000). *Esperanza rising*. New York: Scholastic.

Ryan, P. M. (2001). *Esperanza rising*. Austin: Holt, Rinehart, and Winston.

Ryan, P. M. (2002). *When Marian sang: The true recital of Marian Anderson, the voice of a century* (B. Selznick, Illus.). New York: Scholastic.

Sachar, L. (1998). *Holes*. New York: Farrar, Straus, and Giroux.

Sachar, L. (2002). *Holes*. Austin: Holt, Rinehart, and Winston.

Salisbury, C. (2002). *Elizabeth Cady Stanton: Leader of the fight for women's rights*. Berkeley Heights, NJ: Enslow.

San Souci, R. D. (2004). *The well at the end of the world* (R. Walsh, Illus.). San Francisco: Chronicle Books.

Schmidt, G. D. (2004). *Lizzie Bright and the Buckminster boy*. New York: Clarion Books.

Schroeder, A. (1996). *Minty: A story of young Harriet Tubman* (J. Pinkney, Illus.). New York: Dial Books for Young Readers.

Scott, R. (1987). *Jackie Robinson*. New York: Chelsea House.

Shuker, N. (1985). *Martin Luther King*. New York: Chelsea House.

Simon, M. L. (1978). *A special gift*. New York: Harcourt.

Simon, S. (2002). *Jackie Robinson and the integration of baseball*. Hoboken, NJ: Wiley.

Spinelli, J. (1990). *Maniac Magee: A novel*. Boston: Little, Brown.

Spinelli, J. (1998). *Knots in my yo-yo string: The autobiography of a kid*. New York: Knopf.

Stanley, D. (1997). *Rumpelstiltskin's daughter*. New York: Morrow Junior Books.

Stroud, B. (2005). *The patchwork path: A quilt map to freedom* (E. S. Bennett, Illus.). Cambridge, MA: Candlewick Press.

Sutcliffe, J. (2000). *Babe Didrikson Zaharias: All-around athlete* (J. Reeves, Illus.). Minneapolis: Carolrhoda Books.

Taylor, M. D. (1976). *Roll of thunder, hear my cry*. New York: Dial Press.

Taylor, M. D. (1987). *The friendship* (M. Ginsburg, Illus.). New York: Dial Books for Young Readers.

Thomas, J. C. (2004). *Linda Brown, you are not alone: The Brown v. Board of Education decision, a collection* (C. James, Illus.). New York: Jump at the Sun/Hyperion Books for Children.

Tolan, S. S. (1992). *Sophie and the sidewalk man* (S. Avishai, Illus.). New York: Four Winds Press.

Vander Zee, R. (2004). *Mississippi morning* (F. Cooper, Illus.). Grand Rapids, MI: Eerdmans Books for Young Readers.

Vaughan, M. K. (2003). *Up the learning tree* (D. Blanks, Illus.). New York: Lee & Low Books.

Voigt, C. (1983). *A solitary blue*. New York: Atheneum.

Voigt, C. (2003). *A solitary blue*. New York: Aladdin Paperbacks.

Walter, M. P. (2004). *Alec's primer* (L. Johnson, Illus.). Middlebury: Vermont Folklife Center.

Walvoord, L. (2004). *Rosetta, Rosetta, sit by me!* (E. Velasquez, Illus.). New York: Marshall Cavendish.

Weatherford, C. B. (2002). *Remember the bridge: Poems of a people*. New York: Philomel Books.

Weatherford, C. B. (2005). *Freedom on the menu: The Greensboro sit-ins* (J. Lagarrigue, Illus.). New York: Dial Books.

Wiles, D. (2001). *Freedom summer* (J. Lagarrigue, Illus.). New York: Atheneum Books for Young Readers.

Wolkstein, D. (1999). *The glass mountain* (L. Bauer, Illus.). New York: Morrow.

Woodruff, E. (2003). *The Ravenmaster's secret: Escape from the Tower of London*. New York: Scholastic.

Woodson, J. (2001). *The other side* (E. B. Lewis, Illus.). New York: Putnam's.

Index

Author

Joy F. Moss has since 1970 been teaching graduate students as an adjunct associate professor at the University of Rochester, conducting professional development courses for teachers in schools in and around Rochester, and serving as a consultant in various school districts in this area. As a teacher educator, Moss has focused on the translation of theories of literary and literacy learning into practice.

During this time, Moss has also worked with the children in the elementary division of a private school in Rochester. After several years as a classroom teacher and then as a reading teacher, Moss introduced a literature program into the school curriculum and has been exploring literature with children ever since as a cross-grade literature specialist.

Moss has drawn from her work with elementary school students and graduate students to write articles for professional journals, chapters for edited texts, and seven books for preservice and practicing teachers.

This book was typeset in Palatino and Helvetica by Electronic Imaging.
Typefaces used on the cover were BinnerD Regular and Slimbach Bold.
The book was printed on 60-lb. Accent Opaque paper by Versa Press, Inc.